REBOUND!

BASKETBALL, BUSING, LARRY BIRD, AND THE REBIRTH OF BOSTON

REBOUND!

BASKETBALL, BUSING, LARRY BIRD, AND THE REBIRTH OF BOSTON

Michael Connelly

MVP Books
An Imprint of Voyageur Press

To the generation of school children who were sacrificed because adults failed to find the middle ground between natural law and judicial law.

To my wife, Noreen, and son, Ryan, who are my blessing; my mom and dad, who guide me with the steady hand of love and support; my brothers and sisters, who aren't just my siblings but my friends.

Library of Congress Cataloging-in-Publication Data

Connelly, Michael (Michael P.)
  Rebound! : basketball, busing, Larry Bird, and the rebirth of Boston / Michael Connelly.
    p. cm.
  ISBN 978-0-7603-3501-7
  1. Boston Celtics (Basketball team)--History--20th century. 2. Basketball--Social aspects--Massachusetts--Boston. 3. Boston (Mass.)--Social conditions--20th century. 4. Boston (Mass.)--Race relations. I. Title.
  GV885.52.B67C66 2008
  796.3230744'61--dc22

                           2008023121

Editor: Josh Leventhal
Designer: Helena Shimizu

Printed in the United States of America

On the front cover, top: Red Auerbach and Larry Bird, June 8, 1979 (AP Images); *bottom:* School buses with police escort, South Boston, September 12, 1974 (photo © Spencer Grant 1974)

Contents

Preface

JUST BEFORE THE ORANGE LINE ARRIVED AT DUDLEY STATION, THE TRACKS BOWED OUT IN A PREGNANT CORNER OVER WASHINGTON STREET. When the subway negotiated this crooked bend, the wheels of the train screeched as if warning the passengers of impending danger. That noise made white riders sitting in seats or standing around poles clench their muscles, suffocate breaths, and avert eyes. On the station's platform awaiting the arrival of the train stood hard-working African Americans. They heard the same alarm and held the same fear and distrust. This was the world that Bostonians lived in during the days of forced busing, a time when tolerances became intolerant, where the line of demarcation was defined by race.

I grew up in a predominantly Irish-Catholic neighborhood of Boston called West Roxbury. It was inhabited mostly by firemen, policemen, and politicians of all sorts. My father, a probation officer, and my mother, an unemployed school teacher, found the means to send my five siblings and me to the safe confines of St. Theresa Elementary School for our education. At St. Theresa, we learned how to bless ourselves and say the Act of Contrition and play games of Relievio at recess and floor hockey in gym. The three Connelly boys were altar boys and played CYO (Catholic Youth Organization) sports; my three sisters learned to sew and spin a flag in the color guard. For the most part, the hostilities that existed just miles from our yellow colonial house on Perham Street were simply events that occurred on the nightly news, not much different than the conflicts taking place in Lebanon or Vietnam.

In the winter of 1978, I reached the ripe age of thirteen and immediately began the dance of independence with my parents. I was the fourth Connelly child to leap into the world of adolescence, and consequently my parents knew better than I how to play the game. Only after weighing risk and reward would they allow me to taste the fruits of freedom. On one such occasion, a tame Sunday afternoon in February, I was allowed to join my friends on a trip to the Boston Garden to watch the Boston Celtics play in a matinee game. In previous seasons, Celtic tickets were scarce and not available to aimless teenagers. Sadly, this edition of the men in green was a pathetic shadow of the glory years. Losses at the Garden, which used to be the exception, were now the norm. Players who wore the shamrock on their chest and squeaked high-top black sneakers around the parquet floor were more likely to be booed than cheered as shots and passes often went wayward from their intended destination. Names like Curtis Rowe, Sidney Wicks, and Marvin Barnes did little to rekindle warm memories of Sam Jones, Bob Cousy, and Bill Russell. The inadequacies on the court only served to further frustrate the fans, who came to the Garden to escape the turmoil that existed out on the streets of Boston.

On this Sunday, the futility of the home team couldn't spoil our fun. On our way home on the subway, we took turns exchanging stories along with the other Celtic fans on that train who laughed and told hearty accounts of the game. That was until the train stuttered, slowed, and then rolled toward the next station. Over the static-filled intercom, the conductor called out, "Next stop, Dudley Station. Dudley Station everyone."

Instantly, a quiet swept throughout the car. Dudley Station was the stop on the Orange Line where confrontation between the races often occurred, as it marked a transition point between a black neighborhood and a white neighborhood. Jovial conversations turned to whispers, and cynical women gripped their handbags. My two friends and I paused in midsentence as we stood around a shared pole. When the train finally came to a halt, the doors to the platform parted left and right, allowing passengers to disembark. But before the departing riders had a chance to clear the doors, an unknown, long-haired, white teenager, who happened to be sharing our pole, yelled with all the anger of Boston in the 1970s, "All niggers off!"

Here we were in the midst of one of the most volatile racial storms in the history of Boston, and one side had just dared the other. White riders throughout the train melted in shame while departing black riders took home with them a reminder of hatred. All, that is, except for the very last black passenger who arrived at the doors. He came to a halt, preventing the sliding doors from closing. This delay annoyed the white teenager, who then advanced his challenge: "That means you, too."

Pushed beyond the limits, the black man spun on his heels and, with a look of both fear and fury in his eyes, withdrew his hand from his coat pocket. In his hand, he held a handgun, which he pointed at a collage of white faces, not quite sure who had offered the ultimate insult.

At that moment, time froze. A man now held my life in the flex of his right index finger. Because he couldn't identify the author of the racist challenge, he shined the gun on all who stood in vicinity of the utterance. When it was my turn to have the gun set upon me, I could only hope that it was the intention of the gun bearer to send a message of defiance to the riders who would continue past Dudley Station to their houses in white neighborhoods. For this brief yet seemingly never-ending instant, our train had become the epicenter of the Boston racial conflict. Finally, the black man stepped backward off the train with the gun held out as if he were still pondering whether to fire his weapon. While he weighed his options, the doors of the car closed and the train rumbled down the tracks.

No one said a word. When we arrived at the Forest Hills station, people dragged themselves off the car, scared and embarrassed. Among us was a voice that didn't represent us but would forever be associated with us. As we walked down the stairs of Forest Hills, my friends and I agreed not to tell the story to our families. There was no harm done, and hearing the account of the racist white teenager and gun-wielding black man would only cause our parents to restrict our freedom. So we climbed into the backseat of my parents' waiting paneled station wagon and made our way back to West Roxbury talking only of missed layups and salty popcorn.

On this day, the two worlds of Celtic futility and racial fury intersected. This was Boston in the 1970s. It was a city of two communities: one that was desperate to protect what it had worked so hard to claim, and another that was desperate to share in what was being protected. From schoolhouse steps to elevated trains to Boston Garden balcony seats, the people of this once-proud city longed for a force that could raise the city from the ashes.

✺

From 1956 to 1969, the Boston Celtics dominated the Boston Garden parquet floor, winning eleven NBA championships. As each title was won, the citizens of the historic seaport town became engulfed in Celtic Pride. The Celtics were a reason to feel special. They were the greatest franchise in the world, and they were ours. Then, almost overnight, the fates of both the team and the city were overwhelmed by radical change and embittered unrest that impacted me as a teenager. Three decades later, I am inspired to chronicle these two distinct but parallel stories that run side by side like the city's train tracks and merge at sublime intersections.

Rebound! is like a scrapbook, moving through time and connecting snapshots of Boston and its basketball team. As I spliced together the narrative, I tried to remain vigilant to the advice of Mayor Raymond Flynn, who suggested, "Michael, tell us what we don't know. We already know that the buses rolled up to the schools."

His other pearl of wisdom was equally helpful in my research: "Get a good pair of shoes, and start walking and talking to people." Walk and talk I did. My journey took me to places I could never imagine. I interviewed four of the city's most prominent black leaders: Deputy Mayor Clarence "Jeep" Jones, the Reverend Michael Haynes, civic leader Paul Parks, and South Boston High School Assistant Headmaster Al Holland. Former Celtic Gerald Henderson caught me on my cell phone when I was out walking with my wife, and I conducted the entire interview while standing at an ATM machine in a bank lobby, transcribing the discussion on the back of deposit envelopes with a pen chained to the countertop. I talked with Jeff Judkins about how it felt, after saying he would take any amount of money to return to the Celtics for the 1980–81 season, to be shuttled off in the expansion draft, only to watch his former team advance to a championship without him—his voice still revealing the pain, nearly three decades later. I talked Irish music and the beauty of South Boston with Senate President William Bulger. (My most memorable interaction for this book wasn't an interview at all. It came when I contacted former NBA star Moses Malone by telephone to introduce myself and the project. In that thirty-second conversation I got an inkling of what it must have been like to fight him for a rebound. When I finished my salutation and my request, Moses replied in his deepest Barry White voice, "Big Mo don't know you!" I never heard from him again.)

In my conversations with people about the events of Boston in the mid to late 1970s, I found that the feelings are still raw and sometimes painful to recount, even with more than thirty years gone by. Parents talked about the helplessness they felt as they led their children onto buses and toward potential peril. The memories of this difficult period in the city's history continue to resonate throughout Boston's diverse neighborhoods.

Most Boston schools during this time served as an arena of chaos and racial division. Right or wrong, many of the stories in this book revolve around South Boston High School, in part because the school on G Street was such a focus of Judge W. Arthur Garrity, of the police, and of the media at the time. The problems that took place at South Boston also occurred at many other schools in the city, but South Boston High School is often held up as "ground zero" in the discussion of Boston's busing crisis and racial unrest.

No race, neighborhood, or school was spared the mayhem brought on by the decision to integrate Boston's public schools through mandated busing. The bus I traveled on, with other white riders to Boston Latin Academy in Dorchester, was often the target of rock-throwers, as were buses carrying black students.

During these times of political, civic, and economic depression, many in the city turned to the Celtics for escape. During the late 1950s and throughout the 1960s, Boston grew accustomed to its basketball team's success. These successes softened the coarseness of every day. That's why the Celtics' demise during the late 1970s was particularly painful. Boston desperately needed them to succeed, but they failed. The Celtics' play on the court mirrored the discontent of the fans that they represented.

The despondent citizens of Boston also turned to city hall, a federal court house, and the headquarters of five Boston School Committee members to lead them. But sadly, those institutions turned their backs on the people of the city as well, leaving Bostonians to their own means to try to navigate through one of the most tenuous times in the city's history.

Acknowledgments

THE LIST OF PEOPLE I WISH TO THANK FOR THEIR SUPPORT AND GUIDANCE ON THIS PROJECT IS LONG, AND I APOLOGIZE FOR ANY INADVERTENT OMISSIONS. I thank the following people:

My wife, Noreen, and mother, Marilyn Connelly, for their tireless editing, reading, and support; my son, Ryan, my life's joy, who sacrificed so that I could write; my father, John Connelly, who served as my agent and accessed his vast network across the city to arrange meetings and interviews, through which I learned about not only the subject at hand but also that my father was one of the most feared running backs in Boston.

Josh Leventhal of Voyageur Press, for believing in the concept and bringing it to fruition.

The Microfiche Department at the beautiful Boston Public Library in Copley Square. The library at the *Boston Herald*, especially Martha Reagan. Dick Lipe, who didn't help my batting average at Bentley College but stepped up for me by arranging interviews and allowed me to knock in a run.

Special thanks to Jan Volk, who gave up an afternoon and was called upon to answer countless e-mails; Dick Johnson of the New England Sports Museum, who filled my car with books and scrapbooks; Massachusetts Senate President William Bulger, for taking the time to review my words; Monsignor Raymond Helmick, who was more than my pastor but also a great source of information and connections; Nicole DeLaria of the Bostonian Society/Boston Historical Society—everyone should be so pleasant and helpful. Same said for Kristen Swett over at the Boston Archives; Maureen Coyle at the NBA; Karen Dmochowsky at *Sports Illustrated*; my Scollay Square experts, the beautiful burlesque dancer Lily Ann Rose and David Kruh; Janet Oberto; Jeff Twiss of the Boston Celtics; Brian Connor; Patricia Lynch, my Charlestown connection; Clarence Jeep Jones, who put together an amazing forum of speakers for me to meet; Rob Raichlen of the Los Angeles Clippers; Mike Murphy of the *Houston Chronicle*; Mike O'Connor of the Boston Police and Mission High School; friend and first-round draft choice Bob Bigelow; and the people listed below, who were so generous with their time to grant me an interview.

Several writers whose works gave me direction and perspective are credited in the sources listed at the back of this book. Some writers' works were so valuable in my research that I feel compelled to single them out here. Bob Ryan, although he didn't return any of my three calls, can be heard throughout this book from his writings as the preeminent basketball writer in the country during the time covered in this book. Writers Larry Whiteside, Dan Shaughnessy, Ray Fitzgerald, Will McDonough, and Mike Barnicle from the *Boston Globe* and Ed Gillooly from the *Boston Herald* are all prevalent in the text, as their descriptions and accounts of those days were invaluable in providing me an understanding of mood and settings in my research.

INTERVIEWS

Celtics and Other NBA Figures

Bob Bigelow

M. L. Carr

Dave Cowens

Mike Dunleavy

Wayne Embry

Hank Finkel

The Honorable Mal Graham

Tom Heinsohn

Gerald Henderson

Jeff Judkins

Wayne Kreklow

Steve Kuberski

Cedric Maxwell

Robert Reid

Rick Robey

Kevin Stacom

Dick Vitale

Jan Volk

Rick Weitzman

Pat Williams

Media

Clark Booth

Steve Bulpett

Joe Fitzgerald

Gary Gillis

Richard "Dick" Johnson, curator of the New England Sports Museum

Leigh Montville

Mike Murphy

Dan Rea

Roger Twibell

City and community leaders and busing advocates

Bishop John Patrick Boles

William Bulger, Massachusetts senate president

The Honorable Raymond Flynn, mayor of Boston

Stanley Forman, photographer

Dr. Charles Glenn, author of Phase I Busing Plan

The Reverend Michael Haynes of the Twelfth Baptist Church

Al Holland, assistant headmaster at South Boston High School

Clarence Jeep Jones, deputy mayor under Mayor Kevin White

Father William P. Joy

Melvin King, state representative and mayoral candidate

Theodore Landsmark

William F. Looney

Thomas O'Connor

Barney Olsen

Paul Parks

The Honorable Judge Michael Redd

Alan Rose, clerk to Judge Arthur Garrity

Dr. Marvin Scott, assigned expert to Judge Arthur Garrity

The Honorable Judge Mitchell Sikora Jr.

Robert "Bud" Spillane, Boston school superintendent

Charles Titus

Eric Van Loon

Father Walter Waldron

PROLOGUE

"Are You the Savior?"

IN THE SPRING OF 1976, THE CITY OF BOSTON WAS NEARLY TWO YEARS INTO A RADICAL AND HIGHLY CONTROVERSIAL PLAN TO DESEGREGATE THE SCHOOLS, AND TENSIONS WERE HIGH IN THIS "CITY ON A HILL." The court-ordered desegregation program mandated by Judge W. Arthur Garrity had polarized the city. Children were being uprooted from their neighborhoods and placed on buses that carried them to schools in other parts of the city. Many parents were outraged at being denied the right to choose where their children would go to learn; others saw it as an affront to a community's right of self-government. But more than two decades after the U.S. Supreme Court declared the practice of "separate but equal" in public school systems unconstitutional, Boston's schools were deeply divided across racial lines, and the resistance to efforts to eliminate racial imbalance was getting fiercer and, at times, violent. Parts of the city were in a virtual police state as the powers-that-be sought to restore an element of peace in the midst of radical change.

On the morning of April 5, 1976, attorney Ted Landsmark was on his way to a meeting at City Hall to discuss the allocation of construction jobs among minority workers. Landsmark, an African American, was working to break down racial barriers in other areas of civic life, separate from the ongoing controversy in the schools—but during this painful time in the city's history, nothing was separate from what was taking place in the schools.

Landsmark traveled by way of the Orange Line train that day to the State Street stop. The glare of the sun and the sting of a westerly sea breeze greeted Landsmark and the other commuters as they emerged from the underground station and marched off to their respective destinations. The weather was warm enough to not wear a coat but cool enough that you wished you had. Some riders emerged from the subway and headed east, with a *Wall Street Journal* under arm, down State Street to the financial district to trade stocks and count money. Others, carrying shopping bags, aimed south to the bustling center of commerce on Washington Street to seek bargains at Filene's Basement or to window shop at the many jewelers that lined the road. Those who stepped north would pass through the brick-lined Washington Mall on the way to the Government Center, where they renewed driver's licenses or met with public officials. On this Monday morning in early spring, Landsmark was among the latter group. Dressed in his blue three-piece suit and Windsor knot, he headed toward his impending meeting, head down and deep in thought.

Earlier that morning hundreds of white students had met with public officials Louise Day Hicks, Pixie Palladino, and Jimmy Kelly at City Hall to express their opposition to forced busing and discuss plans to remedy their plight. At the conclusion of the meeting, the students filed out onto the courtyard of Government Center and made their way to the passageway where Ted Landsmark now walked. It wasn't until the Yale graduate peered up that he became aware of the unruly crowd.

The very sight of Landsmark lit a fuse that connected to the white students. Yells of, "There's a nigger!" and "Get the nigger!" echoed off the buildings. Then, a fraction of the parade separated from the group and approached the lone lawyer. A clenched white fist slammed into the face of the black man. A second punch was thrown, breaking Landsmark's nose and separating him from his glasses. The beating continued. Landsmark was knocked to the ground, where he was kicked and stomped.

Prone on the bricks, Landsmark found himself in a surreal world. Time moved frame by frame, like an eight-millimeter film flashing painful images on a screen. Back on his feet but without his glasses, Landsmark was barely conscious of the lone protestor who stood in front of him like an antagonist in a Shakespearian tragedy. On his shoulder the protestor carried a metal pole to which the American flag was attached—the same American flag that 6,891 Americans died for on the island of Iwo Jima, the same flag that withstood the bombardment at Fort McHenry and inspired Francis Scott Key to write "O'er the land of the free and the home of the brave," the same flag that Sergeant William Carney of the 54th Regiment carried into battle in a courageous charge against Confederate \forces at Fort Wagner during the Civil War. But on this day more than a century later, the flag bearer was not overcome by patriotic inspiration; instead, he looked to the stars and stripes to serve as a conveyer of violence.

It wasn't simply one rage-filled adolescent who stood in front of Ted Landsmark on that fateful morning. When that flag pole was lanced forward at Landsmark, it represented years of frustration, pain, and intolerance. It was a moment that would permanently stain a city that had been a cornerstone in the fight for freedom and liberty two hundred years earlier, connecting with it a horrific and sadly symbolic image: the stars and stripes used as a weapon of hate.

The attack lasted seconds, but the impact would last a lifetime. Landsmark looked down at his blue suit, saw a sanguine stain, and realized he was bleeding.

Police eventually arrived on the scene, but the damage had been done.

One of the spectators to this tragic play that was taking place on the stage of brick outside of City Hall was *Boston Herald* photographer Stanley Forman. Through the years the veteran cameraman had developed an instinct that drew him to the "moment"—and this was a moment. Through his lens, Forman saw images that would forever compromise the reputation of the city. The next day, the image of Ted Landsmark being attacked by the American flag appeared on the front pages of newspapers everywhere. Boston could no longer hide its unkempt secret from the world.

Within the shadows of Boston's landmark Old State House and its New City Hall, the scene depicted in "The Soiling of Old Glory"—as Forman's photo came to be known—cast its own shadow on the city and its people that would take years to clear away.

🏀

From up above, the man looked out over his followers and paused to reflect. It had been two years since he had traversed the long road into the city. When he had first arrived, he sat behind a table and was asked if he was the savior. He had never thought of himself as a savior. He was just a man with heavenly blessings able to lead kings and the common man at the same time. But that long road had now led to this culminating moment. Both satisfied and still humble, he stepped forward to speak to his people. A hush swept across the massive gathering. When assured that he held their undivided attention, he called upon the name of a great prophet and declared: "I look out in the crowd and I see one thing that typifies our whole season: Moses does eat shit!"

It was at that very moment that Celtic Larry Bird forever endeared himself to the city of Boston. He had spoken to the people in the language of the proletariat. Sure, media elites would denounce such vulgarity and do-gooders would pen letters to the editor questioning the worthiness of this new voice of promise, but they didn't represent the masses. For the past decade, outsiders had told the citizens of Boston how to act, where to go, and what to say. The wounds and pain of a tumultuous time had scabbed but not completely healed. Now a force had roused the pulse of Boston, one that showed a disregard for the establishment while at the same time connecting with those who had been disconnected.

For centuries, Boston had been known as a city of tolerance and freedom. Somehow it had lost its way. People from outside the city boundaries watched their evening news or read their morning papers and shook their heads in dismay at a city that seemed to be on the precipice of collapse. But Boston was a city whose backbone was built on liberty and equality. It had always been resilient. It always found a way to rise above.

The team that the masses joined as one to cheer on this May afternoon in 1981 was the world-champion Boston Celtics. This collection of twelve men formed a colorless entity working for one common goal of greatness—six black and six white basketball players working as a team to protect the honor of the Boston Garden's parquet floor and to restore dignity to a once-proud franchise and, by extension, the city it represented. The NBA championship won by the Boston Celtics was more than athletic achievement or just another flag to hang from the rafters at the Garden. The franchise's fourteenth championship served as a metaphor of perseverance for all Bostonians. It gave the people an opportunity to feel good again about where they lived, worked, and raised their families.

In all, an estimated million and a half people had joined together at City Hall Plaza to thank the Boston Celtics for their efforts. In a raw expression of their merriment, the people stared upward with extended index fingers of victory chanting "Larry! Larry! Larry!" In the distance, the bells of Arlington Street Church rang in celebration.

CHAPTER 1

"A Dozen New Year's Eves Rolled into One"

THE BELLS OF ARLINGTON CHURCH RANG AS THE INHABITANTS OF THE CITY—FROM SOUTH BOSTON TO EAST BOSTON, FROM ROXBURY TO WEST ROXBURY—FLOCKED TO THE CITY'S SYMBOLIC CENTER, SCOLLAY SQUARE, TO CELEBRATE. It was August 14, 1945, and President Harry S Truman had just announced the "unconditional surrender" of Japan and the end of World War II. America's sons were coming home, and Boston wanted to consecrate the momentous occasion with a citywide party. So they came— one and all—to Scollay Square.

With the sounds of the Lennon Sisters and Glen Miller emanating from the open windows of taverns and theaters, the city smiled once again. In the skies overhead, a squadron of fighter planes circled in V formation, signaling victory to those celebrating down below. Shoeshine boys did cartwheels; cooks from Joe and Nemo's Restaurant led impromptu parades drumming pots and pans; and sailors enjoyed the fruits of their selective-service status, as written in the *Boston Globe* the following day: "Many the gal was kissed last night that never was kissed before. From missy to matron, none escaped who came within arms' length of a service man."

As afternoon turned to evening, pandemonium overwhelmed the square. For five years, people had huddled around radios, spent many sleepless nights, and sacrificed for the greater good. Now they danced, hugged, kissed, and sang until the sun returned. The festive atmosphere was described by one reveler as "a dozen New Year's Eves rolled into one."

The people came to Scollay Square to celebrate and be one. They always came to Scollay Square. It was the heart of Boston, the lifeblood of a thriving city.

❦

Since the mid-1800s, locals, tourists, and sailors alike converged on Scollay Square. It was Boston's center of commerce, entertainment, and discovery. Scollay Square was a fashionable destination for the upper crust, who arrived by horse and carriage to attend musical performances at the Howard Theater. Operas and Shakespearian plays graced the stages of Scollay Square's theaters; literary giants Mark Twain and Charles Dickens captivated audiences with readings of their world-renowned writings.

By the turn of the twentieth century, the city's changing demographics changed the face of Boston and Scollay Square. Theaters began to feature vaudeville acts and burlesque dancers to attract patrons who were more interested in a beer and a laugh than literary readings and "*et tu, Brute.*" Performers such as Abbott and Costello, Jimmy Durante, Phil Silvers, the Marx Brothers, Milton Berle, and Red Buttons all brought laughs to the stage of the Old Howard. Exhibition boxing matches featuring such pugilistic legends as John L. Sullivan and Rocky Marciano had the crowds standing in the aisles.

In the 1940s, sailors on leave flooded into Scollay Square from the many ships that docked at the Boston naval yards. They came for a hot dog and beer at Joe and Nemo's, followed by a tassel-spinning performance at the Howard, Rialto, or Crawford House by the likes of Ann Corio or Lilly Rose or Sally Keith, who not only danced but wrote lyrics:

> To Scollay Square the swells come down.
> Her tassels have been talked about the whole world over.
> And for seven years she's been there,
> The Crawford House has been in clover. . . .

✇

The front-page headline of the *Boston Globe* on August 15, 1945, read, "Japanese Surrender." The stories below told of the return dates for soldiers, plans for occupied Japan, and stories of wild celebrations in the streets of Boston.

Subsequent to President Truman's announcement, Boston Police Superintendent Ed Fallon called in 1,900 policemen, 700 auxiliary policemen, and 1,000 shore patrol and military police in an attempt to harness the mayhem and detour traffic away from Boston. Fire Chief Samuel Pope put out the call for all firemen to report to their stations, anticipating collateral damage from Boston's "twelve New Year's Eves."

From the moment the words "a date which will live in infamy" were uttered by President Franklin Roosevelt, Americans knew that the sacrifices of their country would be mighty. Now, it was over. Japan had succumbed and pronounced its unconditional surrender. Soldiers were coming home, food rations would cease, and light would return, literally, with the end of blackout rules.

Massachusetts Governor Maurice Tobin declared a two-day holiday. Across Boston, only drug stores and taverns remained open. In Chinatown, firecrackers blew beneath the Beech Street Paifang Gate, and the echoes of the night's exultation reverberated through the streets.

Soon the soldiers would reacquaint themselves with loved ones and make their way to Scollay Square to get that hot dog at Joe and Nemo's that they had dreamed about in foxholes, inside tanks, and on the decks of ships. Little did they know, as they cheered General Dwight Eisenhower's motorcade and tickertape rained down on the streets of Hanover and Court and Tremont, plans were in the works to change the face of Boston forever.

With each passing decade, Scollay Square had lost more of its shine. Moralists saw tassels and neon signs and the overall depreciation of the Puritan values upon which the city had been founded. Opportunists saw a prime location and dollar signs. Change was inevitable. A two-word phrase was sweeping through the offices of politicians, architects, and contractors throughout Boston: "urban renewal."

CHAPTER 2

"Read the Rules"

ST. PATRICK'S DAY 1950 DID NOT BLESS THE BOSTON CELTICS WITH THE LUCK OF THE IRISH. Only seven hundred fans came to the Boston Garden to watch the home team take on the New York Knicks in the regular-season finale. The Celtics lost the game, leaving them with a 22-46 record for the season and out of the playoffs for the second year in a row. The team's most popular player was Tony Lavelli, not because of his basketball skills but because he played the accordion at halftime.

The Celtics finished the season by losing eleven of their last twelve games. Owner Walter Brown could only shake his head at his team and the sparse crowds. Following the final game, Head Coach Alvin Doogie Julian resigned, stating, "I'm not tough enough for professional basketball."

That summer, Brown, with his franchise on the verge of bankruptcy, hired thirty-two-year-old Arnold Auerbach from Brooklyn to be the new coach of the Celtics. Auerbach had been the head coach of the Washington Capitols and the Tri-Cities Blackhawks. Known as "Red" because of the childhood shade of his hair (which had since diminished), Auerbach was a cantankerous, complex, brilliant architect and leader of men. Provided the reigns of the team by the owner along with his spiritual and financial support, Red set the program on a course to greatness. Building through the draft, he would rely on only one trade—sending Mel Counts to Baltimore in exchange for Bailey Howell— throughout the decades of the 1950s and 1960s to enhance the team.

As both a coach and a general manager, Red demonstrated an uncanny ability to perceive talent and potential where others didn't. He would not limit his quest for talent by bias or prejudice. He constructed a team to win and only win. This was apparent in his first draft in the spring of 1950, when he recommended to owner Walter Brown that the Celtics choose Chuck Cooper from Duquesne University. Cooper was black, and no African American had ever been selected in the NBA draft. Two years later, Auerbach selected Major League baseball pitcher Gene Conley in the tenth round of the draft and then applied his power of persuasiveness to convince Conley to play both sports.

In addition to his innate sense of the game and his willingness to take chances, Auerbach was a student of the rules and used this knowledge to make the most of those rules. In 1953, he found a loophole in the NBA draft laws that allowed him to select three players from the number-one-ranked University of Kentucky Wildcats—Frank Ramsey in the first round, Cliff Hagan in the third round, and Lou Tsioropoulos in the fifth round. All three players had graduated, but all were returning to Kentucky to play out their final year of collegiate eligibility. (Red would repeat this strategy in 1978.) At the draft, when the Celtics made their picks, New York Knicks President Ned Irish complained, "You can't do that!" With great satisfaction, Auerbach leaned back in his chair and said, "Read the rules." When Irish was shown the written rules, he grabbed his head and screamed, "You *can* do that!"

During the first half of the 1950s, the Celtics had found consistent success, largely thanks to the wizardry of a player that Auerbach never wanted: Bob Cousy. The Celtics had held the first pick in the 1950 draft but passed on the local sensation from Holy Cross, instead choosing Chuck Share from Bowling Green. Red was afraid that the Boston fans would demand that he play Cousy, whom Auerbach called the "local yokel." The magical point guard eventually came to the Celtics when his team, the Chicago Stags, folded prior to the 1950 season and Boston took him in the dispersal draft.

The Celtics went on to reach the playoffs in each of the next six seasons, but they still lacked the final piece to push them to the top. The team's greatest limitation was its defense, which inspired a bold trade by Auerbach prior to the 1956 draft. The Celtics sent All-Star Ed Macauley and the rights to Cliff Hagan to the St. Louis Hawks for the number-three overall pick. With that pick, Auerbach got center Bill Russell from the University of San Francisco. Red then nabbed two other players who would go on to have Hall of Fame careers. In the second round, he selected K. C. Jones, also out of USF, and then the Celtics invoked their territorial rights and chose Tom Heinsohn from Holy Cross. Red now had his team.

Over the next ten seasons, Auerbach's Celtics would capture nine NBA championships. In the course of this odyssey, the coach managed to infuriate referees, opponents, the league commissioner, Celtic fans, and even his own players. During his time as coach of the Celtics, Auerbach was fined more than any individual in the history of the league. He once punched St. Louis Hawks owner Ben Kerner in the face during an argument over the height of one of his baskets, and he was publicly reprimanded by Celtics owner Walter Brown in response to complaints from Boston fans who sat near the Celtics bench and were offended by the coach's "salty language." New York Knick Vince Boryla said of Auerbach, "Nobody has to get me up to play the Celtics. I just have to look over at that son of a bitch."

In the summer of 1965, Red announced that he would retire at the end of the upcoming season. He wanted to give his detractors "one more shot" at him. With his trademark rolled-up program in hand, Auerbach roamed the sidelines taunting, teaching, and winning all season long.

Auerbach's last game as the Celtics' coach was Game Seven of the NBA Finals against the Los Angeles Lakers. The Celtics were leading by a score of 95-85 with just thirty seconds remaining. Standing on the baseline, Massachusetts Governor John Volpe walked over to Red, with lighter in hand. The game's outcome appeared to be a foregone conclusion, and the governor lit the coach's last victory cigar. In the crowd, the fans roared in delight, and many of them surged toward the court in anticipation of the final buzzer. In the midst of the chaos, the Lakers staged a frenzied comeback. With four seconds left on the clock, the Celtics' lead had been reduced to 2 points. On the Lakers bench and in living rooms across the country, many thought this was the moment that Red would have to eat his presumptuous cigar. For years he had taunted and baited opponents with his victory cigar. Although he claimed that he only smoked them on the bench because of an endorsement deal he had with Blackstone Cigars, everyone knew better. (After Auerbach's retirement, the NBA banned smoking on the bench, not least of all due to the ill will created by Red's victory tradition.)

Fortunately, the Celtics held on to secure a 95-93 victory over the Lakers and another NBA championship. Red was carried off the floor on the shoulders of Celtic fans. In the locker room, the now-retired coach stripped to his t-shirt and was carried into the shower by his players, as was the tradition. Later in the day, his victory cigar was puffed in satisfaction.

Governor Volpe's premature cigar lighting in Game Seven earned him the wrath of the press and fans alike. Six weeks later, the governor would again be subjected to the disdain of many when he penned his name to legislation known as the Racial Imbalance Act, which intended to push forward the desegregation of Boston's schools.

⊕

The retired Auerbach returned to coach the 1967 All-Star Game, as was his privilege as the previous year's championship coach. He was ejected in the first half, becoming the only coach ever ejected from an NBA all-star game.

Seven years later, he again assumed head-coaching duties for one game when then-Coach Tommy Heinsohn fell ill. During his temporary return, Auerbach had the following exchange with longtime referee Richie Powers after a questionable call by the official:

Auerbach: "Richie, that call was chicken shit!"

Powers: "Technical foul on Auerbach."

Auerbach: "You've still got rabbit ears."

Powers: "You're absolutely right. [Another technical foul.] You're outta here."

Auerbach: "What's that for? I didn't swear!"

Powers: "What do you call 'chicken shit'?"

Auerbach: "That's not a swear."

Auerbach's quest to win at all costs spared neither opponents nor Celtic personnel. He once fired longtime Boston Garden time-keeper Tony Nota after Nota's apparent slow hand benefited an opponent during a game. Red was so incensed that he stormed the scorer's table and took a swing at Nota before terminating him on the spot. Auerbach reinstated him the next day.

Such unrelenting competitiveness drew the ire of all who came in his wake. When Celtic strong man Jim Loscutoff was asked about his old coach he said, "I couldn't wait to retire so I could take a swing at him." Loscutoff never took a swing at Red but instead grew to understand his brilliance. And though that brilliance was maddening to many, it made it possible for players like Loscutoff to be part of what was the greatest franchise in the history of sports.

Following his retirement from coaching, Red ascended to the seat of general manager, whence he continued to work his magic. Behind a desk covered with takeout Chinese-food containers and his collection of letter openers, he would lean back in his chair, lit cigar in hand, and work the phones in search of an opposing general manager who was naïve enough to talk with him, the greatest mind in NBA history. In a moment of self-reflection, Auerbach once surmised, "Well, I guess I did all right for a guy who never scored a basket."

CHAPTER 3
Brutalist Modern

ON THE WEEKEND PRIOR TO THE GRAND OPENING OF BOSTON'S NEW CITY HALL IN FEBRUARY 1969, THE *BOSTON GLOBE'S* DAVID R. ELLIS WROTE, "OUT OF THE TUMBLEDOWN RED BRICK DESTRUCTION OF SCOLLAY SQUARE HAS RISEN BOSTON'S PHOENIX." He continued, "Boston for all her faults has always done things with a grace and a touch of boldness."

William Stanley Parker of the Boston Planning Board had first suggested radical change for Scollay Square back in the 1930s. Politicians salivated at the prospect of putting their eternal fingerprints on the city by spearheading such a high-profile project. James Curley, who served four inconsecutive terms as Boston's mayor (1914–18, 1922–26, 1930–34, 1946–50), endeavored to oversee the project, but his efforts were thwarted by the shifting postwar priorities. Curley's successor, John B. Hynes (1950–60), was the next to take up the quest. Mayor Hynes first held the office as a caretaker during Mayor Curley's incarceration for influence peddling in 1947 and later assumed the seat in his own right by defeating the bombastic Curley in three straight elections. Hynes planted the seed of change at Scollay Square, which was brought to fruition by the ensuing mayor, John Collins (1960–68). Joseph Keblinsk of the *Boston Globe* explained this genealogy of change on the eve of the New City Hall's dedication on February 8, 1969: "This is the New Boston—conceived by Mayor John B. Hynes, nurtured by Mayor John F. Collins, and now being baptized by Mayor Kevin Hagan White."

The city hall project was three decades in concept before it finally material-ized in 1960. That year, the Boston Redevelopment Authority (BRA) acquired sixty acres of property, including all buildings and lands that encompassed Scollay Square, through the right of eminent domain. In February 1962, cranes with suspended wrecking balls rolled down Hanover Street and proceeded to raze the entire square, with the exception of the Sears Building, which was preserved only after much debate.

With sixty acres of unencumbered land located in the heart of the city, Edward Logue of the BRA contracted world-renowned architect I. M. Pei to design a new municipal center for the city. Pei's directive was to author a mas-ter plan that would bring together all three levels of government—city, state, and federal—around a central courtyard, which would come to be known as Government Center, "The Gateway to a New Boston." The jewel of the center would be Boston's city hall, the design and construction of which was put out to bid. Two hundred and fifty-six proposals from architects across the world were submitted and then secured in the basement of the Museum of Fine Arts. A jury of experts that included Pei, Logue, and other national authorities was assigned the task of selecting the most worthy entry.

In the end, Columbia University professors Gerhard Kallman, Noel McKinnel, and Edward Knowles won the bid. Their design style, known as Brutalist Modern, had captured the attention of those seeking radical change for the city. The Mucenaean Aztec tones stood in sharp contrast to the traditional Georgian red-bricked Old State House, which would sit in the shadow of this new structure.

When the model for the building was unveiled, it roused polarized critiques of the building's aesthetics and complex layout. In the architectural world, the New City Hall was hailed for its design, which provided generous public space. In an interview with the *Boston Globe*, architect Noel McKinnell praised it for being "robust enough to withstand the good, terrible, funny, and even vulgar events" that take place within a city hall.

Detractors of the design were not so kind. City Councilman Pat McDonough cried, "The only thing missing is the gas pumps outside the building." Another critic stated that it looked like the crate that Faneuil Hall came in.

Bringing the design to reality proved to be more difficult than anticipated. By the fourth quarter of 1968, the construction of the nine-story edifice was two years delayed and $5 million over budget, increasing the cost to $26 million. At Old City Hall, outgoing Mayor John Collins was devastated by the setbacks. In the coming month he would relinquish his seat to mayor-elect Kevin White. Collins' dream of being the first sitting mayor to occupy the building now seemed unlikely to come true. With each day that fell off the calendar, Mayor Collins became more desperate to leave his literal footprint in the building that he had overseen from seed to bloom. In December, the final month of his term, he moved his office to the unfinished and unheated fifth floor of New City Hall. Shortly thereafter, Collins came down with pneumonia. He not only spent the rest of his term in bed but also was unable to attend White's inauguration. Mayor John Collins was the first victim of a cold and complicated building.

✦

The baton of the mayor's office passed to Kevin White on January 1, 1969. White, who grew up in Boston's West Roxbury neighborhood, was destined to enter politics. His father, maternal grandfather, and father-in-law all served as presidents of the Boston City Council. In 1960, the thirty-one-year-old White became the secretary of the commonwealth. Seven years later he was elected mayor of the city in a hotly contested race against Louise Day Hicks, a member of the Boston School Committee and staunch defender of her South Boston. Hicks ran under the platform, "You know where I stand." Her campaign spoke to her undying defense of the status quo in the Boston schools, which had been ruled to be desegregated two years earlier by order of Governor John Volpe.

"Kevin from Heaven" was the tagline for the consummate politician who had learned Boston politics through birthright. The task ahead of Mayor White was viewed by some as unenviable and by others as impossible. He would hold office at a time when every word spoken, every neighborhood visited, every decision made would be dissected and digested. In response, White adopted a reticent public persona, preferring to conduct city business and determine public policy through backroom negotiations at his offsite office of the Parkman House in Beacon Hill. As a result, he was seen by some contemporaries as out front yet noncommittal. As one senior Boston official described, "He was always in the boat. He just didn't always put his oar in the water."

In his book *The Hub*, Boston historian Thomas O'Connor wrote of White: "He found himself pummeled from all sides, caught between the demands of the black community and the fears of the white neighborhoods, between the authority of federal power and the pride of local authority, between the judicial gavel of Judge Arthur Garrity and the rosary beads of Louise Day Hicks."

From the moment he took office, Mayor White knew the storm was coming. And although he would beseech the city to "face reality," he was fully aware that if the city burned, it would be on his watch. At stake was both the future of the city he loved and his own legacy.

Kevin White's first task as the mayor of Boston was to plan and organize the dedication of the New City Hall. The plans were to welcome all of Boston to a weeklong calendar of events. The formal dedication was scheduled for 10:00 a.m. on February 10, 1969. That evening, a black-tie gala was to feature a performance by Arthur Fiedler and the Boston Pops.

On February 9, the mayor stood in his new office on the fifth floor, looked out at the Government Center courtyard, and watched as a snowflake touched down on one of the endless rows of hardened bricks. His week of great promise was in danger of being cancelled. In less than twenty-four hours, the city of Boston was supposed to dedicate its new landmark building, but the weather forecast was ominous.

The sounds of bagpipers drifted into his office through the concrete hallways and stairwells. The mayor was expected downstairs to greet the construction workers who had helped bring the vision of Gerhard Kallman, Noel McKinnel, and Edward Knowles to reality. Before he headed downstairs, White took one last look out his window. Snow started to fill the Boston sky and cover the courtyard bricks.

The nor'easter would continue to blanket the city in snow for two days. It was called the biggest storm in twenty years. More than thirty inches of snow fell on Boston and the surrounding communities. Logan Airport was closed, as were all major freeways, stranding more than two thousand cars in highway lanes. The snow was so heavy and deep that fourteen deaths were reported caused by shoveling the heavy wet snow. The City Hall dedication was cancelled.

Throughout Boston, the city's elite were all dressed up with no party to go to. In the empty corridors of City Hall, lily and tulip arrangements wilted and petals fell to the cold floor. It was Kevin White's hope that the new building would "symbolize a fresh concern with the future of urban America and a new beginning toward resolution of its conflicts and problems." The building, in White's words, could help to "bridge the gap between government and people."

But on the day of the building's christening, there was no government or people to bridge. Instead, the mayor sat in his empty building and announced to the city that Boston was in a State of Emergency. There would be no party, no emptied punch bowls, no sweet sounds of the Boston Pops.

For three centuries, the Athens of America had thrived and prospered. Now a building sat perched on the gravesite of Scollay Square promising to bridge an abyss that was destined only to broaden.

CHAPTER 4

"I'm Through with Basketball"

AS THE SNOW FELL ACROSS THE CITY IN FEBRUARY 1969, THE ATTENTION OF BOSTONIANS WAS DIVIDED BETWEEN THE CITY HALL DEDICATION AT CONGRESS STREET AND THE RETURN OF CELTIC GREAT BILL RUSSELL TO THE BOSTON GARDEN. One week earlier, Russell had suffered a devastating injury in a game against the New York Knicks. He had crashed onto the parquet floor in the closing seconds after desperately throwing his body toward the basket in a failed effort to score and prevent yet another loss. The loss dropped the once-great Celtics four and a half games out of first place, and the wounded warrior was taken by police motorcade to University Hospital.

At the hospital, Russell lay helpless in bed with a throbbing knee and an exhausted body. In one corner of the room, team physician Dr. Tom Silva consulted with Red Auerbach and Russell's wife, Rose. Silva was concerned with not only the acutely strained knee ligaments but also the overall physical condition of the star center. The doctor implored Red and Russell's wife to persuade the stubborn patient to accept the prescribed treatment of seven days of hospital rest and physical therapy.

With his arms folded across his checkered sport coat, Red listened intently to Silva's warnings. Then, heeding the advice, the Celtic patriarch walked over to the closet, gathered the center's clothes, and handed them to Rose. He wished her good night and advised her not to bring a change of wardrobe until Dr. Silva approved. Red then made his way over to the bedside of the injured player, turned to Silva, and declared with a smile, "Now he'll stay."

To Auerbach, Russell wasn't only the cornerstone of the Celtics dynasty, he was like a son. Back in 1956, Red had traded two future Hall of Famers for the draft pick that would net the center. Russell had just led the University of San Francisco Dons to back-to-back NCAA championships and captained Team U.S.A. to a gold medal at the 1956 Olympics in Melbourne.

In Russell's first year in Boston, 1957, the Celtics won their first NBA Championship. In the twelve seasons heading into the 1968–69 campaign, the Celtics had won ten championships. But the music was beginning to fade. The tired, thirty-four-year-old Russell carried more than just the burden of playing forty-three minutes a game; now he also carried the responsibility of coaching. Auerbach had named Russell the team's player-coach in 1967, making him the first black head coach in professional sports history. In Red's estimation, Bill Russell was the only person who could motivate Bill Russell at that point in his career. As teammate Rick Weitzman described Coach Russell, "His coaching was only as good as his best player played—himself."

Motivation and thirst for excellence were never an issue for Russell—just the contrary. The man played the game with such intensity and fear of failure that he routinely got violently ill before a game. When he would reappear in the locker room from his episode of regurgitation, his teammates one and all knew that that "beautiful retching sound" meant that he was ready to play.

This unparalleled commitment resulted in an abbreviated period of convalescence at University Hospital in 1969. One week after Russell's injury, the Celtics found themselves in a five-game losing streak, including three straight losses with Auerbach at the helm in Russell's place. Now six and half games out of first place with only twenty-five games to play, a desperate Auerbach allowed the determined center to strap on his knee brace and lace up his black sneakers.

The night's opponent was the Philadelphia 76ers, featuring All-Stars Billy Cunningham and Hal Greer. Not much was expected from Russell, who limped badly throughout warm-ups. He ended up playing 45 minutes and grabbed 23 rebounds. Just prior to the buzzer at the end of regulation, the gimpy center tied the game with an alley-oop pass. The Celtics went on to win the game, 122-117, in overtime.

The Celtics finished the season in fourth place in the Eastern Division with a record of 48-34, good enough to secure the last playoff slot. They proceeded to upset the Sixers (4-1) and then the Knicks (4-2) in the first two playoff rounds, setting up yet another showdown with the Los Angeles Lakers in the NBA Finals. In the previous seven years, the Celtics had met the Lakers five times—and defeated them all five times. In 1969, however, all indicators pointed to a Lakers championship. Prior to the season, Los Angeles had acquired Wilt Chamberlain in a trade, giving them a trio of Hall of Famers in Chamberlain, Jerry West, and Elgin Baylor.

The Lakers had won the Western Division with a 55-27 regular-season record and thus earned home-court advantage in the finals. The first two games were played on the West Coast, and the Lakers won both behind the shooting of Jerry West, who scored 53 and 41 points, respectively. The weary Celtics limped back home to the Garden, where they faced the possibility of being swept. Wounded but not dead, the prideful Celtics, whose average age was thirty-two, somehow summoned the energy to win Game Three, 111-105. They followed that with an 89-88 victory in Game Four, won on a leaning buzzer-beater from the top of the key by clutch-shooting Sam Jones.

The teams split the next two games, each one winning on its home floor, to send the series back to the Forum in Los Angeles for a decisive Game Seven. During pregame warm-ups, the Celtic players noticed that thousands of purple and gold balloons were tied up in the ceiling in anticipation of a postgame celebration. Back in the locker room before taking the floor, Coach Russell read from a piece of paper that Lakers personnel had left on every seat in the arena: "When the Lakers win the championship, the USC Marching Band will play 'Happy Days Are Here Again.' Balloons in the rafters will fall down. And [Lakers announcer] Chick Hearn will interview Jerry West, Elgin Baylor, and Wilt Chamberlain."

Russell stroked his goatee and then set his hands on his hips, as he often did, with his thumbs on his hips and fingers on the back pointed at one other. He lifted his eyes and addressed his team in the recesses of the LA Forum: "One thing that cannot happen, the Lakers cannot beat us. It's not something that can happen. But it will be fun watching the Lakers get those balloons out one at a time."

The Celtics responded to the pregame speech. They outran, outscored, and outrebounded the younger Lakers. By the fourth quarter, they were up by 17 points. The Lakers, with a hurt Wilt Chamberlain on the bench, cut the lead to 1 point late in the game, but the Celtics held off Jerry West and the Lakers. Boston won the game 108-106 to secure its eleventh championship in thirteen years. A record crowd of 17,568 Lakers fans went home without hearing the promised rendition of "Happy Days Are Here Again." In the press box, Celtics

announcer Johnny Most reported, "The Celtics have done it again in spectacu-
lar fashion." Down in the runway leading to the locker room, Red Auerbach
asked ABC announcer Jack Twyman, "What are they going to do with all
those balloons up there?"

In the locker room, Russell was emotionally and physically drained. He
had led the Celtics with 19 rebounds, multiple blocked shots, and unparalleled
leadership. The playoff game was the 165th of his career and the 9th Game
Seven, of which he had won all 9. In the ABC booth, Chris Schenkel closed
out the telecast by declaring the Celtics the "greatest sports dynasty in the
history of athletics."

🏀

After the 1969 championship, Bill Russell had nothing more to accomplish
in the game of basketball. He was a five-time Most Valuable Player. He had
more championship rings than fingers, the last two earned as a player-coach.
He was tired.

That summer, Celtic fans nationwide picked up the August 4 issue of
Sports Illustrated and saw Bill Russell on the cover of the magazine. He was
sitting in a golf cart wearing a short-sleeve yellow mock turtleneck and a
relaxed smile on his face. It was as if the pressures of the world had been lifted
from his shoulders. The headline read, "I'm Through with Basketball—Bill
Russell announces his retirement and tells why."

And with that, he was gone—and glad to be gone. From 1956 through
the spring of 1969, Russell demanded and earned respect playing basketball
in the Boston Garden. Sadly, because he was a black man, that same respect
was not forthcoming when he was off the parquet floor. In a *Sports Illustrated*
article from February 1958, writer Jeremiah Tax described Russell as "desperately sensitive about his height and about being a Negro, about standing taller
than a world of smaller men, and standing out in a world of white men."

Following one of the championship seasons, the town of Reading, where Bill Russell lived (only because he couldn't find proper housing in Boston), toasted the Celtic great at a local country club. Teammate Tom Heinsohn was in attendance and recalled the occasion: "Russell was so touched by the out-pouring of love that when he got up to speak, he cried. It was the only time I had ever seen him cry. When he finally gathered himself, he made a short speech and said, 'This is so nice. I want to live here the rest of my life.' It wasn't long after that that Bill tried to move into a nicer neighborhood in the town, but the people in the town put together a petition to keep him out."

During Russell's time in Reading, his house was broken into several times, including once when the perpetrators destroyed his trophies, defecated on his bed, and wrote racial epithets on his bedroom walls. It was this type of wickedness that caused Russell to build the wall of disdain for the city and its people.

In his book *Cousy on the Celtic Mystique*, Bob Cousy attributed to Bill Russell such quotes as, "I hate all white people"; "Boston is the most bigoted city in the United States"; and "I'd rather be in jail in Sacramento than mayor of Boston."

The hurt and bitterness were profound. Russell could never reconcile the lack of love he and other blacks received in the city. When it came time for his number to be retired in March 1972, he demanded that it be done before the game, with no fans present in the Boston Garden. Auerbach, although unhappy about the request, was sensitive to Russell's feelings and accepted the center's wishes. At 12:55 p.m., prior to an ABC telecast of a Celtics game at which Russell was working as an analyst, Auerbach joined the Celtic legend on the parquet floor, surrounded by only empty seats, as the number 6 was raised to the rafters.

Later during the game, the ABC analyst was saluted with a rousing stand-ing ovation. Russell refused to acknowledge the gesture, and the fans were insulted by the snub. The reasons behind it became clearer a year later when they read Bill Russell's comments in the *Boston Globe* in November 1973: "The years I played in Boston were very traumatic. I didn't enjoy staying here. Racism, bigotry, segregation. I couldn't stay on the court all my life and live in a vacuum that's only 48 minutes of the day."

In 1975, when Russell refused to attend his Hall of Fame induction ceremony, *Globe* writer Ray Fitzgerald had harsh words for the former center: "You can continue to make your living in a sport and at the same time kick it in the teeth, something you seem to be very good at. People cheered you for a dozen years in Boston, and you kicked them in the teeth when they wanted to honor you. You labeled them racists—13,909 racists who merely wanted to let you know they loved the way you played basketball."

Russell's place as both a celebrity and a victim of social injustice in Boston allowed him a rare perspective of the "city on the hill." For thirteen years, he had committed his soul to the green jersey emblazoned with the word *Boston* across its front. He had earned, at the very least, the right to share his concerns about the state of the city. He felt the breeze of an impending storm, and in June 1966 he spoke of this storm as he addressed the graduating class of the Patrick Campbell School in Roxbury, the city's predominant black neighborhood. One year earlier, Martin Luther King had appeared on the steps of the same school with a blow horn and warned, "Some things that are wrong in Alabama are wrong in Boston." Now Bill Russell stood before its outgoing students and offered his own warning: "The fire that consumes Roxbury consumes Boston. The fire will spread."

CHAPTER 5

The Liberator

AS TWO PRO-SLAVERY ADVOCATES DRAGGED ABOLITIONIST WILLIAM LLOYD GARRISON FROM THE ANTI-SLAVERY BUILDING IN OCTOBER 1835, A STIR RAN THROUGH THE CROWD LIKE AN ELECTRICAL CURRENT. It started as a suggestion, turned into conversation, and evolved into a consensus. The mob of five thousand began to roar in such a unified voice that their call could be heard clearly up and down Washington Street: "Out with him! Lynch him, lynch him, lynch him!"

The horde ultimately elected to take Garrison to City Hall and leave it to the mayor to act. So they dragged him along Washington to State Street. In defiance, Garrison declared, "If my life be taken, the cause of emancipation will not suffer."

The crowd arrived with their captive at the back of Old City Hall and demanded that Mayor Theodore Lyman, who was a proponent for slavery, lead the mob in the removal of this voice that was contrary to theirs. The mayor was torn between his beliefs and his duties to oversee the civil obedience of his people. Hoping to save the life of Garrison but still appease the mob, he declaimed that the imprisoned would be arrested for "disturbing the peace" and transported to the local jail.

At the south side of City Hall, a decoy hack and horses arrived at the gate, causing a crowd to swell. Only when assured that the crowd was distracted did the police rush the abolitionist, under the guise of hat and new clothes, out through the north door, where another horse-drawn carriage awaited. As the seconds passed, the crowd at the south entrance grew suspicious and surged across the grounds to the horse and carriage that was carrying the prisoner. Enraged by the dupe, the mob swung open the doors of the carrier and grabbed the reins of the horses. But not for the courage of the skilled driver, who was liberal with his whip, was he able to free his transport. He then galloped across the Cambridge Bridge, which traversed the Charles River and separated Boston from Cambridge, to distract any unwanted pursuers, only to double back and deliver his cargo safely to the Leverett Street Jail. On the following morning, October 22, 1835, Garrison was released and transported to Canton, Massachusetts, where he met his wife and boarded a train to Providence and then Connecticut to find refuge at the home of his wife's family.

William Lloyd Garrison, who was born in Newburyport northeast of Boston, was a tireless advocate of the abolitionist movement for more than thirty years. In 1831, he established the anti-slavery newspaper *The Liberator*, which he would publish for 1,820 straight weeks until the end of the Civil War. In his first publication, Garrison introduced himself to the readers of Boston:

> I am aware that many object to the severity of my language, but
> is there not cause for severity? I will be as harsh as truth, and

as uncompromising as justice. On this subject I do not wish to think, or speak, or write with moderation. No! No! Tell a man whose house is on fire to give a moderate alarm; tell him moderately to rescue his wife from the hands of the ravisher; tell the mother to gradually extricate her babe from the fire into which it has fallen; but urge me not to use moderation in a cause like the present. I am in earnest—I will not equivocate—I will not excuse—I will not retreat a single inch—and I will be heard.

Garrison's courageous paper galvanized those who wished to provide equal rights to all people, as promised in the Constitution of the United States. His unwavering quest also made him the target of many throughout the country. He received hundreds of death threats and had a $5,000 bounty set upon him by the Georgia legislature. A supporter from Philadelphia forwarded him the following warning: "Your life is sought after, and a reward of twenty thousand dollars has been offered by six Mississippians for your head. Be aware of the assassin. May God protect you."

The Liberator was published on Boston's Cornhill Street, which lay in the shadow of Faneuil Hall. Cornhill Street was where runaway slaves sought refuge while traveling through Boston on the way to Canada on the Underground Railroad, and where Harriett Beecher Stowe wrote her international bestseller, *Uncle Tom's Cabin*, which sold more than five hundred thousand copies in 1852 alone. It was also there that Garrison's adversaries placed gallows in an attempt to intimidate him.

After years of unwavering attention to the cause of abolishing slavery, Garrison's dreams became reality when President Abraham Lincoln declared all held in servitude throughout the land emancipated. To celebrate, Garrison and other supporters of equal rights gathered on New Year's Day 1863 at the Boston Music Hall. During this commemoration of the Emancipation Proclamation, a cheer was lifted for President Lincoln, followed by a resounding salute for the fervent leader of the cause: "Three cheers for Garrison!"

Years later, at a memorial service following Garrison's death, runaway slave-turned-statesman Frederick Douglass said of the anti-slavery activist, "[He] moved not with the tide, but against it. His zeal was like fire, and his courage like steel. . . . The man was then and will ever be regarded as the chief apostle of the immediate and unconditional emancipation of all the slaves in America. . . . It was the glory of this man that he could stand alone with the truth, and calmly await the result."

The "chief apostle," as Douglass aptly described Garrison, was not the lone Boston voice to demand equal rights for all. In 1842, more than sixty-five thousand interested parties joined forces in a petition to urge the liberation of runaway slave George Latimer, who had been jailed. This spirit of human kindness was more than a movement; it was a way of life that permeated the streets of Boston.

⊕

Frederick Douglass himself settled in the Boston area to pursue his life of freedom; he raised his family in the city of Lynn on Massachusetts' North Shore. Other prominent runaway slaves and anti-slavery activists were drawn to Boston for its tradition of fighting to protect human rights, among them Harriet Tubman, who frequently traveled through Boston as she led runaway slaves to freedom on the Underground Railroad.

The city's spirit of justice inspired not just rhetoric but action. Bostonians believed in the principle of providing opportunity to all, and that included the opportunity to fight for the country. Three months after the Emancipation Proclamation, Massachusetts Governor John A. Andrew presented and U.S. Secretary of War Edwin M. Stanton approved the proposition that a regiment of soldiers be formed among the black citizens of Boston and nearby communities. The regiment would be led by twenty-five-year-old Robert Gould Shaw, the son of abolitionists from Boston's West Roxbury neighborhood. Shaw, who would be named colonel, was provided with 1,007 recruits, among them Frederick Douglass' sons, Lewis and Charles.

The 54th Massachusetts Volunteer Infantry Regiment fought valiantly for the Union Army. Their defining moment of courage came on July 18, 1863, when the 54th led the charge on the formidable Confederate stronghold of Fort Wagner in Charleston, South Carolina. During the assault, seventy-five soldiers in the regiment were killed, including Colonel Shaw. Among the wounded was Sergeant William Carney, who had been shot three times but still somehow summoned the strength to secure and return the American flag after the bearer of the colors had been shot and killed. When he presented the flag to Union troops, he proclaimed, "Boys, I only did my duty; the old flag never touched the ground!"

For his bravery, Sergeant Carney became the first African American to receive the Medal of Honor. The citation read, "When the color sergeant was shot down, this soldier grasped the flag, led the way to the parapet, and planted the colors thereon. When the troops fell back he brought off the flag, under a fierce fire in which he was twice severely wounded."

On Memorial Day 1897, the 54th Regiment Memorial statue was dedicated in Boston Common with Carney in attendance. The statue's inscription read, in part, "Together they gave to the nation and the world undying proof that Americans of African descent possess the pride, courage, and devotion of the Patriot soldier."

As the struggle for racial equality marched into the twentieth century, Boston continued to nurture and attract proponents of civil rights. William Monroe Trotter, an influential force in the creation of the National Association for the Advancement of Colored People (NAACP) and a longtime activist, lived in the Boston neighborhood of Hyde Park. W. E. B. Dubois, one of the founders of the NAACP and one of the most influential black leaders in the first half of the century, often spoke from the pulpit at Community Church in Boston. Many years later, Martin Luther King Jr. spoke from that same pulpit. King received his doctorate of divinity at Boston University, was a minister at the Twelfth Baptist Church in Roxbury, and considered Boston more than a stop on his journey in the struggle for equality for all. "I have a love for Boston," he said. "It is one of the cities I consider my home." That's where he met his wife, Coretta Scott, who studied music at the New England Conservatory.

In the 1940s, two influential men resided in the city's Roxbury neighborhood: Malcolm Little and Gene Walcott. Little, more familiarly known by his adopted Muslim name of Malcolm X, worked at the Parker House hotel as a bus boy and later at the New Haven Railroad before being incarcerated at Charlestown Prison for grand larceny. There he found the Nation of Islam. Gene Walcott, who attended Boston Latin School and later Boston English, also found peace in the Nation of Islam, where he took the name Louis Farrakhan. Edward Brooke, a native of Washington, D.C., earned a law degree at Boston University, and in 1966 he was elected to the United States Senate for Massachusetts to become the first black senator since Reconstruction and the first ever elected in a northern state.

❦

For more than two centuries, African Americans have influenced, affected, and impacted the city of Boston. From the broken chains of slavery, from the South and the West Indies, blacks have migrated to the Northeast hub of Massachusetts. At the center of the growing community is the neighborhood known as Roxbury. The town was originally named Rocksbury because of the hilly, puddingstone-filled terrain upon which the town was founded in 1630.

Set on a narrow stretch of land known as Roxbury Neck, the town was coveted for its strategic location and for the composition of its land. Travelers wishing to enter or depart Boston three and half miles to the north had to traverse this isthmus. George Washington and his men were entrenched in Roxbury during the Revolutionary War because of its strategic significance in the struggle for independence.

In 1901, when Roxbury was populated mostly by Irish, English, and German immigrants, Dudley Station was constructed as the southernmost point on the Boston elevated railway at the intersection of Warren, Washington, and Dudley Streets in the heart of the neighborhood. Soon thereafter, commerce, housing, and other communal activity gravitated to the Dudley area because of its easy access.

The face of Roxbury continued to change through the twentieth century. A large Jewish population came to the Grove Hall section of the neighborhood in the early 1900s. In the years following World War II, blacks fleeing the Jim Crow South headed to Boston in droves seeking employment at the many industrial plants and naval yards located throughout the city and surrounding towns.

In his book *The Hub*, Thomas O'Connor describes how Boston's black population nearly doubled in just one decade, increasing from some twenty-three thousand in 1940 to more than forty thousand in 1950. By 1960, that number had grown to sixty-three thousand.

This dramatic population shift had a considerable impact on Boston. Money and resources that in the past had been allocated to white communities now had to be divided accordingly. Those who controlled the city's purse strings didn't easily accept this new reality, and tensions escalated throughout the 1960s. The status quo was being questioned. College campuses rebelled, draft cards were burned, women demanded equal standing, and minorities of all races attempted to lay claim to their Constitutional rights.

Boston, like most big cities, struggled to maintain harmony and civil obedience. In an effort to bridge the ever-expanding schism among the varied interest groups, the city called upon Celtic stars Satch Sanders and Sam Jones, who were black, to use their cache as professional basketball players to serve as ambassadors of peace. But most people were less interested in jump shots and more interested in who was getting the teaching jobs and the allocations of city funds.

Even with the dramatic growth of Boston's black community, African Americans still only represented 15 percent of the city's population. They lacked the ability to influence the decision-making voices at the State House, City Hall, or School Committee.

Prominent voices such as the Reverend Michael Haynes of Twelfth Baptist Church in Roxbury sensed a desperate mood beginning to engulf the city. "Boston had this simmering rage that existed in the underbelly of the city," Haynes recalled years later. "Everything was subtle. Boston had an image of a good city, but the Boston black community was being pushed aside. It was like a tumor that kept getting moved from one side to the other that was inevitably going to turn from benign to malignant."

Issues of housing, job initiatives, and transportation were of great significance to Boston's African Americans, but education was a primary concern. Facilities were sorely deficient; students often had to wear winter coats in the classroom because of lack of heating. While books and supplies were also lacking in public schools in many white communities, the greatest discrepancy was in the quality of the teachers. Schools were often rudderless, with vacant principal and headmaster's offices, and the most skilled teachers avoided the poorer neighborhoods, which frequently overlaid the black schools.

As the city of Boston struggled with inferior educational resources, many colleges and school systems throughout the country were reacting, albeit belatedly and reluctantly, to the 1954 Supreme Court ruling in *Brown v. the Board of Education of Topeka*. In that landmark decision, the nation's highest court declared that "separate educational facilities are inherently unequal" and in violation of the Fourteenth Amendment of the Constitution. In Little Rock, Arkansas, at the University of Mississippi, and at the University of Alabama, federal troops and personnel were called in to facilitate integration efforts.

Attempts to integrate the Boston schools, meanwhile, were consistently rebuked. Increasingly frustrated by the refusal of the school administrators to abide by the Supreme Court ruling, the black community decided to take matters into its own hands. In June 1963, the NAACP organized a "Stay Out For Freedom" day, in which eight thousand students did not attend school— "staying out for education and not against it." A second "Stay Out For Freedom" day was held in February 1964, and twenty thousand students were absent from school despite public expressions of disapproval by Mayor John Collins, Governor Endicott Peabody, and Cardinal Cushing, the head cleric of the Boston Archdiocese.

In response to pressure from the NAACP and the people it represented, the state government formed an advisory committee—the Massachusetts State Advisory Committee to the United States Commission on Civil Rights—to measure and chart the racial makeup of the Boston public schools. Their findings were presented to Governor John Volpe in January 1965. Based on a census of the school system—elementary, junior high, and high schools—the committee found that, of the 91,800 students in the school system, 70,703 (77 percent) were white and 21,097 were non-white (23 percent). At the high school level, the citywide student body was 86 percent white and 14 percent non-white across the sixteen schools. East Boston High School and South Boston High School were found to have zero African-American students. The committee further stated that "to the extent that Negro children in Boston are concentrated in predominantly Negro schools as a result of private residential patterns and not as a result of official policies, the result may be described as 'racial imbalance,' 'segregation in the schools,' or 'de facto segregation.'"

The Massachusetts State Advisory Committee concluded that a sound education is adversely affected by racial imbalance in the following ways:

1. Racial imbalance damages the self-confidence and motivation of Negro children.
2. Racial imbalance reinforces the prejudices of children regardless of color.
3. Racial imbalance does not prepare the child for integrated life in a multi-racial community, nation, and world.
4. Racial imbalance impairs the opportunities of many Negro children to prepare for the vocational requirements of our technological society.
5. Racial imbalance often results in a gap in the quality of educational facilities among schools.
6. Racial imbalance in the public schools represents a serious conflict with the American creed of equal opportunity.

After assessing the committee's findings, Governor Volpe introduced the Racial Imbalance Act to state legislators in August 1965. In June of the following year, the governor signed the bill into law, mandating that the Boston School Committee work to eradicate racial imbalance from the city schools or risk losing state funding.

There was no turning back now. Centuries of good intentions and the spirit of tolerance had made Boston a destination for those seeking a new beginning and a better way of life. Now, the city would become a battleground in which the adversaries were identified as much by their race as by their beliefs. The storm that threatened the city the night Garrison was dragged through the streets was sweeping across Boston's neighborhoods again, where the battle cries of "undemocratic" and "empowerment" were heard above the gusting winds that imperiled the Hub of the Universe.

CHAPTER 6

"I'm Never Going to Be a Star"

TOMMY HEINSOHN SAT IN A SEATTLE RESTAURANT READING THE MORN-ING'S NEWSPAPER OVER A PLATE OF EGGS AND BACON. It was January 1959, and the team had just arrived from San Francisco and was taking a moment to eat as a team. They always did everything as a team. They ate together, partied together, and won together. On the previous night, the Celtics had beaten their old nemesis, the Minneapolis Lakers, 109-106, in the first game of a two-game barnstorming tour in which the teams introduced the NBA to the West Coast. For their trouble, the Celtics were paid $10,000, of which $6,000 went to travel and hotel expenses.

While the front page of the paper presented stories of Castro's march on Havana and America's new state of Alaska, the special four-page section on the upcoming night's game is what interested the burley forward from Holy Cross. In each column of the four pages, article after article introduced the readers to the NBA game and the stars of the two teams. One story trumpeted the return of rookie sensation Elgin Baylor, who had been a collegiate All-American at Seattle University; other columns acquainted readers with the magic of the fast-breaking Bob Cousy, the intimidating defense of Bill Russell, the sharp shooting of Bill Sharman, and the wily coaching of Red Auerbach—but none referred to Heinsohn. To get noticed, he would have to do something special in front of the eleven thousand fans who would attend the sold-out game at the University of Washington Pavilion.

Putting down the paper next to his runny eggs, Heinsohn took a distracted sip of his coffee. He was mildly disturbed by the slight. Sure, his shooting touch had been off, but he had been playing on a bad knee. He wondered what it would take to be recognized as a star. Just two years earlier, in his rookie season of 1956–57, Heinsohn was a major contributor to the team's first championship. The rookie put the Celtics on his back in Game Seven of the NBA Finals against the St. Louis Hawks, scoring 37 points and grabbing 23 rebounds. Following the game, teammate Bill Sharman couldn't restrain himself in his praise of Heinsohn: "What a show Tommy put on. I never saw anyone play like that under pressure, let alone a rookie." Point guard Bob Cousy extended further the praise of the star rookie: "The kid's the greatest. What pressure and how he played under it." He had been selected to the All-Star Game that season and went on to be voted the league's Rookie of the Year—although even that moment had been tainted when Bill Russell walked by his locker at the Garden and teased, "You're lucky I was at the Olympics until December, because that [award] would have been mine."

As quickly as the moment of reflection had clouded his breakfast, Heinsohn allowed it to pass. He dismissed the paper and returned to enjoy what was so special about his team—their genuine regard for one another. All around the tables, players laughed and teased and told embellished tales of basketball greatness and supposed smiles from pretty girls in the crowd.

Later that night, the Celtics defeated the Lakers 117-108. The lead scorer in the game was Celtic forward Tom Heinsohn, who put up 38 points while pulling down 14 rebounds. Playing on a team that had seven future Hall of Famers, he was the star that night.

The following morning, while sitting at a Howard Johnson's with teammates Bill Russell, Frank Ramsey, and Gene Conley, Heinsohn opened up the paper and found a two-page spread on the previous night's events. As he read, he searched for his name, but it was lost among articles recounting tales of Baylor's brilliance or Russell's intimidation at the rim or Cousy's behind-the-back passes. It wasn't until the very last line on the page did he read, "And Heinsohn had 38 points."

Heinsohn set down the paper. Leaning over to whisper in Gene Conley's ear, he confided, "I'm never going to be a star."

Tommy Heinsohn was first introduced to Celtic ways in 1955 when he was a senior at Holy Cross. During his final college season, Red Auerbach traveled to Worcester to scout one of Heinsohn's games. As Auerbach was leaving, in an attempt at both cleverness and manipulation, he shared with the media, "He couldn't play for me unless he takes off that baby fat." The comment was hurtful, as would be many comments from the legendary coach over the next ten years. From the day Heinsohn showed up at his first Celtics camp, he served as the coach's whipping boy, taking the brunt of Red's frustrations while the sensitive Russell was spared the wrath of the man with the rolled-up program.

After the West Coast tour, the Celtics continued on to the 1959 NBA finals, where they swept the Lakers 4-0 for their third NBA championship. Over the next five years, they would sustain their reign of dominance by capturing the crown in each of those seasons. Prior to the 1964–65 campaign, Heinsohn announced that he would retire at the conclusion of the season. That April, the Boston team again found itself in the finals against the team from

Los Angeles. After four games, the Celtics held a decisive three-games-to-one lead and were ahead late in the fifth game by a healthy margin. At the end of the bench sat a perplexed Heinsohn. Coaches, family, teammates, and fans knew that this was the last time the forward would lace up his black sneakers. He wondered throughout the game when Auerbach was going turn to the bench and yell "Heinsohn!" one more time. But the call never came. Instead, the future Hall of Famer sat with his sweat coat still buttoned while Red lit his victory cigar. When the horn finally sounded, the score on the scoreboard over center court read Celtics 129, Lakers 96. Heinsohn wasn't able to thank the crowd from the parquet floor, nor were the fans able to thank him for his nine years of sweat, hook shots, and hard-earned rebounds. He would walk to the locker room with eight championships and a sour taste in his mouth.

Heinsohn and Auerbach never talked about the slight. What they did talk about was the passing of the head-coaching responsibilities after the subsequent season. Red was tired, and the dual duties of coach and general manager were becoming too burdensome. The idea of taking over the coaching job intrigued the newly retired forward. The position would allow him to stay in the game and, more important, remain a part of the Celtic family. In the end, however, he was unsure that he would be able to effectively motivate the team's star center. Instead, Heinsohn recommended to Red that he make Russell player-coach, which he did.

Heinsohn waited three years for the coach's seat to open up again. As he waited, Russell's teams captured two more championships. At long last, in the summer of 1969, Heinsohn was named head coach, conditionally. "You've got the job," he was told, "if Russell doesn't come back." It wasn't until the first day of training camp, when Russell didn't walk through the door, that Heinsohn was officially named coach.

Although it was the job he coveted, Heinsohn was saddled with all the expectations that came with being the custodian of the greatest franchise in sports history. When Auerbach took the Celtics' coaching job in 1950, the team's prospects were modest. In the four seasons previous to Red's arrival, the Celtics had never won more games than they lost. When Russell took over the position from Auerbach, he had Bill Russell. In the fall of 1969, Heinsohn had neither Russell nor Sam Jones, who also had retired. The roster was diminished.

Further complicating matters was the timing of Russell's retirement announcement. By declaring that he was done so late in the summer (August 4), the former center had limited the Celtics' options for the pivot position. In late August, the team acquired center Hank Finkel from the San Diego Rockets. Finkel arrived in town with the awesome responsibility of being asked to fill the shoes of the greatest team player in sports history.

In the *Boston Globe's* preview of the 1969–70 NBA season, Leigh Montville pointed to Finkel as the critical piece in the upcoming campaign: "Henry Finkel, who is the seven-foot guy with the name of the next-door neighbor in a television comedy, will try to be ready. He has to be ready if the Celtics are going to do anything. It's that simple."

Finkel was a hard-working basketball player with limitations. In the previous year, he averaged only 3.7 points and 3.1 rebounds. When Boston forward Larry Siegfried was asked before the season his impressions of the tenuous center position, he candidly remarked, "It all depends on what Hank does. No one can be another Russell. He was one of a kind."

Despite the question mark at center, the Celtics were ready and confident heading into the season. In their final preseason game, new coach Tommy Heinsohn was ejected after receiving two technical fouls. ("It won't be the last time I'm ejected," he declared.) As Heinsohn walked off the court and into the locker room, General Manager Red Auerbach slid into the head coach's chair and took over the team for the rest of the game. Heinsohn soon came to realize that despite his bearing the title of coach, the team was, and always would be, Red Auerbach's. After a tough loss, it was not unusual for Red to come into the locker room to lecture the team on effort and Celtic Pride. During some games, the general manager would sit directly to Heinsohn's left at the press table, offering advice and berating officials, giving people the impression that he, not Heinsohn, was the man at the controls.

On October 17, 1969, the Celtics raised their eleventh championship flag to the rafters. Following the ceremony, they opened the season against the Bob Cousy–coached Cincinnati Royals. Even with the pregame festivities, the Boston Garden was not sold out for the opener, nor would it be for any game the entire season. The Celtics lost the opener to the Royals 110-108. They would lose their first four games of the season and finish the year with a record of 34-48. It was the first time in twenty seasons that the Celtics failed to make the playoffs.

After the final buzzer sounded to end the season, the sparse Garden crowd filed out to Causeway Street serenaded by organist John Kiley's rendition of "Auld Lang Syne." As the organ droned, Coach Heinsohn stood in the locker room trying to reconcile a season of losing in an organization that didn't lose. He was asked what the team needed to be successful next year. He pondered the question and then answered simply, "What we need is Russell."

Although Russell would not be coming back, the Celtics would soon be getting the help they needed. In the upcoming draft, they selected forward Dave Cowens from Florida State with the fourth overall pick. The six-foot-nine, fiery redhead from Kentucky was described prior to the draft as "an underrated center never receiving his just recognition."

Soon, he would be recognized.

CHAPTER 7
"The Do-Nothing Committee"

IN 1972, THE BOSTON SCHOOL COMMITTEE WAS INTERVIEWING CAN-
DIDATES FOR THE VACANT SUPERINTENDENT'S POSITION. As part
of the search, they formed an advisory committee, which interviewed
students. The committee asked the students what qualities they felt were
essential for the overseer of the schools. The students made the following
recommendations: (1) The person should be a good communicator; (2) the
person should care about kids; and (3) the person should be able to get our
parents to get over their "race hang-ups."

✺

On February 5, 1848, Sarah Roberts walked from her home to the neighborhood school. When she entered the building, she was summarily ejected by the
school master because she was "colored." In response, her father, Benjamin
Franklin Roberts, a black printer from Boston, turned to the courts to intervene.
The Roberts family was represented by a legal team of prominent Bostonian

and noted abolitionist Charles Sumner and a young black attorney by the name of Robert Morris.

The Boston School Committee oversaw a segregated school system and defended its right to do so. At the time of the lawsuit, Boston had 161 primary schools dedicated to white students and 2 schools dedicated to "colored" pupils. Sarah Roberts was assigned to the Abiel Smith School on Belknap Street, which was 2,100 feet from her home. Sumner pointed out that the plaintiff's daughter, at great inconvenience, had to walk past five primary schools to get to her assigned school. He also argued that separate schools inevitably create a caste system in which one group is perceived as inferior and the other as superior.

The case of *Roberts* v. *Boston* was heard by chief justice of the Massachusetts Supreme Judicial Court, Lemuel Shaw, in 1850. After hearing arguments from both parties, Judge Shaw ruled that the school committee was within its constitutional rights under the "separate but equal" umbrella to maintain segregated schools. He further stated: "This prejudice, if it exists, is not created by law, and probably cannot be changed by law. Whether this distinction and prejudice, existing in the opinion and feelings of the community, would not be as effectually fostered by compelling colored and white children to associate together in the same schools."

Judge Shaw's ruling would have a long-lasting impact. "Separate but equal" would provide precedence for those who sought to sustain segregated systems over the next century. Although five years later, in 1855, Massachusetts Governor Henry Gardner signed a law abolishing segregated schools, the law and reality were likewise segregated.

🏀

In 1930, Mayor James Michael Curley commissioned a consortium of learned members of the Boston community to author a book chronicling the time period between 1880 and 1930 and also provide the reader a state-of-the-city report on all public issues, including demographic trends, hospital construction, the founding of the Franklin Park Zoo, and the Boston Public Schools. The book was called *Fifty Years of Boston: A Memorial Volume Issue Commemoration Tercentary of 1930*.

In the section on the city schools, the report recorded that the schools admitted students from their respective districts. "In addition to the superior instruction which the students receive in the schools," the book stated, "they have the additional advantage of convenient location and ease of access."

That a student could attend the school in his or her neighborhood was seen as a critical component of the city's educational mission. This "ease of access" allowed students to invest their time in learning and extracurricular activities, and not commuting. And it wasn't just the convenience of a shorter walk to school. The school's close proximity promoted a spirit of community. Often community activities revolved around these schools, as people came together for football games, Christmas pageants, and PTA meetings. Multiple generations of the same family walked those same school hallways with book in hand and dreams in heart.

A neighborhood school produced a spirit of pride and belonging, a feeling of being part of something greater than the insular world that existed within the walls of one's home. To learn and thrive as a young person required a connection to something larger, a link both to the past and to future generations of family, friends, and neighbors. One could find ownership in the crest of an institute's name on a football jersey or an engraving over a school's entrance. It was the neighborhood school that Benjamin Franklin Roberts fought for his daughter to be permitted to attend in the 1840s, and that Oliver Brown fought for his daughter in 1952 against the Board of Education of Topeka, Kansas. They too understood the value of "ease of access" and familiarity in a child's education.

Because the different neighborhoods of Boston were populated by distinct ethnic groups, the corresponding student bodies mirrored the faces that walked the respective sidewalks and played in analogous parks. The enrollment at South Boston High School and Charlestown High School was mostly Irish; East Boston and North End schools were populated primarily by Italian students; and at Roxbury Memorial and English High School, the students were as a majority black.

While "ease of access" provided significant benefits for the children, sociologists and the courts were concerned with the long-lasting effects of "separate" educational facilities and how such a system led to abuse of the practice of "equal" promised by the Fourteenth Amendment. These concerns led to the landmark 1954 Supreme Court ruling in *Brown v. the Board of Education of Topeka*. In the majority opinion, Chief Justice Earl Warren expounded on the virtues of education and the peripheral benefits that stretched beyond reading and arithmetic:

> Today, education is perhaps the most important function of state and local governments. . . . It is required in the performance of our most basic public responsibilities, even service in the armed forces. It is the very foundation of good citizenship. Today it is a principal instrument in awakening the child to cultural values, in preparing him for later professional training, and in helping him to adjust normally to his environment. In these days, it is doubtful that any child may reasonably be expected to succeed in life if he is denied the opportunity of an education. Such an opportunity, where the state has undertaken to provide it, is a right which must be made available to all on equal terms.

Subsequent to this monumental ruling, the bell calling for change rang loudly inside the walls of every school in the country. Some cities and districts refused to answer the bell, while others attempted to adhere to its principles by careful compromise. In Boston, the school committee held tight to its traditions and approached all change with a parochial breath. The ruling by the Supreme Court allowed for interpretation. So Boston interpreted.

In 1961, the Boston school system adopted a policy of Freedom of Choice, or Open Enrollment. School Superintendent Frederick Gillis explained the new policy: "We have had integration, and at the present time any child may go to any school in any grade of any system provided there is a seat vacant for him, after the neighbors have been accommodated, provided the course fits his needs and provided if transportation is necessary his parents will pay the carfare fee."

In theory, this modification to city school policy was a positive step in the direction of desegregation. But in practice, the policy was vague, elusive, and smelled more of appeasement than endorsement. Efforts by black families to gain entrance to a school of choice for their children were often road-blocked by the stranglehold of bureaucracy. Information on available seats in certain schools was scarce, and the phrase "provided there is a seat vacant" was often used as an escape route for those who wanted to maintain the status quo. When representatives from the NAACP walked through the classrooms of Charlestown High School, they found that seats had literally been ripped from the floor, leaving four holes in the linoleum where the seats had once been bolted. If there were no seats, then there were no seats available.

Such practices only added fuel to the fire of a disgruntled black citizenry. The community held boycotts, sit-ins, and other forms of organized action to pressure political representatives. The Reverend Virgil Woods encapsulated the concerns and frustrations of the black community when he stated, "We protest poor and racially imbalanced schools and demand a commitment to a program and time table to end this educational genocide."

In April 1965, the nation's most prominent equal rights leader came "home" to Boston. The Reverend Martin Luther King Jr. came to Boston to support the efforts to desegregate the city's schools. He led a march from Roxbury to the Boston Common with the goal of raising the consciousness of the citizens while rallying the desegregation movement to remain strong and steadfast.

A parade of some twenty-two thousand supporters joined King from Columbus Avenue through the streets of Boston, spreading his message of peace and change. Spectators cheered from buildings, honked horns, and stood ten deep on the sidewalk singing "We Shall Overcome." When the march reached the Boston Common beneath a spitting rain, Dr. King preached from the pulpit in the Parkman Bandstand. "This will go down as one of the greatest days that Boston has ever seen," he proclaimed. "The vision of the new Boston must extend into Roxbury. This is not a battle of white people and black people. It is a struggle between the forces of justice and injustice."

During his thirty-six-hour stay in the city, King met with Mayor John Collins, spoke to a standing-room-only audience at the House of Representatives in the State House, and toured Roxbury. But he never met with the Boston School Committee. When asked why, King answered. "We categorically reject such a meeting. Other Negro leaders have been barred from speaking [by Chairman Louise Day Hicks]." At a dinner that evening, the Reverend King made reference to the school committee and to politicians who were party to maintaining the status quo: "We must remove the Pharaohs who still have hardened hearts."

It was just four months after the civil rights leader's call for change that Governor John Volpe attached his name to the Racial Imbalance Act, thus setting the onus of desegregation on the shoulders of the Boston School Committee and the politicians.

The Boston School Committee was an entrenched organization in the city's political framework, dating back to its establishment on October 20, 1789. More than 175 years later, the committee fiercely protected its sovereignty. The committee continued to serve at the pleasure of its members, seemingly oblivious to the fact that they were obligated to subjugate themselves to the power of the U.S. Constitution.

The five-person Boston School Committee was often more concerned with the benefits of patronage, which superseded the interests of the students who attended the schools and whom they were responsible for overseeing. The phrase "five will get you three" was often uttered in reference to the committee's self-serving, backroom dealings—a nod to the idea that a $5,000 payoff would get you the majority three votes needed to be named principal at a Boston school.

Throughout the 1960s, the Boston School Committee persisted in its efforts to circumvent the collective mandates of the Constitution, the Supreme Court, and the Massachusetts State Legislature requiring the elimination of racial imbalances in the schools. The committee employed acts of defiance that were subtle, such as classifying Asians as whites to show racial balance, as well as not so subtle, such as openly pressuring representatives to sponsor bills to repeal the Racial Imbalance Act (which were routinely defeated). Such actions, however, were merely a forerunner to a blatant act of insolence that would change Boston forever.

In the late 1960s, the State Legislature approved funding for the construction of two schools under the condition that both schools, the Lee School in Dorchester and Hennigan School in Jamaica Plain, would be racially balanced. In exchange for this pledge by the Boston School Committee, funds were made available. On the first day of classes, in 1971, both schools were imbalanced.

The school committee's obstinacy set the city's school system on a course of no return. Those who hoped to overturn the status quo originally sought justice through cooperation. They now came to realize that such a tactic was not feasible. Equality and justice would only be achieved through the radical directive of forced desegregation.

Ever since the 1954 Supreme Court decision declared that the doctrine of "separate but equal" had no place in the field of public education, many sociologists and academics focused their attentions to the question of how to implement desegregation. Tucked behind their insulated collegiate walls, they spread out maps that lacked a pulse and dot-matrix reports without a soul. Master plans were drawn with a mathematician's compass as if school children were merely numerators. Meanwhile, all across Boston, anxious children with packed lunches stuffed in school bags and intrepid parents, who looked to the city to provide a safe learning environment for their children, prayed for Solomon's wisdom to help the tide retreat.

In the end, the proposed solution that emerged from the ivory towers by men with "PhD" at the ends of their names failed to take into account the human chemistry that had been developing in Boston over the past decade or more. The proposal to force segregation by busing students from their own home communities into foreign and ultimately unwelcome neighborhoods to sit in unfamiliar classrooms with unfamiliar classmates was an irrational if not irresponsible solution. Martin Luther King, during his visit to the city in 1965, had addressed his own reservations about busing as a solution to segregated schools. "I would prefer the solution of good faith negotiations," he stated. But good faith was never realized.

From Castle Island in South Boston to the Monument in Charlestown across the Mystic River to Maverick Square in East Boston, cries of "never" from Boston's white communities emboldened their political leaders and a school committee determined to maintain its dominion. Asserting the committee's resistance to the winds of change, member Paul Ellison pledged, "School busing will never be implemented." Committee Chair Louise Day Hicks declared, "The answer to the culturally deprived child will be through education not transportation."

Throughout the white community, however, politicians and their constituents continued to underestimate the momentum and the will of the desegregation movement. For two centuries, the School Committee had been challenged and tested, but time after time it had proven its staying power. Now the black community and its leaders had a new light to rally behind. "When the state legislators stood up and passed [the Racial Imbalance Act]," civil rights leader Paul Parks said, "it set a tone for where we could go. If we could go to the State House, then it was a dawn of a new day. But our work wasn't accomplished there and had to be a real effort to retain what we had gained."

One member of the Boston School Committee, Paul Tierney, did recognize that change was coming, but he couldn't convince his fellow members, who clung to the hope of repeals and legal blockade. In an effort to rouse them from their fixed seats, at a press conference Tierney called out the panel of school overseers and labeled them "the do-nothing committee." His comments echoed those made a decade earlier by another committee member, Arthur Gartland, who said the members "have done nothing to remedy racial imbalance in the schools and have elected to keep imbalance going or to increase it."

The inability of the five-person panel to compromise, and its continuing disregard for the law of the land, inevitably led the issue of school desegregation to be ripped from their hands and placed in the hands of a legal system that would determine the city's fate by the swing of a gavel.

On March 15, 1972, representatives from the Harvard Center for Law and Education filed suit in the First District Court of Massachusetts against the Boston School Committee and extended entities on behalf of fifteen black parents and forty-three school children. The suit was based on the premise that the doctrine of separate educational facilities was accepted, practiced, sustained, and endorsed through action or lack thereof by the committee and its overseers.

The federal district judge assigned to the case was the Honorable Wendell Arthur Garrity.

CHAPTER 8

"Back Where It Belongs"

AFTER A LONG AND TRYING SEASON, TWENTY-SEVEN-YEAR-OLD HANK FINKEL HAD DECIDED HE'D HAD ENOUGH. Sitting across from General Manager Red Auerbach and Coach Tommy Heinsohn in Red's cluttered office, Finkel expressed his desire to retire from the game of basketball. The 1969–70 season had been a difficult one for the seven-foot center. People had expected him to sustain what the greatest winner in team sports history, Bill Russell, had established. The task was unfair, as were the people who sat in the seats of the Boston Garden, who had grown accustomed to Celtic championships, not losing seasons. Looking for someone to blame for the team's ineptitude, the frustrated crowd directed its anger upon Hank, or as the radio announcer Johnny Most called him, "High Henry."

For years, Finkel had played basketball because he loved it. In college he was an All-American who led the Dayton Flyers with his lefty hook shot to two Sweet Sixteen appearances. In his senior season, the Flyers fell to the number one team in the country, the University of Kentucky Wildcats, in the NCAA tournament. (Kentucky would go on to lose in the finals to the first all-black team ever to win the title, Texas Western College.) After graduating, Finkel was drafted by the Los Angeles Lakers in the second round. He played for one season with the likes of Jerry West and Elgin Baylor before being traded to the San Diego Rockets. When Bill Russell retired in August 1969, the Celtics had to scramble for a new center, just weeks before the start of the season. In an effort to fill the massive void, Boston purchased Hank Finkel from the Rockets in late August.

That's when it all changed for Hank Finkel. The Boston fans stole the fun of the game from him; it just wasn't worth it to him anymore. Although he had started to show some promise in his first campaign with the Celtics, he was clearly no Bill Russell, and the crowd's wrath wore on him. At the holidays, Bob Ryan of the *Boston Globe* wrote his annual Christmas list, in which he wished: "For Hank Finkel—a dart board with pictures of the top ten most obnoxious Celtic fans." Finkel was only making $30,000, and he decided there were more rewarding ways to make a living than listening to the catcalls and insults of the home fans. Hank was a New Jersey guy and was cognizant of how "edgy" people from northeast cities can be, but this abuse had exceeded what was acceptable. He had earned his degree in education and now had visions of teaching and coaching high school basketball.

Across the desk from Hank with cigar in mouth and legs crossed at the ankle, the curmudgeon of a man known as Red Auerbach looked the long-legged player in the eye and promised, "Henry, we need you to hold on. We're getting you help real soon. And this thing is going to turn around. I promise." One day later, the Celtics drafted Dave Cowens with the fourth pick in the NBA draft. Scouts called Cowens the best jumping white man they ever saw. The arrival of Cowens would relieve Finkel of his

"The Soiling of Old Glory." The brutal attack on Ted Landsmark at Government Center in April 1976 was captured in this gripping photo by Stanley Forman. The image came to represent the worst of the busing crises and racial tensions in Boston during the 1970s. *Stanley J. Forman, Pulitzer Prize 1977*

South Boston High School, seen here with Dorchester Heights Monument to the left and triple-deckers in the foreground, was ground zero for much of the tumult and violence that plagued Boston in the mid-1970s. The predominantly white, working-class neighborhood of South Boston was thrust into the center of the storm as Judge Arthur Garrity sought to expedite the desegregation of the city's schools through forced busing. *Ted Gartland/Boston Herald*

Dr. Martin Luther King came to Boston in April 1965 to lead a march against racial imbalance in the city's schools and public housing. Seen here speaking before the crowd at Boston Common, King called upon Bostonians to fight injustice in their own community and proclaimed, "some things that are wrong in Alabama are wrong in Boston." *Boston Herald/UPI Photo*

In June 1966, Bill Russell spoke at the Patrick T. Campbell Junior High School ln Roxbury and warned of a "fire" that threatened to spread through Boston. The Celtic star encountered many difficulties as a black man in Boston in the 1960s, but he encouraged the students to respect their white fellow citizens even if they could not love them. *Boston Herald/UPI Photo*

The city of Boston came out to pay tribute to the Boston Celtics on April 27, 1965, after the team won its seventh consecutive NBA championship. Coach Red Auerbach, smoking his traditional cigar, and forward Tommy Heinsohn acknowledge the crowd as the motorcade travels through downtown. Mayor John Collins rides in the front passenger's seat. *Boston Herald/AP Images*

Red Auerbach pumps his fist to rally his team during game action in 1966. To his right is Hall of Fame guard K. C. Jones, who spent nine seasons as a player in Boston and later returned as assistant and head coach. Auerbach led the Celtics to nine NBA championships as coach and seven more from the front office. *Boston Herald*

Bill Russell and Wilt Chamberlain went head to head as the league's best big men for a decade. They met eight times in the playoffs, including twice in the NBA Finals. Russell and Chamberlain faced off for the last time in the 1969 NBA Finals after Chamberlain joined an all-star lineup in Los Angeles, and once again Russell came out on top, as Boston defeated the Lakers in a dramatic seven-game series. *AP Images*

In shades of the classic Russell-Chamberlain matchups, Dave Cowens and his Celtics consistently got the better of scoring sensation Bob McAdoo during McAdoo's time in Buffalo and New York. When McAdoo was traded to Boston during the 1978–79 season, player-coach Cowens had little patience for McAdoo's score-first mentality while the team struggled to win games.

John Havlicek was known to come through when his team needed him. His leaning bank shot against the Phoenix Suns appeared to give the Celtics a win as the clock wound down on the second overtime in Game Five of the 1976 NBA Finals. But one second was put back on the clock, and Phoenix managed to tie it up and send the game into a third overtime. Boston ultimately pulled out a two-point victory in the legendary game. *Dick Raphael/ Sports Illustrated/Getty Images*

Under the ownership of John Y. Brown (second from right), many felt that the Celtics organization lost its mystique. The acquisition of the troubled Marvin Barnes (far left) seemed to epitomize the demise of the once-proud organization. At an August 1978 press conference, Barnes was introduced along with fellow newcomers Billy Knight (second from left), and Tiny Archibald (third from left); only Archibald was with the team a year later. Coach Tom Sanders is at the far right. *Boston Herald/UPI Photo*

W. Arthur Garrity, surrounded by his family, shakes hands with Judge Charles Wysanzki after being sworn in as U.S. district court judge in July 1966. Standing at the far right is U.S. Senator Ted Kennedy, who helped secure the position for Garrity and with whose family Garrity had a long professional relationship. *Boston Herald/UPI Photo*

On September 12, 1974, school buses carrying black students roll through the streets of South Boston, complete with police escort, as they travel through the neighborhood to South Boston High School on the first day of classes following Judge Garrity's decision. Despite the police presence, a few buses were pelted with stones and bricks, and several arrests were made during the tumultuous first week of the forced-busing program. *Spencer Grant*

starting duties and of the pressure that he had been saddled with. Hank decided to stay.

Over the next three years, Auerbach acquired, drafted, and traded until his Celtics were again in position to compete for an NBA championship. He compiled a starting lineup that consisted of four first-round draft picks—Dave Cowens, John Havlicek, Jo Jo White, and Don Chaney—and filled in the missing piece by acquiring Paul Silas from Phoenix in exchange for the rights to ABA player Charlie Scott, whom Red had previously drafted with a seventh-round pick.

Going into the 1973–74 season, the defending NBA champion New York Knicks and the Boston Celtics were predicted as the teams mostly likely to win the Eastern Division. In the previous season the Celtics had secured home-court advantage throughout the playoffs by compiling the best record in franchise history, 68-14, but this advantage was negated when captain John Havlicek hurt his shoulder, and the Knicks were able to beat Boston in a seven-game series on their way to the championship.

The current edition of the Boston Celtics would do their best to seek their own identity. Ever since Bill Russell retired in 1969, those eleven championship flags hanging above them served as both encumbrance and inspiration. To wear the Celtic shirt was a burden. Only one outcome would bring acceptance to the bearers of this burden: a championship. But for the present team to accomplish this goal, they had to first recognize their individual worth, to walk their own path toward the same destination reached by eleven teams before them—to just be Hank Finkel, and Coach Tom Heinsohn, and free-spirited, undersized, big-hearted Dave Cowens, and star John Havlicek, and not the sixth man who once famously stole a ball. The Celtics of 1973 needed to prove to themselves and to the Celtics of the past that they were their own team, who just happened to wear the same shirt and play on the same parquet as Bill Russell and Bob

Cousy and sit in the same seat as Red Auerbach. This team needed to find itself in order to be discovered.

In his annual preseason column, Bob Ryan anticipated a strong season for the home team, except for one deficiency: Head Coach Tom Heinsohn, the reigning Coach of the Year. "A definite Celtic downfall is the incessant bleating about the officiating," Ryan wrote, "a phenomenon which prejudices referees against them more than anyone could imagine." At the All-Star break, Ryan took the opportunity to further his point about the team's perceived shortfall: "Tom Heinsohn's continued refusal to calm down and stop alienating refs and getting costly techs." By the end of the season, Ryan seemed to extend his opinion beyond sports to the personal when he nominated "Little Tommy Heinsohn" for the "Miss Jean Romper Room Crybaby of the Year." But, despite the concerns of the *Boston Globe* beat writer, the Celtic head coach steered his team to an Eastern Conference best 56-26 record, earning them a number one seed and a date with the Buffalo Braves in the first round of the playoffs.

Prior to the closing month of the 1973–74 season, the Celtics had an indomitable record of 22-0 against the Buffalo Braves, dating back to the expansion team's inaugural season in 1971. But in the final weeks leading to the 1974 playoffs, the Braves had defeated the Celtics twice in a three-day span, setting the foundation for an intense and competitive playoff series. Buffalo was led by the league's top scorer, Bob McAdoo, and its Rookie of the Year, Ernie DeGregorio.

Brimming with confidence, the Braves weren't intimidated by the first-place Celtics, who were bent on intimidating. The Celtics came out forceful and physical early in the series, causing concern within the Buffalo locker room. The Braves' game was built on finesse, and after the Celtics' Game One win, Buffalo started a war of words in the press in an effort to influence the officials. In the following day's newspaper, a quote by Braves General Manager Eddie Donovan complained that John Havlicek "hit everyone in the building tonight and just missed me twice and only because I was in the balcony." Later in the series, Buffalo Head Coach Jack Ramsey announced that he might activate backup center Bob Kauffman, a rough-and-tough well-traveled player whose shooting eye had diminished but not his right hook. In the past, Kauffman had squared off with Cowens and scored a technical knockout by opening a five-stitch cut above the Celtic center's eye with a well-placed punch.

The teams split the next two games, and in Game Four, McAdoo submitted a masterpiece, scoring 44 points and pulling down 16 rebounds. The fact that the series was now tied 2-2 was shocking, not only to Celtic fans but to writer Leigh Montville, who penned a column after the game titled, "Hey, Buffalo, read the script."

Bob McAdoo possessed skills and athleticism that were unparalleled in the league. These gifts, though, often manifested themselves on the court in the form of points and rebounds and not necessarily wins. By contrast, the man defending McAdoo in the series possessed skills that were a function of just one gift: the ability to will himself to conquer, succeed, and achieve. Dave Cowens came to the Celtics with the body of a power forward and the ability to jump and run. His coach believed this skill-set could be used to exploit the other team's lumbering centers and thus moved him to the pivot. McAdoo was one of these players whose desire to shoot and score sometimes superseded his will to win, and this weakness played into the Celtics' hands.

❀

Four years later, the two would cross paths again when Cowens became McAdoo's coach in Boston. At that time, no different than the 1974 playoffs, the two men would attempt to exert their wills upon the other—one wishing to win and to fulfill, the other to shoot and fill. Even after time had passed to allow reflection, Bob McAdoo still didn't fully understand the value of winning over scoring, as demonstrated by his quote in the book *Selling of the Green*. "[Coach Cowens] tried to embarrass me, totally insult me. I wasn't going to accept that. He of all people should've been the first one to say, 'McAdoo is playing forty minutes,' the way I destroyed him on the court. Go back and look, I probably had some of my greatest games against Boston."

Cowens didn't care if McAdoo scored 44 every night as long as the Celtics won. It was Russell vs. Chamberlain all over again.

⊛

In Game Five of their playoff matchup, the Celtics responded with a 100-97 win to push Buffalo to the brink of elimination.

In Game Six, the team of upstarts fought and scratched in an effort to survive. With 0:00 left on the clock at the end of regulation, the game was tied, 104-104—but Jo Jo White was standing at the foul line with a chance to win the game after Bob McAdoo (who scored 40 points on the night) fouled the Celtic guard at the buzzer. As is the rule, all players were removed from the lane, leaving White alone to focus on the matter at hand. Around him bottles, cups, and boos rained upon the floor and officials. The 18,119 rabid Buffalo fans expressed their displeasure with the officials, who had allowed the game to be determined at the free-throw line. White missed the first free throw but was successful on the second, giving the Celtics a Game Six win and a series victory.

After the game, the Braves players and fans were incensed, chasing officials Mendy Rudolph and Darrell Garretson from the floor to the security of their locker room. But as they took a deep breath of relief safely behind their locked door, a loud knock and cursing came from just outside their sanctuary. The officials tried to ignore the taunts, but the intruder continued to yell and curse. "Mendy, the clock ran out, you asshole. That's a helluva way to operate a league!" Having his fill, Rudolph yelled at the interloper, "Get outta here, or I'll call security." From the other side of the door, Braves owner Paul Snyder yelled back, "It's all right; I own the place."

Following his tirade, Snyder filed a protest with the league about the game, but it was denied. The Celtics had won a hard-fought victory over the Braves and were headed to the Eastern Conference Finals to face the defending champions, the New York Knicks.

⊕

For years, Boston held the Big Apple and its omnipresent superiority complex in contempt. Throughout the boroughs of New York, citizens smugly counted their Yankees World Series flags while disregarding Boston as a little city up north. Since the 1920s, the likes of Ruth, DiMaggio, and Mantle circled bases while Red Sox pitchers hung their heads in failure and Bostonians hung their heads in frustration. Now that refrain was being played in the basketball world, as Willis Reed and his Knicks team had forced their will upon Boston in 1972 and again in 1973.

In 1972, the Celtics and their fans were subjected to a blasphemous celebration on their own court after the Knicks eliminated the Celtics from the playoffs at the Boston Garden. Following the final buzzer, college students from New York, who had attended the game, stormed the Boston Garden floor to celebrate with their team, committing sacrilege on the fabled parquet in the eyes of the Celtic faithful.

A year later, the Celtics appeared to be on the road to their twelfth NBA championship. They had carried the regular season with a league-best 68-14 record and subsequently vanquished the Atlanta Hawks in the first round of the playoffs, leading to a rematch with the Knickerbockers. With the series tied 1-1, Celtic superstar John Havlicek was caught in a "blind pick" set by

New York's Bill Bradley and then was sandwiched by Dave DeBusschere, leading to a devastating shoulder injury for the Celtic captain. Boston went on to lose the series in seven games despite a valiant effort.

Now, facing New York in the playoffs for the third year in a row, the Celtics were seeking redemption. Boston was healthy while the Knicks were nicked. DeBusschere was suffering from an abdominal strain, and Willis Reed was dragging an ailing knee. In the first two games, the Celtics took advantage of their younger legs and ran the Knicks off the floor to take a 2-0 lead. Following the second game, New York reporters asked Celtic forward Don Nelson if the wins were tainted because of the sub-par health of their opponents. Nelson would have none of that. "I don't recall anybody shedding a tear for us in the playoffs last year when Havlicek got hurt. As it was, we almost beat them without him. We've been waiting for this series all year because last year we thought we should have won. Our guys are really souped up." In the Knickerbockers locker room, guard Walt Frazier grabbed onto the injury excuse. "If we had a healthy Willis Reed, if we had a dominant center, this was where we could have taken over."

Injuries or not, the Celtics won the series in five games. In the final two games, Havlicek showed that he was the difference from the previous year, scoring 36 and 33 points in games four and five. Boston was going to the NBA Finals to face the power of the league: the Milwaukee Bucks and their superstar center, Kareem Abdul-Jabbar.

❡

During the Eastern Conference Finals against the Knicks, Red Auerbach had declared, "The team that wins this series will be the NBA champion." On the West Coast, the retired Bill Russell held a contrary opinion. He predicted that the Bucks and Jabbar were too much for his former team. The teams had split their regular-season series 2-2, which included a notable fight in which Dave Cowens hammered forward Bob Dandridge to the ground with a left hook.

Milwaukee secured home-court advantage for the playoffs by compiling the NBA's best record, 59-23. During the season, they were simply dominant at home, amassing a record of 31-7 at Milwaukee Arena. The Bucks were led by their sky-hooking center, who when drafted out of UCLA was known as Lew Alcindor but had converted to the religion of Islam and took the name Kareem Abdul-Jabbar. In his first five seasons in the NBA, the seven-foot-two Jabbar had won the Rookie of the Year and three Most Valuable Player awards (including that season's) and led his team to their first championship title. Over those five years he averaged 30.5 points and 15.5 rebounds.

The young Jabbar had a complete game. To go along with his scoring prowess, he was selected to the All-Defensive team three times as the anchor to Milwaukee's defense, which many observers branded as an illegal zone defense. Jabbar would patrol the lane and help out on players other than his own.

In the finals, it was going to be essential for the Celtic center to do his best to wear down Jabbar. To accomplish this, Cowens would run nonstop from tip-off to buzzer on offense. On the defensive end, he would make a point of meeting Jabbar at the free-throw line for the first of three forearms that would be placed in the Bucks star's back as they danced down to the low box in a war of attrition.

Playing a supporting role to Jabbar was NBA legend Oscar Robertson, who at the age of thirty-five was slowed but still effective. The fact that Robertson had slowed in his later years was apparent to the Celtics, who hoped to exploit this weakness by pushing an up-tempo game. They would look to fast break as much as possible on offense and not allow Milwaukee's zone to get set, while instituting a defensive strategy in which Celtic guard Don Chaney would pressure Robertson from baseline to baseline.

The opening game was played in front of 10,938 fans at the Milwaukee Arena. The Celtics smothered the high-scoring Bucks offense for a 98-83 Boston victory. Jabbar scored 35 of the Bucks' 83 points in the losing effort, prompting Bob Ryan to write the following day, "So much did Milwaukee rely on Abdul-Jabbar to stay even close that the thought occurs that if Milwaukee wins the series he should acquire a new name—Allah."

The Bucks evened the series in Game Two when they outlasted the Celtics in a 105-96 overtime victory for Milwaukee. Bucks forward Cornell Warner scored the key basket in the waning seconds of the extra period even though he had been instructed to pass the ball and not shoot. The play had been designed for Jabbar first and Robertson second, but Warner decided to take advantage of an opening to dunk over Dave Cowens.

After the game, Bucks Coach Larry Costello was asked about Warner's deviation from plan. "My first thoughts?" he said. "As he drove, I said 'Our Father who art. . . .'"

The series was now even, but Robertson's veteran legs had been severely tested. He had played fifty-two minutes in the overtime game. This inspired the Celtics to run faster and press harder in Game Three. Back in the cozy confines of the Boston Garden, the home team suffocated the Milwaukee offense, again holding the Bucks to 83 points against Boston's 95. The star of the game was back-up center Hank Finkel. High Henry had played sporadically throughout the season and playoffs but was now called to defend the league's MVP in Game Three after Dave Cowens got in foul trouble.

Four years earlier, Finkel had contemplated walking away from the game, but he didn't. He stayed for just such an opportunity, and he was determined to realize redemption—and redemption he realized. Up and down the court, he outran, outfought, and outplayed the great Jabbar. The statistics don't do his performance justice. In addition to his 8 points and 5 rebounds, Finkel played stellar defense, took charges, and dove to the floor for loose balls. The crowd stood and cheered. His moment had arrived. Destiny had brought him to the Celtics for a reason, and that reason was Game Three of the 1974 NBA Finals. It was on that day that the calls for "High Henry" were made in appreciation and not derision.

The exhausted Oscar Robertson, who averaged forty-seven minutes through the first three games, was growing increasingly irritable and uninterested in answering questions about his weight or his age. In Game Four, he controlled the game like only a veteran could, leading the Bucks to a series-tying win, 97-89. After the game, Coach Costello told reporters, "It's now a best two out of three series, and we'll take our chances with two of the last three games on our home court. That's why we played an eighty-two-game season to get the best record in the NBA."

Back in Milwaukee, the sold-out crowd wasn't able to motivate the home team more than John Havlicek inspired his own team. In the third quarter of Game Five, as the momentum started to shift back in the Bucks' favor, the Celtics captain gathered his teammates together and implored them, "Let's go out and run our plays as hard as we can. Let's push up our lead and make them work. Then we can take a victory back to Boston, and we'll only need one more to take it all." Looking into their eyes, he concluded, "We have to keep playing hard, and if we do, we can take all summer to relax." The Celtics would carry the day and for the second time in the series win in Milwaukee. With a three-games-to-two lead, Coach Heinsohn was feeling confident and bold. "We're going to win it. Even if they play well and win Friday, we're still going to win it."

The series returned to a wild Boston Garden for the Friday night game. The fans came to celebrate a championship on the parquet floor. Instead, they witnessed one of the great games in NBA history. At the end of regulation, the game was tied 86-86 to force overtime. At the end of the first overtime, a clutch follow-up basket by Havlicek tied the game, sending the teams to a second overtime and 15,320 Boston Garden fans to the ledge. In the second extra period, Dave Cowens fouled out, leaving the game in the hands of the Celtic captain. With just eight seconds on the clock, Havlicek delivered a jump shot from the right corner while avoiding a charging Jabbar to give Boston a 101-100 lead. Throughout the Garden, the fans began surging toward the edge of the parquet to form a human wall around the court. On the Celtics bench, a disqualified Cowens rose to his feet, and Don Nelson, Art Williams, and Steve Kuberski moved off the edges of their seats to take a knee.

As he had in Game Two, Coach Costello designed a play that his players would fail to execute. When Milwaukee inbounded the ball, the intention was to set up sharp-shooting guard Jon McGlocklin for the winning shot. But the play broke down, and Robertson was forced to lob the ball to the right of the key, where Hank Finkel tightly covered Jabbar. With the clock ticking down, Finkel pushed the Buck out of his comfort zone to fifteen feet from the basket. Passing lanes were cut off by the Celtics defense, leaving the fate of the Bucks season in the hands of their future Hall of Fame center. With his back to the basket, he rocked toward the key and then rocked back. He then dropped his left arm parallel to the ground to serve as a buffer between him and the defender, turned toward the baseline, and raised the ball to the sky with this right hand, feathering his famous hook shot toward the basket. As the ball traveled through the air, the Garden went still. The ball seemed to move in spliced frames as it proceeded on its downward arc toward the basket. Instead of bouncing wayward off the rim and sending the Garden crowd into exultation, it swished cleanly through the net, stifling the dreams of the Celtics and their fans. Jabbar's sky hook gave the Bucks a dramatic 102-101 double-overtime victory and new life heading back to Milwaukee.

The lead had changed hands twelve times during the two overtime periods. Jabbar, Robertson, and Havlicek each played fifty-eight minutes in the grueling game. Broadcaster Pat Summerall declared it the greatest sporting event he had ever seen. Around the court, the fans who had assembled to storm the floor in celebration stood in collective shock.

In the Celtics locker room, ball boys hustled to remove buckets of champagne while the demoralized Celtics dragged themselves off the court. A disconsolate Dave Cowens sat in front of his locker on the verge of tears. For the night, he had shot an erratic five-for-nineteen from the field before fouling out. Bucks Assistant Coach Hubie Brown, looking forward to Game Seven, suggested to Head Coach Larry Costello that the "white guy," Cowens, wasn't playing anymore.

Some parties felt that the Celtics had their chance, and it had now passed. In the Milwaukee locker room, guard Mickey Davis suggested, "They've beaten us twice at home. But I don't think they can do it a third time."

After the game, Tommy Heinsohn, Bob Cousy, and Red Auerbach retreated to the general manager's office. They stayed until three in the morning eating Chinese food, discussing the heartbreaking game, and exchanging ideas on strategy for Game Seven. In the fog of Red's cigar smoke, they devised a plan to diminish Jabbar's game. The strategy called for the Celtics guards to put even more pressure on the Bucks' dribblers in the backcourt while Cowens, who stood six inches shorter than the Milwaukee center, would guard Jabbar from the front and eliminate him as an escape option for the under-siege guards. To support Cowens in this physical mismatch, forward Paul Silas would sag from his man to help defend Kareem in a double team.

On the plane out to Milwaukee, a re-energized Heinsohn advised Assistant Coach John Killilea to be prepared to get drunk. He then justified his confidence by describing the double-team strategy that had been concocted in the wee hours following Friday's game. In his book *Heinsohn, Don't You Ever Smile?*, the Celtic coach recounted the conversation with his assistant. "In the seventh game of the championship, on national television and in Milwaukee, instead of letting Jabbar shoot the ball, we're going to give Cornell Warner [the hero of Game Two] the opportunity to achieve greatness."

The anticipation for Game Seven was uncontained. Thousands of fans lined the streets that encircled Milwaukee Arena in search of tickets that didn't exist. All 10,938 tickets had already been secured. Police were called to the scene with tear gas to disperse unhappy fans who would have to watch the game on television. Tommy Heinsohn was guaranteeing victory; Larry Costello countered, "I'll take the percentages."

From the moment that the ball was tipped to start the game, the Celtic guards exerted intense pressure on the Bucks ball-handlers. In the first quarter, Jo Jo White's blanket defense on Jon McGlocklin led to punches being exchanged but neither player ejected. In the front court, the Celtics' new defensive strategy surprised the Bucks and frustrated Jabbar, who was held scoreless for one eighteen-minute stretch. During that stagnant period, the Celtics took advantage and raced out to a 17-point advantage. Throughout the game, Cowens out-hustled and outfought his opponent. At one point in the final period, Cowens was playing at such a fever pitch that he hit his head on the floor and knocked himself unconscious. After being given smelling salts and a ninety-second timeout, the Celtic center stormed back on the court to do battle. In the end, the "white man" that Bucks Coach Hubie Brown thought was dead was instead a warrior. A day removed from tears and disconsolation, Cowens was the hero. He scored 28 points and secured 14 rebounds while holding Jabbar to "just" 21 shots and 26 points.

As the clock ticked down, Coach Heinsohn pulled his starters to celebrate their 102-87 victory. Red Auerbach lit his trademark cigar, ignoring the signs posted throughout the Milwaukee Arena that forbid smoking. After the game, the winning coach reveled in the cooperative strategy that he had implemented. "We caught them by surprise. . . . They didn't know what hit them." Don Nelson chided the one-time Celtic great on his pre-series prediction: "Bill Russell should have known better." And Red received his traditional dousing in the showers.

It was the Celtics' twelfth NBA championship and the first in the post-Russell era. In the locker-room a soaked Auerbach rejoiced, "This is where it belongs." Pausing to puff on his cigar he continued, "This club has desire—desire and the old Celtic Pride."

Celtic Pride and hard work allowed them to defeat the Bucks on the toughest home court in the NBA three different times. In all, Boston was 8-1 on the road in the playoffs. Owner Bob Schmertz, who danced among the flowing champagne and fog of cigar smoke, joked, "We won because of away-court advantage." In the *Chicago Tribune*, Bob Logan wrote, "Milwaukee is a great place to visit, but you wouldn't want to have your home court advantage there."

Throughout the locker room were smiles of satisfaction and redemption. Dave Cowens had proven critics wrong by playing center at a championship level. Coach Tom Heinsohn also found validation in victory, which was affirmed by the *Globe's* Larry Whiteside, who wrote, "This was Hiensohn's team." Even longtime Heinsohn critic Bob Ryan called the coach a "hero."

But there was no bigger smile in the locker room than that of Hank "High Henry" Finkel. His start in Boston had been more than difficult; it had been hurtful. He was put in the untenable position of following the most successful center in NBA history. In the finals, Hank had stood up. He was a contributing member to the World Champion Boston Celtics. Ryan wrote in the *Boston Globe*, "Most satisfied man: Sure there's Red Auerbach, but I'm voting for

Hank Finkel who answered the critics with his outstanding (and necessary) play against Kareem Abdul-Jabbar."

Finkel held no ill will toward the fans and critics in the media. At the post-game celebration, all the bad memories were forgotten: "All's I know is that when I was traded here it was the best day of my career. Who knows, I might just play forever."

CHAPTER 9

A Temporary Solution

JUDGE W. ARTHUR GARRITY ENTERED HIS CHAMBER AND REALIZED RIGHT AWAY THAT SOMETHING WAS AMISS. A man of great detail and routine, he knew that his office wasn't as he had left it. Lifting his thick bifocals from the bridge of his nose, he inspected his workplace and discovered that his black robes had been stolen, and he immediately contacted the Boston field officer of the Federal Bureau of Investigation. Three weeks later, the FBI, after expending significant man-hours on the case, terminated the investigation, failing to apprehend the thief or recover the missing robes, much to the displeasure of the persistent judge.

For Judge Garrity, it wasn't the robes as much as the principle. It wasn't as if he was Lieutenant Commander Queeg (played by Humphrey Bogart) in the movie the *Caine Mutiny* turning his ship inside-out in search of his missing strawberries. It was that his courtroom and, by extension, his chambers needed to be a sanctum of civil obedience in order for him to properly administer justice.

In his eyes, the courtroom was at the core of the American democratic system, and it deserved respect.

⊕

Wendell Arthur Garrity Jr. was born in the central Massachusetts city of Worcester, on June 20, 1920. The name Wendell was chosen by the Garrity family to honor the great Boston abolitionist Wendell Phillips, which spoke profoundly to the family's belief system. The oldest of four children, Garrity was nurtured in a house cloaked in the world of jurisprudence and tolerance. His father was a prominent lawyer, director of the Massachusetts Bar, and member of the NAACP. Wendell attended North High School, where he was an honor student and a member of the debate team. His teachers would say that he "never knew how bright he was" and that he was a "terrific ballroom dancer."

Six months before the attack on Pearl Harbor launched the United States into World War II, Wendell graduated from Holy Cross College in Worcester. In his college yearbook, he was described as a "rare blend of 'know-what-to-do,' surprising frankness, and good old-fashioned horse sense—and how the lad can concentrate!" Soon thereafter, he joined the Army and ascended to the rank of staff sergeant in the Signal Corps. He participated in the D-Day landing at Normandy in June 1944 and earned five battle stars for his courageous efforts.

Following the war, Garrity entered Harvard Law School and graduated in 1946. After serving as a clerk, he joined the private practice of Maguire, Roche, Garrity and Maloney. During this time he married a school teacher named Barbara "Bambi" Mullens. They would go on to have two sons and two daughters. In the 1950s, Wendell, a liberal Democrat, became active in politics and participated in both of John F. Kennedy's senatorial campaigns before taking a leadership role in the politician's quest for the White House.

In 1961, his affiliation with the Kennedy family developed further when now-President Kennedy sought out Wendell Arthur Garrity to become the U.S. attorney for the District of Massachusetts. He was presented to the Senate and approved upon the recommendation of Attorney General Robert Kennedy. His predecessor, Elliot Richardson, was none too pleased and had to be "removed" by order of Attorney General Kennedy. With the office finally vacated, Arthur Garrity took possession of the office on the eleventh floor of the Federal Building in Boston's Post Office Square.

After serving six years in the position, he was again sought out by a Kennedy. This time it was Senator Edward Kennedy, who presented W. Arthur Garrity to the Senate Judiciary Committee for the position of U.S. District Court judge. "He's a man with a strong sense of fairness," Senator Kennedy said, "and I feel certain he will serve on the federal bench with distinction." His presentation was approved and so nominated by President Lyndon B. Johnson on June 24, 1966.

✿

Arthur, Bambi, and the Garrity children lived at 40 Radcliffe Road in the affluent town of Wellesley, Massachusetts. The home was only fifteen miles west of Boston, but the abyss that separated Wellesley from the city in ideology, income, and social standing was much wider.

Garrity was a sturdy man, which would belie his grandfatherly appearance. He had a dry wit and would use words such as *crackerjack* and *concomitantly*, but never would his vocabulary include words of inappropriateness. He stood six-foot-one and wore thick glasses that extended to generous ears, which bordered a balding scalp adorned by wispy remnants of graying almost white hair on each side of his head. By all accounts, he wasn't a good man but an exemplary man. Even his later detractors wouldn't question the man himself, only his decisions.

It was W. Arthur Garrity's lifelong dream to be a judge. Behind the bench, he was known to be a fair and conscientious man who was thorough to a fault. His monotone dissertations, interpretations, and rulings were boring but precise. A legal literalist, he occasionally seemed incapable of blending common sense with the words that were written in black script between the leather-bound covers of his legal textbooks. Former Boston School Superintendent Robert "Bud" Spillane described the jurist as a "brilliant mind who could have been one of the finest judges in the country, but he would often get lost in the minutiae of the matter."

In 1972, Judge Garrity found himself on the front pages of the city newspapers after spending an unannounced night in the Charles Street Jail in Boston. He had not been incarcerated but rather was personally assessing the condition of the facility to get insight into a prisoners' civil-rights case he was sitting on. For Garrity, the essence of his position was to educate himself, which meant dissection, an understanding of application, and edification.

The photo of Judge Garrity ducking through a jail cell made good copy but was of limited interest to law-abiding citizens. And while the lawsuit involving inmates and their rights was of little concern to the public, case number 72-911-G—*Tallulah Morgan et al. v. James W. Hennigan et al.*—certainly captured the attention of the city, the country, and the world.

The case was assigned to Judge Garrity by random selection, as was the policy in order to prevent "judge shopping." Garrity reflected on this arbitrary selection: "The case came to me by lottery, and it is my duty to sit on it. I'm not particularly glad or pleased that I was the one who drew the case."

Some speculated that Judge Garrity had been "chosen" to sit on the case because of his integrity, stamina, ability to interpret and apply constitutional law, and capacity to withstand the pressure of public and media scrutiny. Institutional cases of this magnitude would call for a lengthy trial and decision-rendering period. To have a judge who was nearing retirement or otherwise unreliable take on a case of this scale and consequence would make a random assignment irrational and irresponsible.

Some even suggested that Garrity was "chosen" because he had the ability to interpret, render, and defend without reproach. These attributes would be critical in the resolution of an issue of great concern to presidential hopeful Senator Edward Kennedy. Since the 1950s, Wendell Arthur Garrity's life had been intertwined with the family of politicians from Hyannisport. Some observers connected dots that would allow the desegregation line to be drawn between the judge and the senator. The theory was, if the liberal Edward Kennedy was to be successful in his quest for the White House in 1976, it was imperative that segregation in his own "backyard" be eliminated.

⊕

In 1973, as the winter snows melted and crocuses peaked with the arrival of spring, the case—which Judge Garrity's team called "Tallulah"—was heard over a three-week period. Prior to arguments, the judge had assembled the plaintiffs' and defendants' legal counsel in his chambers. The two sides were positioned around the judge's conference table, and when all were settled, Garrity passed around a copy of a letter. He asked them to take a minute to read its contents, and then they would discuss it. When they had finished, nobody said a word.

Without the knowledge of the lawyers, Joseph Lee of the Boston School Committee had sent a letter directly to the judge that suggested that there was value for both blacks and whites to be separated, as each race is distinct and possessing different skills and capabilities. The letter was written evidence, by itself, that a school policymaker held a belief that was contradictory to the principles of the U.S. Constitution.

In addition to the infamous letter, the plaintiffs also gained access to the minutes of the School Committee meetings, which transcribed every discussion, vote, and ruling. These minutes presented evidence of disrespect for the law, the Constitution, and human obligation. African Americans were sometimes referred to as "immigrants" within the text of these minutes.

At the conclusion of trial arguments, Judge Garrity took the case under advisement and retreated to his chamber, where books filled with laws and precedent-setting cases covered his desk and conference table. This was the setting in which Judge Garrity thrived. With his daily apple in his inbox and his chin-up bar between office and side room, he would call upon his power of concentration to consume massive piles of information. With sleeves rolled up and neck bent, he peered through his bifocals at words that would dance off the pages to be pieced together in a puzzle of resolution. This puzzle, when complete, would translate into a decision of great consequence and historical significance; a decision that would attempt to reconcile matters of biblical proportion; a decision that would impact a city of tradition, ritual, and institutional pattern formed through the drips of time. For more than three centuries, the quilt that mapped Boston had been sewn and mended to allow for distinctness, which some interpreted as segregation while others defended it as community.

The day his decision was completed, Garrity took time from his possessed world to blow out birthday candles at his Wellesley home. The fifty-four-year-old family man had a life of fulfillment, with a lovely bride, four healthy children, a home of substance, and a position of meaning. Usually a birthday is a time for reflection and self-examination, but not this birthday. After the final notes of "Happy Birthday" drifted away, the judge sat down in his library and read and reread his 152-page decision. It had taken him fifteen months to compose. He had suffered and agonized over every word. The decision was direct and succinct, lacking adjectives but filled with meaning; it was a composition that, he anticipated, would be tested and prodded for years to come. On his lap sat words on paper that when read, on the following day of June 21, 1974, would change the city of Boston forever.

In the courtroom at the Federal Courthouse in Post Office Square in Boston, not an empty seat was to be found. Media members and sketch artists were stuffed into the jury box, while school committee members and plaintiffs alike anxiously awaited the ruling.

The decision found that the plaintiffs "proved beyond question that racial segregation exists in parts of the Boston public school system" and that "the rights of the plaintiff class of black students and parents under the Fourteenth Amendment to the Constitution of the United States have been and are being violated by the defendants in their management and operation of the public schools of the City of Boston." It continued:

> The court concludes that the defendants [Boston School Committee] have knowingly carried out a systematic program of segregation affecting all of the city's students, teachers and school facilities and have intentionally brought about and maintained a dual school system. Therefore the entire school system of Boston is unconstitutionally segregated. Accordingly, the court will contemporaneously with this opinion file a partial judgment permanently enjoining the city defendants from discriminating upon the basis of race in the operation of the Boston public schools and ordering that they begin forthwith the formulation and implementation of plans to secure for the plaintiffs their constitutional rights.

Judge Garrity and the court ordered the School Committee to "eliminate every form of racial segregation in the public schools of Boston, including all consequences and vestiges of segregation previously practiced by the defendants." They were obligated to dismantle the "dual system" by "whatever steps might be necessary," including busing, pairing of schools, redistricting, or involuntary student and faculty assignment. The decision acknowledged that some of these approaches would be "distasteful" and that "the remedy for such segregation may be administratively awkward, inconvenient and even bizarre in some situations."

To illustrate the mindset that had corrupted the Boston School Committee during the period of noncompliance, Judge Garrity inserted as a footnote in his decision a statement made by an unidentified committee member at a 1971 meeting: "I think the facts of the matter are that the Negro immigrants from the South are disinclined to put the effort into our northern type of education."

In the eyes of the unbiased, the decision was fair and accurately applied the law to the case at hand. Distinctness had melted into the realm of "separate," causing Constitutional rights to be violated. The School Committee and city politicians had been provided ample opportunity to adhere to the Supreme Court's *Brown v. Board of Education of Topeka* ruling of 1954 as well as the state's Racial Imbalance Act of 1965. Their failure to do so left the task of determining a solution in the hands of the courts and one federal judge.

Tragically, the proposed solution was not human but mechanical. Years of avoidance had led to an intolerant and impatient presiding judge who chose immediacy over incremental change to rid the city of Constitutional violations.

It had been well over a century since Sarah Roberts was ejected from her neighborhood school because she was "colored." Judge Garrity was determined to rectify that injustice, and all that followed, prior to the first day of school—a mere eleven weeks away.

⊕

Because the administration of his directive was time sensitive, Judge Garrity opted to employ the plan that the Massachusetts Board of Education had written the previous year. This "temporary" solution, which was authored primarily by Dr. Charles Glenn, called for twenty thousand of Boston's approximately eighty-seven thousand public school students to be bused from the neighborhoods where they lived (and played and went to church) to a cross-city neighborhood.

Two of the neighborhoods that would be most severely affected by so-called Phase I of the school desegregation plan were the mostly black-populated Roxbury and the predominantly Irish-Catholic community of South Boston. For years these two communities existed independently but relatively congruent. Both neighborhoods held subtle and not so subtle layers of mistrust toward the other. Now Judge Garrity's plan linked the two entities as virtual protagonists, leaving them to fight over the scraps of a decrepit educational system.

Within the black community, the ruling and plan of implementation were widely hailed as heroic, although many families were concerned about the safety of their children on the buses and inside the schools. In South Boston and other white neighborhoods so impacted, families were outraged by what they saw as the judge's callous disregard for parents' right to protect and choose for their children.

South Boston's own Louise Day Hicks wrote about Judge Garrity and his decision in the *South Boston Tribune*: "He has ignored the wisdom and advice of the professional educators of Boston and the wishes and pleadings of its people. This unjust justice has gleefully swung the ax that sounds the death knell from his lily-white sanctuary West of [Route] 128. He has effectively tied a garrote around the neck of Boston."

Throughout the summer of 1974, concerned white leaders and parents protested the ruling. In Southie streets, the judge was burned in effigy, while in Charlestown his figure was carried in a casket in front of parades. Marches through the streets, appeals for repeal, and horn-beeping motorcades past Judge Garrity's Wellesley home were all conducted but with little effect.

Such exhibitions led federal authorities to assign U.S. Marshalls to provide the judge with twenty-four-hour protection, at a cost of $150,000 a year. Twice, would-be assassins were arrested in route to the Garrity home. One Dorchester man grabbed his shotgun and said goodbye to his wife, adding as he walked out the door, "I'm going to kill Garrity." Another man was arrested in Wellesley carrying a bomb, which he intended to affix to the undercarriage of the judge's car. Police had been alerted to the threat by the suspect's mother after her son had threatened the judge, asserting that Garrity was "worse than Hitler" and "guilty of taxation without representation."

The volatile reactions were of concern to many. Charles Glenn recommended that Phase I avoid combustible neighborhoods and instead allow the remedy to ease its way into the fabric of the city. This recommendation was rejected under the premise that it would violate the law as written. Others, such as Paul Parks—a city official, prominent black leader, and former chairman of the Boston School Committee—felt that certain parties of authority were more interested in "breaking Southie" than in bringing equality to the school system. Still others saw this "death knell" as just punishment for the neighborhood's support and votes for intolerant school committee representatives all these years.

Whatever the motivation, the wheels of change—literally and figuratively—would soon be in motion. On September 12, 1974, the buses would roll from black neighborhoods to white neighborhoods and white neighborhoods to black neighborhoods. The fire that Bill Russell had spoken about years earlier was about to spread.

CHAPTER 10

"Practically Ignored by this City"

DESPITE WINNING ELEVEN CHAMPIONSHIPS IN THIRTEEN YEARS, THE BOSTON CELTICS HAD FAILED TO FULLY CAPTURE THE ATTENTION OF THEIR CITY. Boston was a hockey town. By the time the Celtics played their inaugural season in 1946, the Bruins had already won three Stanley Cups and appeared in six championship finals. Boston sports fans had already committed their attention, discretionary income, and time to the established franchise in the city; they had little interest in a team playing a sport that was unproven and confusing to the post–World War II sports fan.

Diehard Bruins fans, who were known as the "Gallery Gods," filled the Garden night after night to watch the great "Kraut Line" of Bobbie Bauer, Milt Schmidt, and Woody Dumart. This fanatical following was sustained with the arrival of a handsome defenseman from Parry Sound, Ontario, by the name of Bobby Orr. Number 4 transcended the sport with his end-to-end rushes with the puck, his blond locks blowing in the breeze as he skated by mere mortals.

Orr's radiant presence only served to further entrench the team with the "B" on the front of their hockey sweaters as the team of choice during Boston's cold winter months.

The Bruins' hold on the community made it difficult for the Celtics to claim market share, and interest in the world's greatest basketball team was constrained. During the 1960s, the average attendance at Celtics games was only 8,229—54 percent of capacity at the Boston Garden—even though the team won nine championships in the decade.

During the championship season of 1974, season tickets for the Celtics accounted for only 4,000 of the 15,320 seats that the facility had available for basketball. The building had been built in 1928 by boxing promoter Tex Rickard for the purpose of hosting boxing matches, using New York's Madison Square Garden as its model. The arena had significant limitations for viewing a basketball game. Many seats were set beyond the baselines of the court, affecting sight lines and proximity to the action. Many seats were obstructed by cement pillars that encircled the stadium to support the balconies above.

The disrespect for the team by the community and disdain for the building were the source of much frustration for Red Auerbach. This frustration often manifested itself in the form of petty revenge. Often the Celtic patriarch would blackout television coverage to local viewers, even for critical playoffs games, if a game wasn't sold out within seventy-two hours before tip-off. Boston fans, infuriated by Red's tactics, asked Congress to intervene. In Washington, the Celtics were found guilty of manipulating their interpretation of a "sell out" by including obstructed seats in the count. To Red, Congress was just another referee making a "chicken shit" call.

⊛

At the annual Greater Boston Chamber of Commerce dinner following yet another Celtic championship season in 1968, former team president Dick

Greibel was the invited guest speaker at the Boston Sheraton. Greibel wasn't from Boston, so he spoke with a reserved tone: "It seems unbelievable to me that the Celtics, after winning ten world championships and two division titles during the past twelve years, have failed to gain the recognition of the city's fathers. Here is a team that has brought so much pride and honor to the city of Boston while achieving unprecedented feats, but still fails to gain the recognition of lesser competitors."

Years later at the same Chamber of Commerce function, the principals assigned the responsibility of securing a speaker for the function made the mistake of choosing Red Auerbach. In his speech, Red was far less restrained than Dick Greibel had been. "This isn't quite the honor—my being here— that you might think it is. I haven't had too much regard for the Chamber of Commerce over my years in Boston. When the Celtics won eleven championships in thirteen years we were practically ignored by this city. How could I feel otherwise?"

This frustration with being treated as second-class citizens extended beyond the box office and to the tenant-landlord relationship. The sovereignty of the Bruins wasn't limited to fan interest. The Boston Garden was a hockey arena run by hockey people. The Bruins' parent company owned the world-famous facility that both teams called home. Ever since the Celtics first became a tenant, the arrangement was less than satisfactory. As landlord, the hockey team received priority on all matters concerning the facility, including locker rooms, scheduling, and practice time. The Celtic locker room was described as two rusty nails to hang up your clothes; one working shower head in the bathing area that would often plug and overflow into the locker room; and one toilet that lacked a door, which as Tommy Heinsohn would say, "could make things unpleasant." Practicing at the Garden was out of the question for the Celtics, and the team first had to use the Cambridge YMCA, until robberies of the players' personal items led the team to switch to the Tobin Gym in Roxbury. Game scheduling was another challenge. Organizing dates with the Boston Bruins' schedule and with the NBA was further complicated by visits to the Garden by Ringling Brothers and Barnum & Bailey Circus, ice skating shows, and concerts. Because of such restrictions, the Celtics would have to sacrifice five to ten home games a year, and "host" games in Providence, Rhode Island; Portland, Maine; and Hartford, Connecticut.

The acrimonious relationship between tenant and landlord was as much a function of the golden rule—"he who owns the gold, rules"—as it was the hockey team's jealousy. Along with the monthly rent the Celtics paid to the Boston Garden, the landlord also charged a fee that infuriated Auerbach. Before every Bruins game, Garden personnel were required to roll up the Celtics' championship flags that hung in the rafters. The manpower cost for this was passed on to the basketball team. Red believed that the Celtics' winning legacy was embarrassing to the hockey team and its owners.

The Celtics were so dissatisfied with their playing environment that they endeavored to build their own facility at various sites around the city and greater Boston, including at the Suffolk Downs racetrack. The Bruins tried to force their tenant to sign a long-term lease that would make the Celtics remain at the Garden. This strong-arm tactic led the Celtics to file a lawsuit against the landlord, the New Boston Garden Corporation, claiming they were in violation of anti-trust laws. The suit read, in part: "New Garden has refused to enter into any agreement with Celtics under terms which the Boston Celtics would be permitted to play home games in the Boston Garden during the 1980–81 season except under terms of which are extremely unreasonable and so burdensome that New Garden will succeed in maintaining such monopoly position in the market." In conclusion, the suit alleged, "New Garden has abused its monopoly position by failing to make the Garden available to all competitors on reasonable and non-discriminatory terms and conditions."

The basketball team hoped that a positive court decision would compel the New Boston Garden Corporation to provide them with a one-year lease. The shortened lease would allow them to play the impending NBA season while building their own facility. But the ruling wasn't positive. The suit was quashed by Federal District Judge W. Arthur Garrity, who drew the ire of Celtics ownership for his lack of regard for their needs and concerns.

CHAPTER 11

"Southie Is My Hometown"

LORD LIEUTENANT OLIVER CROMWELL ARRIVED IN IRELAND ON AUGUST 15, 1649, AND PROCEEDED TO LEAD A SCOURGE OF ETHNIC CLEANSING AND LAND-TAKING THAT WAS UNPRECEDENTED IN EUROPE. In his report back to England, he wrote about his massacres of Catholics, adding, "And it may be wished that an honest people would come and plant here."

Prior to Cromwell's arrival, Catholics had owned 60 percent of the land in Ireland; less than a year later, they possessed only 8 percent. The Catholic religion was outlawed, and those who practiced it were denied political rights and representation. An estimated 618,000—or 40 percent of the Irish population—perished during England's invasion of Ireland. Irish soldiers, priests, and friars were ordered killed on sight. Those who weren't killed were sold and sent to the West Indies for a life of servitude.

The murder and pillage of Ireland left the country devoid of resources. Every tree, livestock, and fertile piece of land was stripped from the Irish.

Farms, homes, and estates were gifted to English soldiers as part of the "Cromwell Plantation," while Irish commodities were sent back to England. This led to an Irish dependency on the potato as a main source of food. Two centuries later, when a fungus blanketed Ireland's potato crop, some one million Irish people died from famine, and one million more emigrated from the country.

Many of the Irish who emigrated from Ireland secured passage on "coffin ships" destined for the port of Boston in the "New Country," carrying dreams of a new beginning in the land of promise. Sadly, when they arrived, the Irish were subjected to similar prejudices from which they fled—notwithstanding the pledge of the "Mother of Exile" (Statue of Liberty) who stood in New York harbor to welcome the "huddled masses yearning to breathe free." Proper Bostonians, whose roots traced back to the English, went to great lengths to deny the Irish immigrants their basic rights and impeded their efforts to procure work and decent housing. Signs in the windows of Boston businesses warned, "Irish need not apply." Available work was limited to the mills, cleaning homes, and hard labor. Living quarters were restricted to overcrowded boarding houses, where they settled according to their county of origin back in their Irish homeland.

Despite the bigotry that the Celtic immigrants were subjected to, ships carrying cargo of Irish continued to arrive in Boston ports. During the 1840s, Boston's Irish population grew exponentially, nearing one hundred thousand by the end of the decade. This dramatic change in the city's demographics only increased the fears and prejudices among Boston's established citizens. Desperate and unwanted, the Irish immigrants migrated to the far corners of the city, where they could find jobs at the docks and other manual labor while remaining in close proximity to Boston proper.

By the late 1800s, the peninsula known as South Boston was populated predominantly by Irish immigrants, who joined with Polish, Italian,

Lithuanian, and Albanian immigrants to build a community. Insulated from the rest of the city, these new inhabitants welcomed the cold breezes of the Atlantic that swept through their neighborhood. The ocean connected them with their homelands and provided them with work and recreation.

In the final decade of the nineteenth century, that same ocean helped to change South Boston from a colony of unwanted immigrants to the most popular destination in the city. In 1892 a walkway was built from City Point, the easternmost point in the neighborhood, across the bay to Fort Independence, on the site known as Castle Island. Situated at the mouth of Boston Harbor, Fort Independence (previously Fort Williams) served as the last line of defense for Boston's vital port, and its critical role in the protection of the city dated back to pre-Revolutionary times. British troops were banished to Fort Independence following the Boston Massacre in March 1770.

After the fort was decommissioned, it was transferred to the Boston parks system. Located at the crest of four sloping grassy knolls, the fort provided the perfect setting for those seeking respite from the turmoil that at times engulfed the city. The new walkway, which was constructed for $13,973.06, provided easy access.

The rising popularity of the South Boston neighborhood sparked the construction of the L Street Bathhouse and, later, the aquarium, both of which sat along the shores of the Atlantic. The further demands for travel to the peninsula led the city to lay tracks for the electric train that would carry riders back and forth to Dudley Station in Roxbury.

It was not unusual for tens of thousands of people to journey to South Boston on a Sunday afternoon to swim at L Street or picnic on a grassy slope at Castle Island, from where they could listen to the floating notes of patriot songs emanating from the bandstand at City Point across the walkway. It was this experience that the Irish had dreamed of from the steerage compartments of ships during the difficult journey across the ocean from their starving homeland. They had built a new community in a new land with hard work and pride. This spirit of ownership inspired the word *my* in the famous song "Southie Is My Hometown." It was theirs—a neighborhood of streets named after letters and numbers feeding from the main thoroughfare of Broadway to the Atlantic Ocean.

As many Irish generations before them had come to realize, however, their position on the ladder of society's caste system always left them vulnerable. For centuries, the Vikings, then the English, and now the Boston Yankees had imposed their will upon poor Irish, who had no option but to acquiesce. When they were newcomers to this country, they submitted when told that they weren't welcome in the Back Bay and Beacon Hill. They accepted substandard wages so they could put food on their tables. They were forced to settle in a primitive peninsula town, which they, in turn, built into a thriving community.

But when the federal government came to South Boston to commandeer Castle Island, first for a lighthouse station and later an immigration depot (similar to Ellis Island), the people of South Boston had had enough. Those on the rungs above them were attempting to take their jewel, and they would have none of it. The people of South Boston had struggled but persevered, and it was here that they made their stand. Organized and represented, they lobbied Congress and ultimately staved off the imperialistic efforts of an "outsider" to determine the fate of their neighborhood. The successful effort to preserve Castle Island had a long-lasting affect on the community, as it illustrated the value of representation and organization.

By 1894, South Boston had a population of ninety thousand. Such numbers brought both power and needs. While Castle Island and the bathhouse were sources of great pride, the residents of South Boston realized that for their children to make real gains up the ladder of success, it was essential that they receive an education. South Boston was the only neighborhood in the city that didn't have the resource of a high school. A Reverend George was quoted in the *Boston Globe* as making the following statement in support of a high school for South Boston: "I want to speak from a moral point of view. . . . If you had a high school there the children would take advantage of it and it would elevate them. What we want to do is to elevate South Boston. Our children should have the same opportunity to receive a high school education as the children living in the Back Bay, Roxbury, and other places." So, once again the community organized and formed the "High School Committee" with the objective to secure $125,000 in funding to construct a school within the neighborhood boundaries.

This effort, though sincere, was saddled by the community-held belief that it was hard to get the Boston School Committee to give anything to South Boston. This conviction was given credence by a story in the *Globe* on January 30, 1894, that stated, "The School Committee gave the opinion of that body, that a high school in South Boston was inexpedient and unnecessary."

The ruling discouraged many in the neighborhood, but they were buoyed by the subsequent recommendation of Alderman Thomas Flood, who advised the people of South Boston, "If the people earnestly desired a high school in the district, they would have to work hard and impress upon the School Committee that they must have such an institution."

The people of South Boston took to heart the recommendation and did work hard. Organized and resolute, the High School Committee waded through the bureaucracy and through the tenor of discrimination against their neighborhood. Eleven months later, in November 1894, their perseverance was rewarded when the school committee voted to appropriate a sum of $50,000 for the purpose of acquiring a half acre of land and buildings at the intersection of East 4th Street and G Street.

Upon this directive, the Boston land-development agency know as the Street Commissioners commenced negotiations with the owners of the nine properties that composed the subject site. The landowners' counteroffers exceeded $60,000 and were deemed prohibitive, so the committee turned its attention to an unencumbered lot at the edge of Thomas Park, which sat at the peak of South Boston looking out over the Atlantic Ocean to its east and the city of Boston to its west. Following the land purchase of $15,877, a bid of $236,966 was accepted to construct the school. South Boston was going to have its high school.

On March 18, 1901, while construction of the school was ongoing, South Boston took pause from community development to host its first St. Patrick's Day parade in honor of the 125th anniversary of the evacuation of British troops from Boston during the Revolutionary War. It was said that more than one hundred thousand people traveled to South Boston to watch the parade, which marched up Broadway before steering its way down G Street to salute the blooming high school. The *Boston Globe* reported that the neighborhood fulfilled its duties as host: "All along the route of the parade in South Boston, red, white, and blue bunting was to be seen, and the arrangement of the many portraits of national heroes of the past and present. . . . Many of the clubs and local organizations kept open house and South Boston hospitality was extended with open hand and but few doors were closed to the strangers."

The following autumn, South Boston High School was completed. It had been a decade since the High School Committee had appealed to the Boston School Committee. Now the community was complete. The headline on the front page of the *Boston Globe* read: "Proud Day for South Boston Folk." And a proud day it was. The school represented exactly what had compelled the Irish and other immigrants that inhabited these parts to leave their homeland: opportunity.

The school's brick colonial design extended east and west with wings of classrooms. The center façade was crowned with the seal of Boston, which was underlined by the engraved title, "South Boston High School." Beneath the engraving were four Greek pillars framing three entrance doors reached by fifteen ascending granite steps.

Through the threshold was a vestibule constructed with Italian marble and walls painted a Pompelian red. The foyer led to marble stairs that conveyed students and teachers to the second floor, which consisted of offices, classrooms, bathrooms, and the library. On the third floor, laboratories were readied to challenge the minds of young scientists. In the basement, the school had a massive gym, a drill hall, locker rooms, and a cafeteria.

At the school's unveiling, dignitaries were greeted in the auditorium by the student body, which sang a beautiful rendition of "The Song of Peace." Following the student salutation, Headmaster Augustus Small welcomed the guests. He spoke eloquently to the potential of the great school and the obligation of those bestowed with the responsibility of shaping the minds of the youth of South Boston:

> I receive with particular satisfaction these keys and with them the responsibility. Great is the power of the keys, which, by the little circumstance of adjustment, open and close the doors. They admonish us to open them for the innocence and bloom of youth, and close them against insidious assaults.
>
> On this patriotic height we have established an institution of highest patriotism. The public schools of America have ever been the bulwark of liberty. We intend to make this a school to uphold liberty, but to oppose license. Here we will educate both sexes of all races and religions without partiality, with malice toward none and

charity for all. All are here alike welcome, from him of the greatest pedigree to the lowest immigrant, from the child of the oldest
faith to the one belonging to the latest discovered truth.

Send us your children then as God shall provide ability for
you to provide for their welfare and we will endeavor to return
them with higher and loftier patriotism, with proper self-control,
with honest citizenship and an ascending career.

On December 11, 1974, Charlie Titus, a black community counselor, was
wading through his daily workload at Lena Park Community Development
when his phone rang. It was his friend Al Holland, the assistant headmaster
at South Boston High School. In the background, Titus could hear screaming
and the sounds of chaos. He soon learned that the school was in the midst of
a race riot. A white student by the name of Michael Faith was lying motionless in the second floor hall in a pool of blood after being stabbed by a black
student named James White. Throughout the school, police in riot gear were
forcibly escorting white students out onto G Street, while administrators and
teachers frantically yelled for black students to lock themselves in offices for
their own safety.

On the other end of the phone, Charlie Titus shook his head at the sense-
lessness of it all and wished Al good luck. But Al wasn't finished. A collection
of angry and concerned parents had started to assemble outside the high school
after receiving word that a resident of South Boston had been killed. Standing
at the cast-iron fence that protected the grounds were white students who had
been extricated from the school, mothers filled with disgust for having lost
their natural right to choose for their children, and fathers who walked off their
jobs at the docks and the Gillette factory to join the movement of solidarity to
protect what they had fought so hard to gain.

The crowd had swelled to two thousand and now grossly outnumbered the Boston police. The state police barracks in Framingham and Concord received calls for reinforcements. Louise Day Hicks, the daughter of South Boston and school committee leader, was rushed to the scene. Looking out at the very people she had stirred in the past, she shouted through a blow horn for the residents of her great neighborhood to return to their homes. "My friends and neighbors," Hicks announced, "Mickey [Faith] is stable. His condition is good. The school is closed." The last statement drew boos from the crowd. "You and I love South Boston and have lived here our whole lives," she continued. "We have a serious situation. We are going to take care of this assault. The only thing I ask you to do is allow these black students to go home to Roxbury." The mob's response was a unified, "Hell no, we won't go!"

It was too late for reason or compromise. Hicks was booed from the steps. Next to her, City Councilor Ray Flynn said to the other politicians and police, "Garrity should be here to see this."

Back in Dorchester at the Lena Park offices, Charlie Titus was consumed by feelings of empathy and helplessness. He, like many blacks who had grown up in Boston, had dreamed of a day that the people from his community would be welcomed throughout the city. But somehow it had all gone wrong.

Holland shared with Titus a plan that had been concocted by the administrators and police: four buses would form a convoy and navigate their way through the swelling crowd and flying bricks to the front of the high school. The purpose of these buses was not to transfer students from peril to safety, but instead to serve as decoys to draw the wrath of the crowd-turned-mob long enough to allow the black students to be snuck out the side door of the school, where other buses would be waiting with police escorts.

In Titus' eyes, the plan was suspect, but he wished his friend good luck and went to hang up when Holland pleaded with the six-foot-six former college basketball player. "Charlie, I need you to be on one of those buses." A confused Titus replied, "Al, I can't drive a bus." "You don't understand," Holland explained. "If they don't see a monitor on the buses, they'll know something is up."

Appreciating the gravity of the situation, the outreach worker accepted the assignment. He drove over to the Bayside Complex, where buses mustered for the delivery and pick-up of bused students. The ride to South Boston High School would take five minutes but could last a lifetime. Before boarding the yellow carrier, Titus looked toward the west. Above the triple-deckers and projects and tenements he could see the steeple of the Dorchester Heights Monument, which sat in the backyard of the high school. He walked up the steps of the bus. Behind him the door was pulled closed, and the bus driver maneuvered out of the parking lot and headed north on Day Boulevard. The street ran parallel to the ocean on the right, where white caps now danced, while to the left the tide was surging. The road then bent east before arriving one mile down the road at I Street, where the bus negotiated a sharp left, placing the ocean in the rearview mirror and bringing them one turn closer to potential danger. Standing between the rows of the black upholstered seats, Charlie Titus inhaled and thought to himself, "This is what the kids suffer through every day—the same fear, the same pounding of the heart, the same confusion."

The buses traveled north up I Street in the direction of East Broadway until the convoy came upon the intersection of East 6th, where they had to turn left. Reluctantly, the driver steered the transport onto the narrow thruway. The tight squeeze caused the buses to pause. Up the hill through the windshield, the brick high school could be seen hiding behind the American flag.

With the path cleared, the buses shifted gears and bounced ahead. With three hundred yards to ascend, the buses were effectively boxed in by the triple-decker homes that lined each side of the street. The shadows of the rooftops met ominously in the middle of the road.

The buses crossed over the intersecting H Street and for the first time passed parts of the crowd, which was spilling down the hill on the sidewalks. From both sides, the bricks, bottles, and stones assaulted the buses. Glass shattered, and the noise of disdain echoed throughout the street and into the buses. Within the furor of the attack, Titus looked to the sidewalk, where he locked eyes with an older woman. In those eyes he saw a hatred that shook his very being. It was a look that would stay with Charlie Titus the rest of his life.

Titus soon felt the bus begin to list. Turning his attention back to the front of the bus, he saw the driver had ducked beneath the steering wheel in an effort to avoid the shattering glass and the falling bricks that rained down on his windshield. Running between the rows of seats littered with glass, Titus yelled for the driver to sit up, which he did just as they crested the hill. Looking left and right, Titus was awestruck. On the street, police on horses galloped back and forth as tactical police swung their batons and dodged projectiles. When space was cleared, the buses took a slight left and parked on the right curb in front of the school, where they waited and waited and waited—thirty minutes in all. Strangely, the buses brought calm to the mayhem, as the mob rationed their rage for the black students, whom they presumed would soon appear at the three doors of the school's front entrance.

At the front of the bus, Titus could hear scrambled voices over the walkie-talkie. Next to the bus on the left, mounted police bounced past as Titus continued to wait and ignored the insults that slipped through the broken windows. Then, the call came over the walkie-talkie: "They're all out." Instantly, the buses were set into gear and accelerated down the hill of G Street back toward the shores of the Atlantic. Titus didn't look back. He didn't want to. He only wondered what would have happened to those students if they had walked down the school's granite steps and into the angry mob.

⧎

Southie Pride was not a bumper-sticker slogan but a palpable condition that connected the people of the peninsula. South Boston High School was much more than a school building; it was a symbol that represented different ideals for two sides now engaged in a bitter fight—first philosophical, now physical—over that very building. For the residents of South Boston, the school that they had built from scratch was a symbol of neighborhood solidarity and community, a neighborhood to which they had once been exiled. For the black community, South Boston High School represented the ever-present struggle for equality. For decades the black enrollment at the school had been *zero*, even though union training was conducted at the building on G Street.

Following the stabbing of Michael Faith, the school was closed for two weeks. Although only three arrests were made in the ensuing chaos, twenty policemen were hospitalized, horses had their tails lit on fire, and the abyss that separated the two groups broadened.

From the first day that buses had rolled across the city that September, it was apparent that the resolution of the "dual school systems" would not be achieved as initially conceived. Of the 1,300 students that were assigned to South Boston High School, only 124 reported to the opening day of classes. The students who did attend class found that there was little learning, only survival. Classrooms were locked down, and police patrolled the hallways. Teachers didn't teach but instead broke up fights and counted the days to their pension. Hallways, cafeterias, and bathrooms served as stages of confrontation. At the beginning of each day, teachers paid special attention to the footwear of the white students. If they were wearing sneakers (which was uncommon for white students in the mid-1970s), then the teachers would prepare for a long day of fights and mischief.

In the classrooms and the cafeteria, students determined their seating assignments not by the alphabet but by race. Students had to be careful not to interact with individuals of the other race and risk the scorn of "their own people." Teachers and administrators organized walking patterns by which the black students walked in one direction in the hallways and whites in the opposite, to keep shoulders from bumping and books from dropping. During the Pledge of Allegiance, whites would stand while blacks would sit. Separate detention and holding areas were set up in the basement near the basketball court, which went unused while Judge Garrity selected a neutral gymnasium in which the players could practice. At the end of each day, whites were corralled inside the school and not allowed to depart until blacks were led to their buses and were safely aboard.

Demonstrations against the forced busing were held in South Boston throughout the fall. The protestors targeted Judge Garrity's home and marched through the city's neighborhoods. An estimated eight thousand to ten thousand people gathered at South Boston's Marine Park on October 28, 1974, to protest the perceived occupation of their community by outside forces. The American-flag-waving crowd posted banners displaying proclamations such as "Better Not to Be Educated Than Not to Be Free" and "The Family Is More Sacred Than the State." One banner outlined the similarities between the Boston of 1974 and the Boston of 1774: "The city is occupied. A boycott exists. A tyrant reigns. Law is by decree. The people are oppressed."

❀

The lack of a stable learning environment in the schools, the unrest on the streets, and the overall effect on the perception of the city were all devastating to Boston. Citizens, parents, and politicians were desperate to save the city. These concerns impelled Louise Day Hicks to telegram President Gerald Ford with the following plea: "President Ford, Come to Boston at once so that you can personally view the tragedy and trauma that now engulfs our beloved and no longer peaceful city."

President Ford didn't come to Boston, but he did offer his support to those who railed against busing by issuing a controversial opinion on the deteriorating state of the city and its cause. "The court decision in that case wasn't the best solution to quality education in that city," President Ford stated. "I respectfully disagree with the judge's order."

In addition to offering his opinion, Ford also placed the 82nd Airborne Division, based at Fort Bragg, North Carolina, on alert for deployment. Federal troops had been used in the desegregation efforts in Alabama and Mississippi a decade earlier. The stigma connected to such an act was one that Boston would prefer to avoid.

Federal troops were never deployed to Boston, but unwanted "reinforcements" from the South did land in the fall of 1974: the Ku Klux Klan. Traveling by bus, the white supremacists arrived in South Boston, expecting to be greeted with a tickertape parade and warm welcome. Instead, they were greeted by City Councilor Ray Flynn's warning, "Get the hell back on the bus. You're not welcome here."

The Klan members were surprised but not deterred. While in Boston, they decided to go door to door to spread their gospel of hate. When they walked into the Clock Tavern on Broadway, the patrons set down their beers and turned in their seats to face the solicitors. The leader of the group walked up to the bar and introduced himself to the bartender known as "Irish." After listening intently to the out-of-towner's appeal, Irish placed his bar towel on the bar and inquired in a curious tone, "Aren't you the assholes that wear those stupid white hoods and hate Catholics?" Hearing no response, Irish answered his own question, "So screw!" The paying customers cheered wildly, and the KKK left, not to return.

It was this type of tragic circus that brought disgrace to the city. Boston was divided and searching for direction and guidance. Judge Garrity's ruling was not serving its purpose of breaking down racial barriers but rather seemed to be building them up. In a 1974 *Boston Globe* op-ed piece, Senate President William Bulger wrote, "Forced segregation is an evil. It is a social sickness. But the medicine of forced busing is demonstrably not its cure here. In fact, it is poisoning us. To persist in large dosages is, in a moral sense, to carry folly to the edge of a felony."

CHAPTER 12

The Greatest Game Ever Played

"IT RESEMBLED AN ANTI-BUSING DEMONSTRATION. A NEAR RIOT CAUSED BY A GROUP OF FANS WHO WOULD HAVE CHEERED THE BOSTON STRANGLER." That's how Barry McDermott of *Sports Illustrated* described the chaos that enveloped the Boston Garden after Game Five of the 1976 NBA Finals. During that memorable contest, the parquet was littered with fans; announcers were placed under armed protection; and the Phoenix Suns players and coaches feared for their lives. The busing reference was an obvious analogy for a national writer who only saw Boston as the rest of the country did: torn, violent, and sad. Not even the greatest game in NBA history could separate Boston and its basketball team from the imagery that clouded the city.

❧

The Phoenix Suns were only eight years removed from being an expansion team when they won the Western Conference in 1976, shocking the Seattle Supersonics and then the defending-champion Golden State Warriors in the playoffs. Throughout the 1975–76 season, the "Sunderellas" had been inconsistent performers as they stumbled along to a humble 42-40 record. Tucked in the middle of the season was a winter swoon in which they lost 18 of 24 games. But they peaked at the right time and battled their way to the NBA Finals, where they would face the heavily favored Boston Celtics. Boston—led by All-Stars Dave Cowens, Jo Jo White, and John Havlicek— won all four of their meetings with the Suns during the regular season. In the face of such seemingly long odds, Phoenix's rookie center, Alvan Adams, set as his primary goal not victory, but keeping Cowens from winning the series' Most Valuable Player award.

Despite the one-sided results of the regular-season encounters, Phoenix did hold two distinct advantages over Boston heading into the finals: youth and health. The average age of the Phoenix team was twenty-six; the Celtics' veteran legs averaged thirty-one. Complicating matters for Boston was the fact that their captain, John Havlicek, had torn his plantar fascia, limiting his ability to jump and run.

Entering the playoffs, only two teams in the league made Boston uneasy: the Washington Bullets and the Golden State Warriors. The Bullets' Wes Unseld and Elvin Hayes and the Warriors, with Rick Barry and Phil Smith, created match-up problems for the Celtics. Fortunately, both teams were eliminated prior to potential match-ups with Boston. The Celtics earned their passage to the championship series with victories over the Buffalo Braves and the Bill Fitch–coached Cleveland Cavaliers, both in six games.

As holder of the superior regular-season record, Boston earned home-court advantage in the Finals. In the first two games, the health restrictions of Havlicek didn't hinder Boston's ability to impose their physical will upon the finesse-driven Suns. The Celtics beat the visitors twice on the Garden floor, first 98-87 and then 105-90, giving them a two-games-to-none lead and sparking talk of a sweep.

The series then traveled to the booming southwest city of Phoenix. Game Three was played on Sunday morning to accommodate CBS television, whose main audience was on the East Coast. (Suns management formally apologized to the city's church-goers for the unavoidable conflict.) The early tip-off seemed to favor the young Suns, who held the weary Celtics scoreless through the first five minutes of the game. Phoenix's early lead grew to 23 points, thrilling the 13,304 fans at the Memorial Coliseum. Then, a fistfight between Suns guard Ricky Sobers and Celtic guard Kevin Stacom ignited the team in green to a rally that reduced the lead to 2 points. That was as close as they would get, however, and Phoenix earned a physical, hard-fought 105-98 victory, proving to the Celtics, the nation, and themselves that they could play with the great franchise.

The fisticuffs and overall physical play in the previous game convinced the officials that they needed to take control early in Game Four. Within the first ten minutes of the game, the refs called 21 fouls. When it was all over, the Suns evened the series with a 109-107 victory.

The deadlocked finals headed back to Boston, where an enraged Red Auerbach was waiting. The general manager was furious with the media for what he perceived as biased coverage, which in turn was influencing the impartiality of the officials. Auerbach focused his finger-pointing at the CBS broadcasters: play-by-play man Brent Musburger and color analysts Rick Barry and Mendy Rudolph, a former NBA official. Red had been down this road before and knew exactly what he was doing. He needed to minimize the referees' impact on the game so that Dave Cowens and the other Celtics would have the freedom to assert their will on the court.

Because the NBA was drawing meager television ratings, the games were held at whatever time CBS felt would bring maximum viewership. Game Five in Boston was scheduled for a late Friday-night start, to allow West Coast viewers to arrive home in time to tune in. When Suns Coach John MacLeod made his way onto the court before the game, he could feel the electricity in the crowd. He later surmised in the *New York Times* that this energy might have been artificially enhanced. "I remember walking out onto the floor of the Boston Garden at 9:00 p.m. on a Friday night. There was no air conditioning, it was hot, and there was already a lot of Boston spirit in there because instead of going home [after work] people went right to the taverns and had a couple beers and then came to watch the game."

The CBS broadcast table was situated at center court. Seated with microphone in hand was Brent Musburger, who welcomed the viewers: "Good evening, everybody. It's so nice you could come along and watch this game." Next to him sat a self-conscious Rick Barry with his newfound hair and unbuttoned shirt exposing his chest for all to see. Filling the void where the shirt is customarily buttoned hung a sizable crucifix, as if Barry hoped that the symbol of Christ would ward off the Satan-like Boston fans. Barry, who had a Hall of Fame career with the Golden State Warriors, never could separate his jealousy of John Havlicek and dislike for the Celtics from his job as an announcer. His veiled and subtle aspersions were transparent to the Celtics and their fans. Musburger, who had been accosted by fans when he entered the Garden, attempted to appease the viewers at home. "There's some passionate fans here in Boston," he announced during the broadcast. "I think they thought that maybe Rick [Barry] and Mendy [Rudolph] had favored the Phoenix Suns a little bit in the last two games, but not so folks."

After Musburger's attempt at reconciliation, the camera switched to center court, where Boston's redheaded center was geared up and ready to go. The energy that engulfed the Garden was fueling the Celtics, and especially Dave Cowens, who exploded into the air on the opening jump and tapped the ball to Jo Jo White. Cowens then sprinted for the basket, where he ripped a rebound off the backboard and laid the ball back in for the first points of the game. The Celtics would build off the opening basket to control the pace and the ball. They pushed the lead as high as 22 points during the first half. By intermission, the Celtics had scored 61 points, and the young Suns were reeling 16 points down.

Halftime adjustments by the Suns and long beer lines conspired to slow down the Celtics and their crowd in the second half. A frenzied comeback by Phoenix carried them to a 1-point advantage with just 23 seconds remaining in the game. The Suns' first lead of the night would be short lived, however. A hobbled Havlicek tied the game at 95-95 with a free throw to send the game into overtime.

Defense dominated in the first extra period, as the two sides managed to score just 6 points apiece. The most memorable moment was a controversial non-call by the referees in the waning moments of the overtime session. With the game tied 101-101 and just three seconds on the clock, Boston's Paul Silas pulled down a defensive rebound and signaled for a timeout. Veteran referee Richie Powers looked at Silas but ignored the request and ran up court. Time ran out, and the game headed to a second overtime. The Suns were furious. In the heat of the moment, Silas had forgotten that the Celtics had used all their allotted timeouts. If Powers had acknowledged Silas' request, he would have been obligated to call a technical foul, and the Suns would be granted a technical free throw for a chance to win the game. Years later, Powers confessed that he saw the appeal for timeout but chose to ignore it because he didn't want the game to be decided at the free-throw line. (Suns Assistant Coach Al Bianchi never forgave the referee for his failure to properly officiate the game. In honor of the "stolen victory," Bianchi had a championship ring made for himself, which he had inscribed, "Fuck you, Richie Powers.")

High above the court, thirteen Celtics championship flags hung from the rafters, swaying back and forth with every nervous breath from the collective Celtic crowd. The last time the Boston Garden had hosted an overtime postseason game, Kareem Abdul-Jabbar broke the hearts of these same fans with his famous skyhook in 1974. With that painful moment etched into their memories, the Boston crowd crossed fingers and summoned the blessings of God, the wisdom of Red, and the glory of past Celtic heroes.

The Celtic ghosts appeared to be listening, as the current Celtics opened up a lead in the second overtime against Phoenix. Whereas the first overtime had been controlled by the defenses, the second extra period was ruled by offense. Back and forth the teams ran, until referee Richie Powers appeared to make amends for his earlier decision to ignore Silas' timeout. With the Celtics leading by 3 points, the ball was fed into the low post to Dave Cowens, who was covered by Suns backup center Dennis Awtrey. Cowens, sensing his superiority, turned to face the basket and leaned in to shoot a five-foot jump shot, which sailed through the basket. Underneath the hoop, official Richie Powers looked down on the floor and saw the six-foot-ten Awtrey laid in a heap. Born in Hollywood, the Suns center had sold his acting performance. Powers waved off the basket and called Cowens for an offensive foul. It was Cowens' sixth personal foul, resulting in disqualification. He was furious. If there was one thing Dave Cowens hated more than anything, it was a player that flopped. (On one occasion, after being called for two questionable offensive fouls, the redhead got so incensed that he ran the length of the court yelling, "If you want to see a Goddamn foul, I'll show you a Goddamn foul!" He then proceeded to de-sneaker an opponent before turning to the referee and declaring, "Now *that's* a foul!")

But with the outcome of such a big game hanging in the balance, Cowens simply marched over to the bench and grabbed a towel. On the other end of the floor, John MacLeod relished Cowens' disqualification. Sensing a momentum swing, he called a timeout. With his team trailing by 3 points and only nineteen seconds left on the clock, the Phoenix coach kneeled down in front of his team and with chalk in hand diagrammed a play on the green paint that outlined the parquet floor. As he drew circles signifying players and dotted lines representing potential passing lanes, he looked up to see guard Ricky Sobers attempting to fight a fan behind the bench. Sobers was restrained by his teammates as the Celtic booster reminded Sobers to take a look at the scoreboard.

Within the maelstrom of the Boston Garden, the Suns were able to compose themselves before taking the floor—and then they proceeded to turn the game upside down. In the span of fourteen seconds, Phoenix scored a basket, stole the ball, and scored a second basket, wresting the lead from the home team. The scoreboard showed a mere five seconds remaining for the Celtics to save themselves from what would be the losing end of the greatest comeback in NBA history.

On the sideline, Coach Tommy Heinsohn's complexion went from pale to ashen. He called a timeout and drew up his own play in the hopes of salvaging what would otherwise be a devastating loss—the kind of loss that requires a full offseason of hibernation to recover from. Forward Don Nelson took position out of bounds just over the midcourt line. He accepted the ball from official Dan Murphy and proceeded to slap the ball with his left hand to set the play in motion. From the weak side, Havlicek ran toward Nelson, who placed the ball in the able hands of the team captain.

For fourteen years, the man who was called Czech by his teammates and called Hondo (after the John Wayne movie) by his fans had found a way to win championships. He famously stole the ball during the Eastern Conference Finals in 1965, and nine years later he earned the Finals MVP award against Milwaukee. During the week leading up to this pivotal Game Five in 1976, he spent every waking hour when he wasn't on the court icing his injured foot. Prior to the night's game, he gingerly shot baskets with his son, hoping that he would be able to drag his tired and sore thirty-five-year-old body onto the parquet. Did the captain have another memorable play left in him? His heart said yes, but would his feet allow?

Having received the ball from Nellie, Havlicek put it on the floor with his left hand, once and then a second time and then a last. Arriving at the extended left elbow of the free-throw line, he pushed off his foot, lifted forward, and released the ball from his fingertips. The ball arched through the smoky Garden air and toward the glass backboard. It was a shot he had practiced thousands of times—a running, leaning bank shot. The ball met the backboard and darted down and to the right. As the ball hovered over the hoop, mouths were set ajar on the benches and in the balconies. At home, people stood from their seats or couches. And then the ball smoothly fell through the orange cylinder and the white net.

He had done it again. In living rooms throughout Boston, viewers jumped for joy, while in Phoenix they melted back into their seats. Brent Musburger exulted, "He's done it! John Havlicek won it. It's all over!" But in the midst of such demonstrations, a voice was shouting a conflicting opinion. The man with the unbuttoned shirt indignantly beseeched, "No, there's two seconds to go."

Unaware of Barry's pleas, fans streamed onto the parquet court—as was the Boston Garden tradition after victories of great consequence, and this game had great consequence. For Celtic fans, the custom of rushing the floor was as much a part of Garden history as were the championship flags hanging from the rafters. In 1974, with the championship in the balance, the pressing crowd along the baseline had been thwarted by Jabbar's skyhook. They would not be robbed of the opportunity this time. As a mass, the fans blanketed the floor as the players desperately serpentined their way down the midcourt runway to the locker rooms. The exhausted Celtics fell into their seats and removed sneakers, socks, and tape. It was off to Phoenix.

Back on the floor, in the midst of the pandemonium, official Richie Powers was desperately signaling that the game was not over, that there was one second remaining in the game. He determined that the ball had passed through the hoop with time still on the clock. An incensed fan attacked the graying referee. They wrestled each other to the floor until police, ushers, and Phoenix Suns players separated the official from the mad fan.

This wasn't the first time that Richie Powers proved to be a thorn in the side of Celtics basketball. In his book *Give 'Em the Hook*, Tommy Heinsohn described Powers as a little Napoleon who "just didn't like me." During the 1965 Finals in Los Angeles, Powers called six fouls on Heinsohn in sixteen minutes. On several of those calls, Powers had overruled his partner, who had made the opposite call. Disqualification in such a critical game incited Heinsohn, who ranted and raved all the way to the bench and kicked the scorers' table. After the game, Powers mocked the disgruntled forward: "I let him do his little dance, and then he called me names that couldn't be printed on asbestos paper. . . . He's like a petulant little boy when he doesn't get his way."

After Havlicek's apparent game winner, the Celtic players back in the locker room were busy disrobing and preparing to shower. Then came word that there was one second remaining on the clock, and the game still had to be completed. Reluctantly, the players returned to the floor, some without tape or socks. One second was put back on the clock, and Powers walked the ball to the baseline under the Suns' basket. Phoenix would have to traverse the full length of the court and shoot, all within one tick of the clock. Instead, Suns player Paul Westphal concocted a plan for the team to call an illegal timeout.

They would be penalized with a technical foul, but they would then receive the ball at half court following the Celtic free throw. Coach Macleod agreed with the plan, and he called the timeout. Jo Jo White successfully shot the technical free throw to give Boston a two-point lead.

On the Celtics bench, Paul Silas looked at the scoreboard and saw that his team still hadn't committed the requisite number of fouls to earn the Suns free throws on a non-shooting violation. Silas made his way to Coach Heinsohn and argued that the team should foul whichever Sun got the ball, thus killing the clock and securing victory. Heinsohn rejected the idea. For one thing, he didn't think Phoenix would have ample time on the clock to catch and shoot. But more important, Heinsohn didn't trust Richie Powers. A foul on the floor could be interpreted as a shooting foul, putting a Suns player on the foul line with a chance to tie the game.

Now trailing by 2 points, the Suns looked to enter the ball to a cutting Paul Westphal, who would catch the ball in front of the Celtics bench, turn, and shoot—all in one second. But as he broke, the Celtics anticipated Westphal's cut and took away his lane. Instead, the ball was sent by chest pass to the top of the key, where Gar Heard caught the ball with his back to the basket. Heard pivoted on his left foot and pushed a turnaround jump-shot that rose high above the height of the backboard. The ball reached its pinnacle and descended, landing on the back edge of the front rim, where it bounced off the cylinder to the back rim before dropping through the hoop. The game was going to a third overtime period. At the CBS table, a stunned Musburger proclaimed, "I don't believe it." Next to him, Brent's partner Rick Barry couldn't contain himself as he rejoiced with a whelp of, "Yeahhhhh! Unbelievable!"

(The process of catching, turning, and releasing the ball seemed to take more than one second. Someone in management agreed, and the timekeeper was never heard from again.)

On the floor, Silas fumed for not being allowed to take the foul. Up in the front row of the Garden's first balcony, Suns radio announcer Al McCoy reported the "shot heard around the world" to ecstatic listeners back in Phoenix—even though a fan had fallen into his lap and passed out. It was the same fan that had been punching McCoy in the shoulder throughout the game every time the Celtics had made a good play.

With the game extended into a third overtime, the Celtics turned to a little-known rookie from Long Beach State named Glen McDonald. With fresh legs, the guard was able to run and jump at speeds and heights that other players could no longer muster. This energy provided a spark for the home team. In all, McDonald scored 6 of the Celtics' 16 points in the seventh period. Over the airwaves, Musburger praised the seldom-used rookie: "He has been a disappointment to the Celtics this year but here when they most needed him."

McDonald's heroics helped to build an insurmountable lead, and the Celtics held on. In the final moments, Jo Jo White, who had played sixty minutes in the game and had to sit on the floor during timeouts and free throws, dribbled out the clock on the Celtics' two-point victory.

For the guard from Kansas, Game Five was his greatest moment. In the scorebook, White had accounted for 33 points, 15 in the overtime periods.

The game had started on Friday but ended on Saturday. John Havlicek, who had not been sure if he would be able to play at all, logged fifty-eight minutes. In the locker room, Coach Heinsohn fell unconscious from dehydration and had to be given an IV to replenish his fluids. According to former Celtic Steve Kuberski, Heinsohn lost twenty-five pounds of fluids during the game. This was actually the second time Heinsohn had lost consciousness after a game. Following an earlier playoff game against New York, he fell to the ground, and many feared he had suffered a heart attack. The training staff revived him by packing him in ice while he recovered.

It was after 12:30 a.m. when Brent Musburger signed off to the TV audience, "Saying goodbye from the Boston Garden, where you have just watched the most incredible game in the history of the NBA: Boston 128, Phoenix 126 in triple overtime."

In the Suns locker room, the team was devastated. They had played the Celtics shot for shot despite the hostile environment on and off the court. In the following week's issue of *Sports Illustrated*, Barry McDermott recounted the hardships the Phoenix players were subjected to throughout the game: "Phoenix General Manager Jerry Colangelo all but suggested that the Suns needed either more police guards or machine guns to protect themselves. Besides suffering an agonizing defeat, the Suns had to endure the attentions of a mob of sloshed crazies." Coach Macleod had to weed Boston fans out of the Suns huddles during timeouts, and he suspected that the chaos in the arena intimidated the players more than the Celtics did.

The Suns may not have been intimidated, but they were facing elimination as they headed across country for Sunday's sixth game. The tip-off was scheduled for 10:00 a.m. Phoenix time. Months earlier, the Church of Jesus Christ of Latter-day Saints had reserved the arena for their annual assembly. The convention had been scheduled to commence services in the morning, but the church agreed to amend their time to 2:00 p.m., only after CBS and the NBA agreed to pay all expenses.

On the plane ride to Arizona, Jo Jo White sat with backcourt mate Charlie Scott. In 1968, the two guards had been teammates on the U.S. Olympic team that won the gold medal in Mexico City. White had left that experience with a negative opinion of Scott, whom he felt was a selfish player and had a penchant to talk when he should be quiet.

The Celtics management was aware of White's disdain for the shooting guard, but the team acquired Scott anyway. The player they traded for him was the unhappy Paul Westphal, who had been looking for more playing time. When the media asked Tommy Heinsohn about the reported tense relationship between White and Scott, Heinsohn snapped, "It doesn't disturb me one damn bit about his compatibility with Jo Jo."

But it did bother Jo Jo. The disdain he held for Scott carried over to their Celtic partnership. The two guards spent the first half of the 1975–76 season fighting for control of the ball and for turf. It wasn't until midseason that the two met somewhere in the middle, and White learned to tolerate the boisterous off-guard.

Scott was considered a head case during his time in Phoenix, and he had been offered around the league as trade bait but only drew interest from three of the league's seventeen other teams. When the Celtics agreed to take him in exchange for the young Westphal, Bob Ryan expressed his surprise at the transaction in a column in the *Boston Globe*: "Charlie Scott—who once ranked with Arthur Fielder, Gilles Gilbert, and Patty Hearst as the unlikeliest inhabitants of the Western World to ever become a Celtic—believe it or not, is a Celtic." In a neighboring column, Ray Fitzgerald expounded further on the subject: "I like the trade, if only for the fun of watching to see if the leopard can change his spots."

Scott was raised in Harlem, New York, but had moved with his family to North Carolina as a youth. Coach Dean Smith offered him a scholarship to play at the University of North Carolina, making Scott the first black player in either the Atlantic Coast Conference or the Southeastern Conference to be bestowed with such a grant. It was a difficult time for Scott, who was subjected to great hatred wherever he played. In South Carolina, a fan held up a sign that read, "Go back to Harlem, nigger." While playing against North Carolina State, an opposing player spit in his face.

After leading North Carolina to two NCAA Final Fours, Scott matriculated to the free-wheeling American Basketball Association, where he averaged twenty-six field-goal attempts a night. After throwing up thousands of shots with the red-white-and-blue basketball, he jumped from the fledgling league to the NBA. Following three years of discontent in Phoenix, he arrived in Boston preceded by his reputation.

Through the first five games, Scott's performance in the finals had been subpar. The guard with number 11 on his jersey had fouled out in each of the five games and shot an erratic 11 for 44 from the field. The fact that he had spent so much time on the bench in foul purgatory is what drew Jo Jo White to take the seat next to Scott's on the plane ride after Game Five. On this trip from Boston to Phoenix, White's policy of tolerance evolved into one of encouragement. Pointing to Scott's fresh legs, White knew that Scott was in prime position to take over Game Six. Scott agreed; he was always up for taking over a game.

The next morning, the players were roused by a 6:00 a.m. wakeup call. The Celtics then unrolled a dominating performance over their foes. Although the game was tied 66-66 in the third quarter, the Celtics never felt threatened on their way to an 87-80 victory and the franchise's thirteenth NBA championship. The star of the game was Charlie Scott, who scored 25 points to go with 11 rebounds, 5 steals, and 3 assists. CBS and *Sport* magazine named Jo Jo White the MVP of the series. His reward was an AMC Pacer (which *Time* magazine later rated one of the fifty worst cars in history). The team received a playoff bonus of $250,000 to divide as they saw fit.

In the corner of the locker room, veteran John Havlicek was asked by a reporter if winning a championship was getting old. With champagne in hand, he shook his head no and said, "It never gets old. It only gets old if you lose."

CHAPTER 13

Phase II

IN THE SPRING OF 1976, BOSTON WAS IN THE MIDST OF PHASE II OF SCHOOL DESEGREGATION BUT WAS NO CLOSER TO RESOLUTION THAN IT HAD BEEN ON THE DAY OF JUDGE ARTHUR GARRITY'S RULING IN JUNE 1974. Since that time, appeals to reverse the ruling were denied by both appellate and supreme courts. This confirmed the brilliance of the written judgment but also raised the ire of the anti-busing contingency. In all, sixteen appeals were made to the Circuit Court and six to the Supreme Court. Judge Garrity was 22-0.

Incensed by the court's repeated support of the original decision, Boston School Committee member Pixie Palladino offered a harsh critique of the highest court's collective make-up: "The Supreme Court is a pack of flaming liberals who are definitely out of touch with reality, out of touch with the people of Boston, and out of touch with the times. I would expect this type of political oppression in Russia or Cuba or China."

In spite of the turmoil that simmered throughout the city, life went on. The Celtics were winning basketball games, and Boston was in the midst of a massive redevelopment program that would reassert the "Hub of the Universe" as a world-class destination. The new hotels, government buildings, and roadways stood out in contrast to the struggles taking place in the streets and courtrooms. The Reverend Martin Luther King Jr. had argued a decade earlier that this very development should include Roxbury and its people.

King's message led to organized efforts to pressure the city to establish job initiatives and redevelopment programs for all of Boston's people. One such effort in April 1976 led to a meeting at City Hall to discuss job allotment in the city's many construction projects. Ted Landsmark was the attorney representing the interests of minorities at the meeting. He arrived at the State Street subway stop and made his way up the stairs of the Old State House, the basement of which served as a subway station. Just outside the swinging doors of the city's oldest government building, the fate of a young country had been profoundly affected two centuries before.

⍧

"The said Michael Johnson was willfully and feloniously murdered at King Street in Boston. . . . On the evening of the 5th—instant between the hours of nine and ten by the discharge of musket or muskets loaded with bullets two of which were shot through his body by a party of soldiers."

That's what the death certificate read following Michael Johnson's killing on March 5, 1770. Johnson, whose given name was Crispus Attucks, was the first American to die in the colonists' uprising that protested England's occupation of Boston. Attucks' cause of death was described as "killed by two musket balls striking the victim in the right and left breast." Five patriots were shot dead by British troops that day in a slaughter that would come to be known as the Boston Massacre.

The *Boston & Country Gazette Journal*—which boasted "Containing all the freshest advice Foreign and Domestic"—reported that the bells from Boston, Charlestown, and Roxbury rang, and shops were closed as the caskets of the martyrs were carried through the streets of Boston to the Granary Burial Ground, where the five men were buried together as a symbol of their collective act of heroism.

Calling himself Michael Johnson to avoid recapture by bounty hunters who roamed the streets of Boston, Attucks stood shoulder to shoulder with his fellow colonists, leading the charge that would ignite a rebellion. In the shadow of Boston's State House, five men died in a quest for basic human rights—rights that would be promised to all but accessible to only some.

Crispus Attucks made history as the first American to die for the cause of independence. The fact that he was also a runaway slave had added symbolism two centuries later, as the struggle of his people continued on these same streets. From the doors of the historic Old State House, commuters now surfaced from subway cars to face their everyday tasks and responsibilities, detached from the historical significance of where they tread.

❦

Back in 1969, Boston's New City Hall was constructed mere blocks from the Old State House, more than 250 years its senior. The two buildings represented the city's past and its future, and they lay at the physical and figurative center of Boston.

When the New City Hall was first introduced to Boston, architect Michael McKinnell commented on the special arrangement of the mayor's office, which looked out onto Washington Street. In the *Boston Globe*, McKinnell described the office's location as offering "a sort of dialogue with the hiving life of the city." It was at this window that Mayor Kevin White stood with his newly assigned deputy, Clarence Jeep Jones, on April 5, 1976. They watched a group of white students, fresh from a meeting with public officials to protest the busing of students into their neighborhood schools, making their way across the courtyard. White and Jones grew concerned when they noticed a lone black man moving toward the students in the brick passageway below.

Ever since he took office, White's ultimate, self-absorbed fear was that if the city "blows up," it would be on his watch. For years, the officials who occupied this building, including White himself, had been unable or unwilling to find compromise that could resolve the racial strife that had plagued Boston for the better part of a decade. Now, from his window, the mayor was about to witness his fear become reality.

White could only stand and watch as the angry white students unleashed their rage on the innocent and unsuspecting Ted Landsmark. Committing the ultimate indiscretion of using the American flag as a weapon of hate, the attackers represented the darkest culmination of years of conflict that had generated such tension among the city's people, its officials, and the principles of liberty that had been so central to Boston's growth and vitality over the centuries.

In the aftermath of the attack Mayor White could make no sense of the senseless. "He [Landsmark] was taking no part in any demonstration, yet he became a victim because he was a black man who came in contact with a bunch of hooligans," White said. Calling the attack "an affront to common decency," he continued: "Violence will not be tolerated in this city. Guilty persons will be punished to the full extent possible regardless of color. I was nauseated."

The crime of incomprehensible violence could not be explained by white or black. For the black community, the attack was a painful reminder of a struggle that seemed to have no end in sight. The Reverend Taylor of Ebenezer Baptist Church remarked, "It seems like war is being declared on black people in Boston, and we are helpless victims." From the City Hall steps, State Senator William Owens expounded further: "People of color are not safe in Boston; people of color from other parts of the nation should stay away from Boston; people of color must unite against the climate of racism in the city; people of color in Boston should ask for federal protection because the city has failed to protect them."

Shortly after the attack, *Boston Globe* columnist Mike Barnicle wrote, "When you take a good close look at what happened two days ago, you realize it wasn't really about busing at all. It was about race, about the basics, about calling people 'niggers' and laughing as they hit the ground, nose breaking, and clothes spattered with blood."

❀

The Landsmark attack personified the pain and difficulties that consumed the city throughout the first two years of the desegregation efforts. In the second year of implementation, Judge Garrity removed the word *temporary* from the plan and adopted a formal policy known as "Phase II." This official plan was authored in most part by sociologists Marvin Scott and Robert Dentler of Boston University. From within the walls of their faculty offices, they concluded that the city needed to intensify the scope of desegregation by eighteen thousand to twenty-five thousand.

Included in the Phase II plan was an expanded role for the community of South Boston and its high school. This directive was ordered even though the peninsula neighborhood had borne the brunt of Phase I and continued to reel from its effects. Dr. Charles Glenn, who had devised the original plan, urged Dentler and Scott to leapfrog South Boston, but his pleas were ignored and openly mocked. Dentler chided Glenn, "I could write a better plan than you with both hands tied behind my back."

In addition to South Boston, Dentler and Scott focused on two other neighborhoods where the high school populations were more than 95 percent white and were thus in need of "balancing": East Boston and Charlestown.

Police Commissioner Robert DiGrazia reported that his department had received threats that if East Boston High School was chosen as the school to desegregate, then the tunnels that lead from downtown Boston to East Boston (and Logan Airport) would be blown up. While some saw DiGrazia as a man obsessed with television cameras and an alarmist who overreacted both on the street and behind a microphone, the threat was taken seriously enough that Judge Garrity made the decision to bypass the neighborhood on the east side of the harbor: "East Boston High School, which is 95 percent white, is across the harbor and adjacent to Logan Airport. To desegregate these eleven schools [including elementary and junior high schools] would require transporting four to five thousand children through the tunnels with the gassy air and heavy traffic hours." In translation: East Boston would be allowed to "voluntarily" integrate. The onus of Phase II thus fell on Charlestown.

✺

Annexed by the city of Boston in 1874, Charlestown is situated at the northern end of the city, in the inner harbor. It long served as a port of commerce and was formerly the site of the bustling Charlestown Navy Yard, once a major source of employment for the neighborhood residents prior to the yard's closing in 1974.

Charlestown's storied history dates back to John Winthrop's first steps on these shores in the 1600s. The Battle of Bunker Hill was waged here on June 17, 1775, as the colonists fought valiantly against the British forces at Breed's Hill. The town constructed a monument to honor those who fought and died. The cornerstone of the memorial was laid by General Marquis de Lafayette in 1825 and was dedicated by statesman Daniel Webster in 1843.

The 221-foot-tall Bunker Hill Monument is a source of great pride for the community that financed and built it.

During the Civil War, the Union Army turned to Charlestown to fortify the fight to preserve the union, and the people of the proud town answered. A son of the community, Edward Foss, was inspired to write, "The men, who in the darkest hour of the country's peril, went manfully to the struggle to resist aggression, put down rebellion, and defend the stars and stripes, which to us are the choicest of the American legacies."

Charlestown was the birthplace of Samuel Morse, inventor of the telegraph, and home to many prestigious people, including five men who established institutions of higher learning: John Harvard (Cambridge, Massachusetts), Charles Tufts (Boston), Gardner Colby (Waterville, Maine), William Carleton (Northfield, Minnesota), and Thomas Doane (Crete, Nebraska).

While these distinctions are a source of great pride for the neighborhood, Charlestown was also the victim of persecution. In June 1775, British troops burned the city to the ground, leaving its inhabitants to rebuild homes and stores brick by brick. A half-century later, in 1834, the Ursuline Convent in the town was torched by anti-Catholic forces that condemned the religion that was heavily practiced in the community.

Protected by the merging waters of the Atlantic Ocean and the Mystic and Charles Rivers, Charlestown is connected to Boston proper by a network of bridges. The blue-collar neighborhood used its physical isolation to sustain an ideological separation. This predominantly Irish-American neighborhood, like South Boston, deeply valued its right to protect the community that had been molded to conform to the beliefs, morals, and desires of its residents.

❦

Judge Garrity would spare no expense to facilitate the implementation of Phase II in Charlestown. He did not want a repeat of South Boston—nobody did. To ensure this, the neighborhood was transformed into a virtual police state; Boston police, U.S. Marshalls, and the National Guard were summoned with the task of "peace keeping." Helicopters hovered above the streets while the National Guard marched below, and police flexed their muscles and snapped their batons on street corners and in school hallways.

The occupation of Charlestown greatly affected the quality of its inhabitants' lives. Parents were forbidden access to their children's schools; nighttime curfews constricted movement through the neighborhood; ordinances that outlawed the congregation of three or more people made a walk to the corner store with siblings an act of defiance; and Hail Mary marches comprised of mothers pushing baby carriages were seen as riotous and thus disbanded by forces dressed in riot gear.

Initially, many of the police sympathized with the plight of the residents. But sympathetic or not, their mere presence was burdensome. It didn't take long for tensions between residents and police to bubble into conflict.

Reports of police brutality and free-swinging batons led frustrated residents to seek revenge. At night, mattresses and cars were set on fire to lure responding police and firefighters into the range of hurled bricks and Molotov cocktails. During the day, police were occasional targets of propelled potatoes laced with razors or of piano wire that stretched between telephone poles across the narrow streets, awaiting unsuspecting motorcycle police. Reprisals even targeted horses from the mounted patrol, which were found grazing on poisoned apples.

Such demonstrations didn't discourage the authorities but instead led them to step up the efforts at control. The manpower required to maintain such a presence placed great constraints on the police and its budget. In the first four years of busing, Boston paid more than $20 million in police overtime. At City Hall, these excesses roused the never-shy City Councilor

Dapper O'Neil to suggest that busing was nothing more than "a racket to make a buck."

Police were required to work twelve-hour shifts and be on call seven days a week. For their efforts they would receive overtime checks that could be as much as $7,000 a month. With this newfound discretionary income, some law enforcement officers parlayed the tragedy playing out in the streets of Boston into a new boat or a second home; others invested in the weekly high-stakes card games that took place in the back of the Charlestown precinct. (Cash pots would often climb as high as $25,000.)

Ultimately it was the duty of these police officers to ensure that the yellow buses that rolled into Monument Square were able to deliver their passengers to the high school. Every day, students filed past tactical police and into the school, passing through metal detectors in the entrance lobby. They were not greeted by words of Thoreau or Socrates or Frost but by a reminder of their current crisis— a list of prohibited items, which included: firearms, knives, razors, or sharpened objects; any athletic equipment (baseball bats, hockey sticks, karate sticks, or ropes); pipes, brass knuckles, and other metal objects (screwdrivers, wrenches, hammers, other metal tools); chains, whips, or ropes; combs with metal teeth or rat tails; scissors, metal nail files, or hatpins; mace and other chemical sprays such as spray paint and spray deodorant; bottles; and all other instruments not listed above that may inflict bodily harm.

In the classrooms, cockroaches outnumbered students, and truants exceeded attendees. Students soon discovered that presence in class was not a prerequisite for promotion. Students who opted to miss months at a time would still receive their assignment for the next grade because schools became more concerned with balancing than with teaching. A sign at one of the many Charlestown protests summarized the effects of Phase II: "School used to be fun. Now it's a riot!"

In reviewing the harmful effects endured by grandmothers, students, husbands, and wives, James Coleman of Chicago, the man who had originated the concept of busing for integration, came to realize that the basis for his doctrine had failed. In his words, South Boston and Charlestown became "innocent third parties." Busing had served to separate the races further, while also negatively impacting the quality of education being offered to all. Progress in the schools was now measured not by median test scores or college acceptances but by the number of police assigned to a school's hallway.

As School Committee members and city officials were busy posturing to ensure the security of their positions, the schools were in a state of disrepair. Facilities were unkempt, teachers lacked training, and counseling was sub par. The parents of black students who were going to be driven halfway across the city to attend these schools shook their heads in disbelief upon arriving at open houses at South Boston and Charlestown high schools, which they had assumed would be institutions of grandeur.

As Louise Day Hicks once said, the answer was in "education not transportation." Sadly, steps were never taken to enhance one, which would have prevented the need for the other.

CHAPTER 14

Celtic Outsiders

WALTER BROWN, AN NBA PIONEER, ESTABLISHED THE BOSTON CELTICS FRANCHISE IN 1946 AND REMAINED OWNER OF THE TEAM FOR TWO DECADES. During that time, he supported the team financially and spiritually. He was the lifeblood of the franchise, and along with Red Auerbach, he set the franchise on a path toward greatness. After Brown's death at the age of fifty-nine on Labor Day 1964, the Celtics honored their patriarch with black arm bands and dedicated the season to him, which they concluded with the franchise's seventh championship. Following the season, Brown was inducted into the NBA Hall of Fame and would later have the NBA championship trophy named in his honor. In the rafters of the Boston Garden (and its successor, TD Banknorth Garden), he is honored with the retired jersey number 1, as he was the number-one Celtic.

After Brown's death, ownership of the team changed hands eight times in fourteen years. The jewel known as the Boston Celtics was owned by outsiders who possessed the team not as an extension of the community but as a trophy to boast about at cocktail parties. These individuals, as a collection, would prove to be clouded by ego and limited by both moral and financial restrictions that would adversely affect the team on the court and in the front office.

BOSTON CELTICS OWNERSHIP, 1946–1983

Walter Brown and Boston Garden Arena Corp.	1946–1949
Walter Brown and Lou Pieri	1950–1964
Majorie Brown and Lou Pieri	1964–1965
Rupert Knickerbocker Breweries	1965–1966
Marvin Kratter	1966–1968
Ballantine Brewery	1968–1969
Trans National Communications	1969–1971
Investors Funding Corporation	1971–1972
Robert Schmertz	1972–1974
Robert Schmertz and Irv Levin	1974–1975
Irv Levin and Harold Lipton	1975–1978
John Y. Brown and Harry Mangurian	1978–1979
Harry Mangurian	1979–1983

For the 1964–65 season, the team was controlled by Brown's wife, Marjorie, along with Lou Pieri, who had been a part owner with Brown since 1950. The following summer, the two parties sold the team for $3 million to Ruppert Knickerbocker Breweries, which in turn was purchased by New York real estate developer Marvin Kratter and his corporation, National Equities. Kratter, who once owned Brooklyn's Ebbetts Field, became known around the Boston Garden for his lucky green jacket and his good-luck ring, which he'd ask the players to rub before games, causing Bill Russell to wince. In a column in the *Boston Globe*, Ray Fitzgerald wrote of Kratter's years in ownership: "In those days, Kratter supposedly had several zillion dollars, but his fortune always seemed to be tied up in silver mines or plutonium or hula-hoop production. Marvin sat next to the bench at home games, and since he was roughly the size of the Goodyear blimp, the bench always seemed crowded, even with half the team in the game."

Kratter sold the franchise in 1968 to the Ballantine Brewery for $4 million, a deal that netted the real estate developer a significant return on his investment. In the 1950s Ballantine was the third-leading beer distributor in the country; such celebrities as Ernest Hemingway, John Steinbeck, Joe DiMaggio, Marilyn Monroe, Frank Sinatra, Jim Thorpe, and Rocky Marciano enjoyed the tasty brew. Throughout the 1960s, however, the brewery faced declining market share and so acquired the team in an effort to enhance the brand. Dick Greibel, president of P. Ballantine and Sons, announced to the Greater Boston Chamber of Commerce that the company "purchased the Celtics because of their winning tradition, and we don't intend to let it falter. The company wants to be associated with a brand name image throughout the country." The brewery intended to "invest a great deal of money into the Celtics organization, to bring in the best talent available so that Boston can have winning teams for a long, long time."

One year later, Ballantine sold its interest to a conglomerate known as Trans National Communications Inc. for $6 million in cash and stock in their corporation. Part owners in the conglomerate included former football greats Pat Summerall, Dick Lynch, Earl Morrall, and Jim Katcavage, and Yankee Hall of Famer Whitey Ford. The organization was a media giant that owned the radio broadcast rights to the football Giants and Jets and the baseball Mets. The principal owner of the corporation was Ellis Woody Erdman, whose motto was, "Our only limitation is that there are only twenty-four hours in a day."

Soon after Trans National took over control of the team, it was discovered that the corporation was cash poor. Bills for airlines and hotels went unpaid, and cash receipts at the box office would go missing. More than once Red Auerbach had to reach into his own pocket or rally friends to raise sufficient funds to meet payroll. In the 1971 draft, the Celtics had to skip over more talented players and settle for Clarence Glover, whose contract would be more manageable. The owners were so constrained by limited cashflow that, in desperation, they attempted the unthinkable. In the middle of the 1971–72 season, Celtics Chairman Woody Erdman summoned Coach Tommy Heinsohn to New York. Erdman informed the coach that ownership was planning to go in another direction and had decided to make Heinsohn both coach and head of basketball operations, while part-owner Dick Lynch would assume the role of general manager. A confused Heinsohn asked Erdman what Red Auerbach's role would be with the team. Erdman responded matter-of-factly that Auerbach would no longer be involved with the Boston Celtics.

When Heinsohn returned to Boston, he sat down with Auerbach and alerted him of the New York group's plans. But Auerbach was a step ahead and had already been talking to the Philadelphia 76ers about taking control of their basketball operations. Before action was taken to fire Auerbach, however, Trans National Communication turned insolvent. Ownership reverted to the majority stockholder, which was Ballantine Breweries.

Ownership was transferred again when a group of New York bankers known as Investors Funding Corporation assumed control of the team as a quasi custodian/investor, until they came to an agreement with the Hollywood partnership of Irv Levin and Harold Lipton. The NBA voided the agreement, however, because an entity related to Levin and Lipton already held an ownership interest in the Seattle Supersonics. This allowed third-party Robert Schmertz the option to purchase the team for $5.1 million, which he accepted.

Schmertz was the owner of a $60 million real estate development corporation in New Jersey named Leisure Technology. The company built retirement communities and boasted General Alexander Haig as a board member. The jetsetter from Jersey, who considered himself a collector of sports teams, also owned the New England Whalers hockey team and the New York Stars of the World Football League, and previously maintained an interest in the Portland Trailblazers. He bought the Celtics as a "hobby," well aware that a sports team is not a good investment. At the press conference held at the First National Bank of Boston, which financed the acquisition, the financial institution announced that the loan would be in default if the team was relocated to another city. At the same press conference, Red Auerbach compared Bob Schmertz to Walter Brown. "Victories came first with Walter, everything else was secondary, and I can see that same trait in Bob. For the last two years we've been in limbo, and the year before that it was worse. There've been a lot of times in the last few years I've been ready to quit. I've been down, real down. The only thing that's kept me here is all the years and all the emotion tied up in this thing. But now we're ready to go."

Schmertz loved to surround himself with athletes and beautiful women. With his private plane and closetful of leisure suits, he was often seen squiring head-turning dates to games and functions. On one such occasion at the Hartford Civic Center (where the Celtics occasionally hosted home games), Schmertz entered the arena with his shapely significant other, and the couple proceeded to take a seat at the scorer's table, located directly across the court from the team benches. The table lacked an apron, and players and fans were treated to a different kind of hand checking, one that offered bored substitutes a titillating distraction from the bench.

Schmertz's regular girlfriend at the time, Phyllis, would later become his wife and was twenty years his junior. Schmertz often said about her, "I don't know whether I should adopt her or marry her." During one nationally tele-vised Celtics game, an ABC cameraman couldn't help but fix his camera on the owner's box seats, inducing announcer Chris Schenkel to report to the viewers at home, "There's Red Auerbach, Bob Schmertz, and—wow, who is that pretty thing?!"

Schmertz owned the Boston Celtics from 1972 to 1974, until Levin and Lipton filed suit against the New Jersey developer alleging that the Celtics owner had reneged on a verbal contract in which Schmertz agreed to sell them 50 percent of the team after they divested themselves from the Seattle fran-chise. At the trial, Levin's attorney, Frank Rothman, whispered into the ear of Schmertz witness Red Auerbach, "Be careful about what you say, Red. You never know who your boss is going to be when this is all over." In the end, Levin and Lipton were victorious and were awarded a 50 percent stake in the business. In February 1975, Bob Schmertz was indicted on bribery charges related to a retirement project that he was involved with in New Jersey. Five months later, the forty-nine-year-old Celtics owner had a stroke and died. Phyllis later sued Presbyterian Hospital in New York for malpractice and was awarded more than $5.7 million. Irving Levin, who came to be known as "Swerving Irving" for his slick demeanor, meanwhile wrested complete control of the team from the Schmertz estate.

Now in command with his partner, Harold Lipton (whose daughter Peggy starred in the 1960s television series *The Mod Squad*), Levin treated the team like a movie production. In the 1950s, Levin, a former World War II fighter pilot, had started a movie production company called National General Corporation (NGC). With that company he produced films such as *Divorce American Style*; *The Cheyenne Social Club*, featuring Henry Fonda and Jimmy Stewart; and *The Getaway*, starring Paul Newman and Ali McGraw. It was also with NGC that he wooed British actress Carol White to Hollywood to star in the film *Daddy's*

Gone A Hunting. The subtitle of that movie was apropos: "When the Love Story Ends, the Nightmare Begins." According to the book *Fallen Stars: Tragic Lives and Lost Careers*, Levin and White had an extra-marital affair that would end White's marriage and lead Levin's wife to attempt suicide.

⊕

Just days away from raising the flag to commemorate the 1976 championship, the Celtics were still without their star power forward, who was holding out for a better contract. Red Auerbach walked onto the practice floor and gathered the team around him.

In the fall of 1972, Paul Silas had come to the Celtics from Phoenix in exchange for the rights to ABA star Charlie Scott. At the time, the six-foot-seven forward was coming off an All-Star season in which he averaged 16 points and 11 rebounds per game. Silas wasn't happy about being traded to Boston but said he would "go where the money is." Four years later, during which time the Celtics won two championships, he was again in search of the money. After the 1975–76 season, the team held an option on the forward, and it was their intention to execute that option. As was standard practice at the time, Auerbach's secretary mailed out a boilerplate contract to Silas, who advanced the document to his agent, Larry Fleischer. The agent found a loophole in the contract that allowed his client to become a free agent. The league's collective-bargaining agreement stated that team options are only enforceable if the contract offer was at least as favorable as the terms contained in the last year of the prior contract. In Silas' case, his previous contract had been prepared by the Phoenix Suns, who had added the phrase "this is a no-cut contract" to the last page of the document. Because the Celtics had failed to include this additional clause in the contract offer to Silas, it could be construed as "less favorable" terms, thus allowing the player to seek alternative employment.

Auerbach knew that the contract error placed the team in a difficult position. For years he had manipulated every covenant, codicil, and clause in NBA regulations to assert leverage on the league, other teams, and his own players. Auerbach made sure that he held the position of power in contract negotiations and only paid a player or coach or trainer the minimum possible. But now he lacked leverage in the negotiation with Silas. The Celtics offered Silas a salary of $250,000, but the forward, in the position of power, was seeking $330,000. In the end, the $80,000 difference was an amount that owner Irv Levin was unwilling to part with, and the Celtics had to part with Silas.

So, prior the start of the 1976–77 season, Auerbach stood on the practice floor with the players and informed them that the team had a chance to acquire Detroit forward Curtis Rowe in exchange for the rights to Silas. Lurking in the back of the semi-circle, Dave Cowens went red. During their four years together, Silas and Cowens had combined to average 28 rebounds a game. Silas was a leader and a positive presence on and off the floor. His contributions to two championships could not be measured by just his domination around the basket; he was a galvanizing force that put the Celtics in the best position to succeed. An enraged Cowens slammed a basketball to the floor and raved at Auerbach, "Pay him the fucking money, and we'll win another championship!"

In the midst of the negotiations with Silas, Levin had called Coach Tommy Heinsohn and asked his opinion of the player. Heinsohn didn't care about the money; he only cared about the players and their contributions to the team. The coach implored the owner, "I don't know what you're paying him or what he's asking for, but I can tell you he's the second most important player on the team, and you should pay him whatever you have to pay."

Ignoring the recommendations of both the coach and the team's best player, Levin refused to pay Silas the money. Instead, the Celtics acquired

Rowe in a three-way trade the day before the season opener. In the following day's paper, Auerbach was careful to separate himself from the deal. "Irv Levin is the one who pulled it together," he was quoted as saying. At the press conference introducing the new player, Rowe shared his excitement in joining his new team: "Anyone who has ever played the game of basketball has had the ultimate goal of playing for the Celtics." From that moment on, his partnership with the Celtics only depreciated.

In addition to Rowe, the Celtics purchased the contract of his UCLA teammate Sidney Wicks from the Portland Trailblazers to fill out the roster. Wicks was made available after a trade between Portland and the New Orleans Jazz turned contentious as Wicks refused to accept a contract offer from the Jazz. Subsequent to the failed trade, New Orleans General Manager Barry Mendelson offered, "Sidney Wicks thinks he's a superstar. But as far as I'm concerned he isn't half the player Pete Maravich is, or the human being."

This opinion didn't deter Irv Levin. He figured that if Rowe and Wicks were good enough for John Wooden at UCLA, they were good enough for the Celtics. Prior to the opening game, Levin boasted to Coach Heinsohn, "We got two players for less than what we would have paid the other guy [Silas]."

The loss of Silas was devastating to the team and profoundly affected Cowens. The All-Star center was so upset with the team's failure to bring back his friend and rebounding partner that he took a leave of absence eight games into the season. He was not interested in playing with teammates who, in his estimation, were more concerned with the statistic of field goal attempts than with wins. Cowens would return later in the season, but he missed thirty-two games in all. Heinsohn would do his best coaching job to lead a distracted, aging team to the playoffs, only to be eliminated by the Philadelphia 76ers in the second round.

Describing the Celtics under Levin's ownership, Ed Gillooly of the *Herald* wrote, "The team went from one of the strongest to one of the weakest in two years." After winning the championship in 1976, the team spiraled into a freefall that was sparked in large part by the failure to retain the services of Paul Silas, combined with the acquisition of mercenary shooters and the declining health of captain John Havlicek and Jo Jo White.

🏀

At the beginning of the 1977–78 season, the Boston Celtics roster featured seven former All-Stars. The task of leading such an ensemble fell upon a coach who recognized that the league was changing along with society. The absence of respect for authority, the increasing influence of selfish play, and an increase in drug use all conspired to impact the coach's role. Heinsohn himself used this analogy to illustrate the evolution of the coaching vocation: "The job has gone from dictator to Henry Clay the Great Compromiser." Duties that used to consist of teaching, diagramming, and leading were reduced to acting as custodian of men with great financial means yet a seeming inability to govern themselves. While on the road, Heinsohn followed players into the bathrooms at airports to make sure that their intention was relevant to restroom activities and not the consumption of drugs, which had became prevalent throughout the league.

The loss of Silas and the addition of players who didn't fit the mold of the prototypical Celtic infected the program on the court. Boston started the season 1-8 and never recovered. Blame fell mostly on the shoulders of the team's head coach—not the players, or the general manager who chose the players, or the owner who refused to pay the necessary money to keep Paul Silas, but on Heinsohn.

In the past, even success on the court could not completely silence the whispers of discontent. During the 1974 championship season, Silas was quoted as saying that the players had "fallen out of love" with Heinsohn. Two years later—when Boston beat Phoenix for yet another championship under

Heinsohn—an aging Don Nelson had grown unhappy with his diminished role and became a divisive presence in the locker room. He stirred up other players, including the captain, John Havlicek, whose relationship with the coach had always been tenuous. Havlicek had voiced his displeasure about the coach when Heinsohn failed to protect veteran Celtic and former Ohio State guard Larry Siegfried, whom the team released following the 1969–70 season. Havlicek also questioned Heinsohn's professionalism, viewing the coach as uncouth and tactless at times. In the press, he questioned the sophistication of the offense that the coach had implemented.

If winning could not hold back the simmering dissension, the losses brought it to a full boil. Those whispers of dissent blew into the ear of *Boston Globe* beat writer Bob Ryan. For years, Ryan had held Heinsohn and his ref-baiting, bombastic coaching style in contempt. Ryan's columns now began to resemble the grumblings that were heard in the corners of the Celtics locker room. Such stories began to sway public opinion and, in turn, management's opinion. It was becoming apparent to Heinsohn that a campaign was underway to expedite his departure. This view was crystallized when friends around the league told him that even his Assistant Coach John Killilea was expressing anti-Heinsohn sentiments.

Heinsohn was a realist. He understood the hazards of the job but still believed that his two-decades-long contribution to the team had earned him the right to a dignified exit. Instead, his former coach and current boss opened up old wounds. For years, Auerbach had made Tommy Heinsohn his whipping boy. Now the whip would be cracked harder and deeper than ever before.

The team was in the midst of a prolonged streak of futility when the players were summoned to the gym at Lexington Christian High School for a between-game practice. Heinsohn walked out onto the floor to lead his team in the scheduled practice when Auerbach pulled him aside and told him to take a seat on the sideline while he took over the practice. Embarrassed, furious, and insulted the old power forward dragged himself to the bench and took a seat. As he sat there contemplating whether to quit, he couldn't help but reflect on all that he had done for the Celtics organization. In his playing career, Heinsohn had been an integral contributor to eight titles. As head coach, he had led the team to its greatest regular-season record (68-14) in 1972–73 and guided undersized, aging squads to unexpected championships in 1974 and 1976. Through it all, the coach rarely received the full credit, as the media would point to Auerbach's silent guidance as the true mastermind behind the success. Following the 1976 championship season, Heinsohn commented on this burden. "It's an ego-busting job," he said. "Whatever buildup there is, is going to be attributed to someone else [Red]. Whatever goes wrong is going to be attributed to me. I've known this from the beginning."

So, he sat on the bench deep in thought and smoking a cigarette while Auerbach ran the team through some drills. There Heinsohn decided, with still one year left on his contract, "If they're going to make me sit or let me go, then they will have to pay for that pleasure."

On January 3, 1978, Auerbach, with the full support of an impatient Irv Levin, informed Tommy Heinsohn that his services were no longer needed. Ten rings and more than two decades of excellence were not enough to give Heinsohn the chance to try to reverse the team's fortunes and climb back from its 11-23 record.

Bob Ryan, "Swerving Irving" Levin, and the disgruntled players got their way. For a replacement, the Celtics turned to the quiet and dignified Tom "Satch" Sanders, whose number 16 hung in the rafters with Heinsohn's number 15. A warrior in his thirteen seasons as a Celtic forward, Coach Sanders and his steady hand had little impact on a team that exhibited little interest in steering in the direction that the green uniform was accustomed to.

In the midst of the futility, John Havlicek announced that he would retire at the end of the season, at age thirty-seven. The thirteen-time All-Star was tired. He had been a pivotal part of eight championships. He had stolen the ball against Philadelphia in 1965, won the Finals MVP against Milwaukee in 1974, and hit the running bank shot against Phoenix in 1976. Red Auerbach said he wished him for a son. Bill Russell called him the best player he had played with in thirteen years as a Celtic. Dave Cowens recommended that the entire league retire Havlicek's number. Paul Westphal said that number 17 "never made a mistake." Exiled coach Tom Heinsohn suggested that the NBA enshrine him in the Hall of Fame as both a guard and a forward.

On the Friday before Havlicek's final game, the *Globe*'s Ray Fitzgerald wrote a column reflecting on the long-absent spirit of Celtic Pride. "Gone for a long time, pride sees no reason to return in anticipation of Havlicek's last game. Who will remember the way it was when Celtic Pride stood for all that was admirable in professional sport? That era from all indications is gone forever."

For his final game, which was broadcast live on CBS, Havlicek arrived at Boston Garden in a tuxedo. During pregame introductions, the crowd serenaded the captain with an eight-minute standing ovation. As the cheers reigned down upon the Celtic great, Havlicek made his way to center court and faced the far baseline, raised both arms in the air, and then genuflected. He repeated the salutation in all four directions.

At halftime, the Celtics honored him with a special ceremony. Because Havlicek was an outdoorsman, the team bought him a camper for his fishing trips. Auerbach, tired of Levin's meddlesome ways, decided to set the owner up by convincing him to make the on-court presentation. Levin, never shy, jumped at the opportunity, only to be ambushed by the Celtic faithful. The fans were in great spirits for their captain's farewell game, but when Levin was introduced, their enthusiasm took the form of boos directed at the owner. Levin forced a smile before sulking off the parquet.

The captain himself went on to thrill the crowd with a 29-point, 9-assist, 5-rebound balanced performance that was representative of his game. Hondo scored 17 points in the fourth quarter alone, but sadly for Celtic fans, CBS broke away from the coverage to show the final round of the Masters. At homes across New England, families ran to their kitchens to listen to Johnny Most declaim over the radio the final minutes of Celtics history.

After the game, Havlicek found a telegram at his locker from John Wayne that read, "Hondo is watching." Donning his tux, Havlicek and his teammates made their way to a party that he was hosting. The liquor was served from sixteen years' worth of nip bottles that he had collected and saved from every flight he had ever traveled on as a Celtic.

Back in Hollywood during the offseason, Irv Levin struggled to reconcile the harsh treatment he had received from the Celtic fans. He had always assumed that they felt graced by his presence. In his own self-adulating eyes, he had more than fulfilled the duties of his position. "I think I'm one hell of a good owner," he said. "Maybe the best in the NBA."

Now seeing that he was no longer appreciated or wanted, Levin met with Buffalo Braves owner John Y. Brown to talk basketball, and anything else that might come up.

CHAPTER 15
Boston Outsiders

ONE OF THE RARE FEATURES OF BOSTON'S GEOGRAPHY IS THAT THE NEIGHBORING TOWN OF BROOKLINE TRAVERSES THE CITY'S BORDERS AND DIVIDES THE NEIGHBORHOODS OF BRIGHTON AND ROXBURY. From the suburb of Brookline, the call for Boston to acquiesce to the desegregation program was firmly voiced by such prominent residents as Governor Michael Dukakis, former Attorney General Elliot Richardson, State Senator Jack Backman, and Congressman Father Robert Drinan.

As long as their own community remained unthreatened by the ripples of change, the virtuous voices from the suburbs felt free to express their disgust about the city's failure to execute the desegregation mandate. But when the desegregation process threatened to cross over onto its own streets, the town of Brookline maintained its right to hedge this conviction. Such was the case when buses carrying Boston school children attempted to broach the Brookline town limits to transport students to and from the neighborhoods situated on either side of it.

The residents of Brookline and other nearby towns were no different than Bostonians. They had worked hard to establish a way of being and weren't inclined to alter it. The hypocrisy of the situation further divided the city's communities—white and black, urban and suburban.

❀

Rising from the streets of Boston, patriots Crispus Attucks, George Washington, and John Hancock, among others, led the charge to end political servitude and drive the English from their streets, churches, and purses. Boston and its surrounding villages were established on the very principle that the people of the land should be allowed to determine its destiny. The people of Boston—and all throughout the American colonies—stood together against a foreign entity to fight for self-determination and the sovereignty of the land on which they worked and raised their families.

Two hundred years later, forces foreign to the streets of Boston again attempted to determine the fate of its people. Jurists and academics who lacked a full understanding of the city's landscapes were given the task of devising solutions that would deeply impact Boston's diverse communities. From the safe confines of courtrooms, political agencies, and academic offices came a plan that was rational in theory but irrational in practice.

It was Boston's disregard for Constitutional principles and Supreme Court rulings that had allowed those unfamiliar with its communities to have the decision-making power affecting the daily life of its citizens. Now the people of Boston looked to voices of power to help them resolve and reconcile.

One such voice was Massachusetts Senator Edward Kennedy. For years, the Kennedy family had come to Boston in search of votes, though rarely did they roll up their sleeves and work directly in the city's neighborhoods. Still, despite a lack of direct access to this leading family, the Irish-Americans of Boston maintained a strong allegiance to the clan in election after election.

Now, when the courts sought to assert their desegregation rulings on the people, these same Bostonians looked to the Kennedy family to reciprocate the years of loyalty. But the campaign promises proved to be largely election-year rhetoric, not a binding contract. Boston's Irish were hurt and offended. Loyalty and brotherhood transformed into disdain and hate. The original Kennedy homestead in Brookline was torched, and a message was spray-painted on the sidewalk outside the burning house: "Bus Teddy."

In Washington, Kennedy was growing concerned over how the busing fallout could affect his future political aspirations. Hoping to temper Boston's venom, Senator Kennedy traveled to Government Center to speak to the public and explain his stance. But he was not allowed to speak; he was booed off the stage. He was showered by eggs and tomatoes and chased through the courtyard to the federal building named for his brother Jack. The anti-Kennedy faction followed in pursuit and continued the onslaught, breaking windows and shouting words of disdain. In the following day's newspaper, Mike Barnicle reported that Kennedy had been punched and was targeted with such comments as, "I hope they shoot you like they shot your two brothers" and "You're a disgrace to the Irish."

When it was suggested that the senator enroll his own children in the Boston school system, the silence was deafening. His children were tucked away behind the ivy-covered walls of Phillips Brooks Academy and Portsmouth Abbey—not riding buses being pelted with rocks and bottles. No longer could the senator deflect by reciting passages from a Robert Frost poem or by conjuring up images of his brothers. The time for rhetoric had passed.

✺

As the Kennedy family observed the rising tensions from the family compound on the other side of the Sagamore Bridge and the residents of Brookline and other secure suburbs sought to keep the desegregation battles out of their backyards, Judge Arthur Garrity continued to seek solutions to the city's woes in the face of increasing antagonism. While some observers saw as heroic the judge's efforts to rid the city of a divided and imbalanced school system, others simply viewed him as an outsider out of touch with the reality of the issues at hand. When Boston School Superintendent Robert Spillane was asked if he felt the judge was courageous, he scoffed. "Anyone can make decisions from behind a bench. Courageous are those kids that keep getting on the bus every day and walking into those schools not knowing what each day will hold."

To the people of South Boston and Charlestown in particular, Garrity was not one of "them." Although he had a shared ethnicity with many in those communities, he was branded a "lace-curtain Irish" whose air of superiority and high moral platform—as well as his home address—separated him from the reality of the urban neighborhoods. Every night the judge boarded the train from downtown Boston to his home in "lily-white" Wellesley, while Bostonians were left to live amid the National Guard and curfews and hovering helicopters. Like those of his friend Senator Kennedy, the judge's children went to private schools where the student population was more than 95 percent white. The Garrity girls rode horses with long combed manes at the Dana Hall School, while Boston kids were trying to avoid being trampled by police horses.

From his "book-lined study in Wellesley" (as Louise Day Hicks described it), Judge Garrity had a firm understanding of the Constitution and its principles, but he didn't fully understand how to properly apply it into a workable solution that was best for a city. One of his strengths as a judge was his willingness to engross himself in the matter before him, almost to the point of obsession. In the desegregation case, however, he had failed to immerse himself in what stood at the core of the legal issue before him: Boston itself. He did not take steps to learn about Boston's neighborhoods. Instead, he chose to rely on two other "outsiders" to dictate the plan for the next phase of desegregation, academics whose own lack of understanding of Boston would do little to acquaint the Wellesley judge with the marrow of the city.

Although Garrity had assigned the highly respected Edward McCormick, a South Boston native, and Jacob J. Spiegel, a graduate of Boston English High School and former State Supreme Court justice, the task of developing a plan for desegregation, the judge ultimately rejected their recommendations to redistrict the school system, reduce the number of bused students to fewer than 15,000, and create citywide magnet schools. Rather, he accepted a more radical and obtrusive plan for Phase II that was developed by two sociologists who were not Boston natives: Dr. Robert Dentler, who grew up in a Chicago suburb and attended a military academy for high school, and Dr. Marvin Scott, from North Carolina.

Dentler and Scott were gifted academics, but they had no understanding of the people who inhabited the city of Boston. To them, the students of Boston's schools were just pawns to be moved around on a chessboard from one square to another in a sociology experiment. "The solutions," Dentler wrote, "come out of developing the collective will of the community." What Dentler seemed to ignore was that the collective will of the community had already been formed and molded over several generations.

The school crisis required a solution that included a micro-understanding of the communities and the human consequences of the desegregation efforts, but Dentler and Scott rejected that approach. When Scott was asked if it would have helped to understand the inner workings of the city and the distinctness of its communities before formulating their plan, he laughed. "The only thing I needed to do was look at a map to realize that the city needed to change."

Dentler and Scott drew their new maps showing yellow buses dissecting the city in a virtual "Chinese fire drill," and then the two academics sat behind their desks with framed degrees on the wall and visions of the future textbook in which this would all be explained. In the end, though, the textbooks would show that the schools came to be more imbalanced than they had been before Garrity's ruling.

The ultimate imbalance of the races occurred not so much from neighborhood to neighborhood within Boston but in the division between city and suburbs. If the Supreme Court's intention had been to expose different cultures to one another as part of the educational experience, it would seem logical that the act of balancing should have included the many suburbs that fed off the breast of Boston for work, commerce, and culture.

When Boston School Committee member John Kerrigan devised an alternate plan that would include the area's predominantly white suburbs, Garrity, Dentler, and Scott hid behind the precedent of the 1974 Supreme Court decision in *Milliken v. Bradley*. That decision, which dealt with plans to desegregate Detroit-area schools through busing across district lines, essentially exempted suburban school systems from participating in cross-district desegregation or the "metropolitization" of the towns' all-white school systems.

The *Milliken* decision did not prohibit suburbs from participating in school desegregation efforts, but only stated that they were not obligated to be a part of them. The busing program had cost the city of Boston more than $100 million during a time of unprecedented inflation. Incentives to get suburban communities to participate would have been prudent. But without any incentives, the suburbs opted out of playing a role in any broader busing program. The town of Lexington, for one—where the first Revolutionary War battle was fought on the town green, and where Robert Dentler and his family now resided—rejected the calls, and the hypocrisy infuriated the Reverend Herbert Adams, who castigated his Lexington congregation. "People do a lot of talking about brotherhood but don't practice it," Adams proclaimed. "We are what we do. People talk more than they act."

In 1974, the Greater Boston suburb of Quincy approached the state to seek funding to support the construction of a new high school. Town officials were careful not to accept any funds that would mandate the enrollment of minority students from Boston into their schools. Six years earlier, a program called METCO (Metropolitan Council for Educational Opportunity) was introduced by the state to give Boston's minority students the opportunity to attend schools in the neighboring suburbs. METCO's mission was to "expand educational opportunities, increase diversity, and reduce racial isolation." In Quincy, the town voted against the initiative and refused to participate.

⊕

From the secure tree-lined suburbs of Brookline, Quincy, Lexington, and elsewhere came collective outrage at the rejection of basic Constitutional principles in the classrooms of Boston. These same voices, meanwhile, were exerting their own rights to excuse themselves from the efforts to increase diversity and bridge the gap between the races in the larger Boston community. The public cries of admonishment from suburban or elite quarters seemed to cloud private prejudices while allowing those admonishers to distance themselves from the unrest and protests being shown on the front pages of newspapers and the nightly news.

An example of this shunning of urban Boston by those on the periphery of the battlefield is apparent in the book *Ever Green* about the Boston Celtics. The author, *Boston Globe* sportswriter Dan Shaughnessy, grew up more than an hour outside of Boston and attended the same private college as Judge Garrity (and Tommy Heinsohn), Holy Cross. The book was a historical account of the city's pro basketball team and included a written tour of the Boston Garden. Shaughnessy describes the Garden's upper seating sections as follows: "The second balcony was often empty during Celtics games. Kids populated this uppermost region, and the bigots from Southie and Charlestown dubbed it 'Nigger Heaven.'"

Shaughnessy's reference to the term *Nigger Heaven* in an almost amused vein while attributing it to the "bigots" of two specific Boston neighborhoods served not only to excuse himself from any culpability but also perpetuated the idea that Boston and racism are inextricably linked. For those personally unaffected by the crisis, but who were within its fallout, the great concern was to avoid being painted by the broad brush of national opinion. People spoke with condescending righteousness to make clear that they were close in proximity but not ideology.

Another book on the Celtics, *The Selling of the Green* by Harvey Araton and Filip Bondy, quotes Spike Lee, the noted African-American filmmaker and New York Knicks fan, as saying, "When I hear the name Celtics, I see this American flag. I see Elvis Presley. I see mom and apple pie. I see the bus with black school children being overturned during the whole busing thing."

While racism in this nation is a deeply complicated issue that has impacted generation after generation, in both the North and the South, the images of "angry white mobs" protesting black children entering their communities on school buses came to represent for many the epitome of racial strife in the United States. The scenes playing out on the Boston streets became deeply imprinted on the minds of observers, shattering the city's image as a bastion of liberty and freedom. The voices from the suburbs and other outsiders tended to sweep aside the complexities of the history of Boston's myriad communities, just as the Boston School Committee and public officials failed to look beyond the impulse of self-preservation and maintaining the status quo. On both sides of the issue, the tendency to point fingers at an "other"—others who were fomenting racism within inner-city Boston, others who were dictating to mothers and fathers where to send their kids to school—perpetuated a narrow vision for solving the city's problems in a way that failed to take into account the reality of Boston's diverse social and economic relationships, from city neighborhood to city neighborhood and from city to suburb.

❦

In the 1960s, when Boston was planning to raze Scollay Square and rebuild the downtown area, city officials turned to outsiders to plan, design, and build one of the most important projects in the city's history. When the design was unveiled, it was apparent that these outsiders had gone to great lengths to create something that was contrary to the historic city. Instead of following a style that was indigenous to the city—such as the colonial brick of the Old State House or granite of the Bunker Hill Monument—the outside architects designed the New City Hall in a style that was cold and alien to Boston's traditions. In turn, it became a fixed symbol of the deficient leadership that occupied the building.

The famous architect I. M. Pei, who was born in China, had been a central figure in the overall plan for the project. When asked why historic buildings were torn down in the reconstruction of Boston, he claimed that he was unaware of their significance. Consequently, amid the rubble of what was once Scollay Square, sat the remains of the building where William Lloyd Garrison produced his influential anti-slavery publication, *The Liberator*, among other historic structures—now waiting to be taken away by a bulldozer.

Boston was a city of great pride and tradition. There was no text-book or map to explain to sociologists, professors, and judges why the people of South Boston or Charlestown would fight so hard to preserve their way of life. There was not enough time on the nightly news to put into context for people in the suburbs and elsewhere in the nation what was motivating the people of South Boston or Charlestown to react so passionately to the winds of change. Instead, the images on television—the rocks, buses, and scally caps—were the images that people latched onto and, in turn, shook their heads in condemnation.

In a *Boston Globe* column, Mike Barnicle described the hypocrisy inherent in those outsiders who felt obligated to pass judgment on the city of Boston. He wrote:

> Nothing guarantees a better feeling than the ability to sit out in the suburbs and shake a head at the troubles that seem to live inside Boston. You can get a nice orange Volvo station wagon, a corduroy jacket with patches on the sleeves, and a superiority complex. . . . In some suburbs, where it is common to gloat over a city's problems, five black people walking down Main Street are enough to shut down the town for a day.

CHAPTER 16

"Trade Was Made over Whiskey"

TWO MONTHS AFTER JOHN HAVLICEK'S LAST GAME, THE BOOS AND CAT-CALLS STILL PAINED CELTICS OWNER IRV LEVIN. "It hurt, and I guess I was disappointed," he said. "I thought we did everything we could to make the playoffs." He always considered himself a great owner and believed he had exhausted all resources in his efforts to recapture Celtic greatness. Levin was a movie producer more accustomed to people bowing at his presence than booing. The relationship between owner and the Celtics family was forever severed, making it impossible for him to return to the Boston Garden.

In June 1978, the owners of NBA franchises assembled in San Diego for their annual meeting. Sitting at the table with Irv Levin was Buffalo Braves owner John Y. Brown. Brown, who was known to be a freewheeling riverboat gambler, was in the process of pursuing the transfer of his franchise to a more lucrative market. At the end of the 1977–78 season, the Braves owner had terminated his lease with the Buffalo Auditorium, exploiting a clause in the contract that mandated a season-ticket benchmark of 4,500, which had not been met. Following the season, he traveled the country fielding proposals from various chambers of commerce and mayors of locations hoping to enhance their city with an NBA franchise. In Dallas, the team would be known as the Express; in Birmingham, they would be second in popularity only to Bear Bryant, football coach at the University of Alabama. In the end, Brown limited his choices to Minneapolis and San Diego.

At the same time, Levin was contemplating moving his franchise. It was his intention to move the Celtics to California, which would bring him home while also allowing him to realize some degree of revenge for the perceived mistreatment he received in Boston. But the NBA simply couldn't afford to allow its most storied franchise to be removed from a big-market city like Boston. Consequently, the league turned to its outside legal counsel, David Stern, to broker an agreement that would allow Boston to retain an NBA franchise and Irv Levin to lead a franchise based in California.

By late June, the deal was agreed on in principle, except for two issues that needed to be resolved. First, the Celtics needed to sign free agents Kevin Kunnert and Kermit Washington, who would then be included in a trade between the two franchises. The second issue was more complicated. Earlier that month, the Celtics had selected two college players in the NBA draft. It was decided that each franchise would attain the rights to one of the two selections. John Y. Brown had no preference, so he gave Levin the option of choosing. Levin consulted with his attorney, Frank Rothman, who years earlier had represented the movie producer in his lawsuit against then-Celtic-owner Bob Schmertz. Now he looked to his attorney as an evaluator of basketball talent. Years later, Rothman recounted this conversation with Levin to Will McDonough of the *Boston Globe*. According to Rothman, he told Levin, "Listen, you can get proven NBA players, but you don't know what this kid

Bird can do. He has another year to play in college; you never know what can happen. And, he's supposed to be slow and can't jump that well. My advice is to let them keep Bird and take the players."

Levin accepted the advice of his attorney and opted for the alternative selection, two-time NCAA leading scorer Freeman Williams of Portland State University. He now had to wait for Celtic General Manager Jan Volk to complete negotiations with the agents of Kunnert and Washington, at which point he could consummate the deal. Volk was successful and returned from those meetings with two signed contracts. Unaware of the agreements that had been brokered behind closed doors, he held in his briefcase the final piece in the biggest transaction in NBA history. When he landed at Logan Airport, Volk called Red Auerbach and informed him that the deals were done. Auerbach then called Levin, who thanked him for the news.

The next morning, Auerbach, Volk, and Celtic fans everywhere would pick up their morning papers to learn that their owner had switched franchises with the owner of the Buffalo Braves and would relocate the team to San Diego, where they would be renamed the Clippers. Irv Levin would now have his California team. As part of the deal, the Celtics sent first-round pick Freeman Williams, Kevin Kunnert, Kermit Washington, and Sidney Wicks to the new San Diego team. The Celtics in return received Marvin "Bad News" Barnes, Billy Knight, Tiny Archibald, and two future second-round picks. (One of those picks the Celtics would use to draft baseball player Danny Ainge in 1981.)

After the deal was announced, the *Globe*'s Bob Ryan wrote, "Nobody matters to Irv Levin but Irv Levin. . . . There will be absolutely no meaning to the uniform of the Boston Celtics. Say goodbye to class and say hello to the minstrel show."

In 1950, Red Auerbach was the coach and general manager of the Tri-Cities Blackhawks. During that season, team owner Ben Kerner executed a trade without Auerbach's knowledge or consent. Subsequent to seeing his authority undermined, Auerbach quit, thus making himself available to the Celtics. Six years later, he punctuated his disapproval of his former boss's actions by punching Kerner in the face prior to a championship game against the now St. Louis Hawks.

Almost three decades later, Auerbach was equally incensed when such a major decision was made without his knowledge. Auerbach weighed whether he wanted to continue working for an organization that he no longer controlled. Brown apologized in the newspapers for the slight, stating that he had wished he could have consulted with the iconic general manager but that he had a gag order placed upon him.

In the pages of the *Boston Globe*, columnist Leigh Montville gave voice to the frustration of the team's loyal fans and the uncertainty of the franchise's future:

> Who is this man Brown? The flagship franchise that he holds in his hand now is our flagship franchise. This toy he has decided to take this time is our toy. Who is he? What does he want? He is unannounced. He is here. The hope is that he will take this back to where it was. Back to playoffs and championships and the best of times. The worry is that he will do what he wants to do and that already there are things going on beneath the surface that we don't even know.

🏀

John Y. Brown Jr. was a good ol' boy from Kentucky. He graduated from the University of Kentucky, where he was a classmate of former Celtics star Frank Ramsey, played on the golf team with future Masters winner Guy Brewer, and loved to gamble. Brown's father was a lifelong politician who served in the

U.S. Congress and in both houses of the Kentucky State Legislature, providing his son with a life of modest entitlement. After graduating from college, Brown earned his law degree at Kentucky. He later served as legal counsel for Paul Hornung when the football legend was brought before the NFL brass to answer charges of gambling on games. Under Brown's representation, the former Heisman Trophy winner and Packer star lost his case and was suspended from the league for the 1963 season. This relationship spoke to the circles in which Brown preferred to travel—fast and famous.

Brown's schooling was in law, but his skill-set was more consistent with sales, and he effectively exploited his innate ability to tell people what they wanted to hear and sell them what they didn't want. He called himself the "greatest encyclopedia salesman" ever and carried with him a sales commission check that proved it. His greatest sales pitch, however, came in 1964, when he borrowed $160,000 and then parlayed that into $2 million in financing. He then used his newfound millions to acquire a blossoming business owned by Harland Sanders called Kentucky Fried Chicken. During his nine-year tenure, Brown and his partner, Jack Massey, grew the business from 600 to 3,500 franchises before selling the fast-food goldmine to Heublein Inc. for $285 million, much to the dismay of Harland Sanders who felt he had been "cheated" years earlier in the sale of his lifelong business.

By age thirty-eight, Brown was worth more than $30 million. He and his wife, Eleanor, used their equity to purchase the Kentucky Colonels franchise of the American Basketball Association (ABA), in which they already held a minority interest. Behind stars Dan Issel and Artis Gilmore, the Colonels won the 1975 ABA Championship. Following the season, Brown bargained with the other ABA owners to allow him to disband the franchise, which would net the Browns a $3.3 million indemnity buyout. With that money, Brown acquired the Buffalo Braves to pursue his dream of winning championships in both the ABA and the NBA. The purchase price for the team was $6.2 million, which he recouped by selling Braves' players Moses Malone to the Houston Rockets and Bob McAdoo to the New York Knicks. He then sold an ownership interest to national furniture kingpin Harry Mangurian.

During this time, Brown and his wife divorced. When asked why the marriage dissolved, he suggested, "Your wife sees you make all this money and she thinks you're really smart. And then she sits across the desk from you and realizes that you're a dumb shit." But the truth is closer to the fact that the marriage's demise was the result of Brown's penchant for fast people and fast women. It wasn't uncommon to see Brown escorting the likes of Angie Dickinson to the jet-setting parties.

🏀

By a vote of 21-1, the league's owners approved the complicated franchise transfer that sent the Braves from Buffalo some 2,500 miles to San Diego and put the storied Boston franchise in the hands of its ninth owner since the death of Walter Brown in 1964. (The Los Angeles Lakers, concerned with the infringement on their California market share, were the lone dissenter in the vote.) Meanwhile, Red Auerbach was left to ponder his own future. In talking with Larry Whiteside of the *Globe*, Auerbach said, "I'm not sure what's going to happen. The whole town is up in arms about the thing. I don't know what I'm going to do either." Days later, Auerbach made a phone call to New York and ironed out a four-year contract with Knicks owner Sonny Werblin to become the president of his team.

In his book *High Above Courtside*, Johnny Most recounts a conversation that he had with Auerbach in which Red reflected on the prospect of leaving a team that he had given twenty-eight years to and taking a position with a long-standing Celtics rival: "Do you think deep down I want to go to the fucking Knicks!? I've been their enemy for more than thirty years. But I can't put up with this amount of pure bullshit. I don't mind taking criticism, but only if I'm the guy making the decisions. I'm not going to be a stooge for John Y. Brown, a guy who thinks he knows more about basketball than I do."

In the end, Auerbach's heart was in Boston. He couldn't bring himself to leave the Celtics, even if it meant turning his back on the most lucrative contract in sports management history. Instead, he returned with the mission to be the last man standing. Celtic folklore gives credit for Auerbach's change of heart to a persuasive Boston cab driver, but in reality it was Auerbach's belief that he would outlast the owner and be sitting in his Celtic office long after John Y. Brown was gone.

For the time being, Auerbach agreed to work alongside his new boss and try to rebuild the Celtics. Following the introductory press conference, *Boston Herald* writer Leo Monahan sat down with Brown and asked him several questions about who he was and what he expected.

How is your relationship with Red?

"I think me and Red can team up and complete some trades. Owners are afraid of Red. I won't be a naïve owner."

How do you see your role?

"I'm an active owner. I want to be in charge of my own destiny. I can be an asset in acquiring talent."

Days later John Y. Brown tried to prove that he was an asset in acquiring talent when he agreed on a deal with the Indiana Pacers for guard-forward Earl Tatum. Excited with his maneuvering, he called Auerbach and informed him that he had just acquired the Pacer in exchange for a second-round draft choice. Auerbach hung up the phone and called General Manager Jan Volk and asked him to contact the Pacers to finalize the deal.

As requested, Volk called Indiana to complete the transaction. During the course of the discussion, however, the Pacers management was surprised to hear Volk talking about a *second*-round pick. In the earlier discussions with John Y. Brown, they had negotiated in good faith to trade Earl Tatum for a *first*-round pick. Volk, not in a position to act on such a significant variation in the deal, told the Pacer people he would have to get back to them. He immediately called Red, who in turn phoned Brown. The owner ordered Red to "do the deal anyways." Auerbach was furious. He had never traded a first-round pick in his career. Auerbach reluctantly gave Volk the go-ahead but was determined to right the wrong. Three games into the 1978–79 season, Auerbach traded Tatum to the Detroit Pistons for Chris Ford, in a return volley at the owner.

The high point in the season came on opening night, when John Havlicek's number 17 was retired. His jersey was raised up into the Boston Garden rafters, joining nine other former Celtics so honored, including the number 16 of the team's present coach, Thomas "Satch" Sanders.

Satch Sanders was widely respected and a contributor to eight Celtics championship teams. Now, five years after retiring as a player, he faced the daunting task of trying to mesh new and selfish personalities into a cohesive unit. He had taken over midway through the previous season when Tommy Heinsohn was unceremoniously dismissed. Sanders' season would end similarly. He lasted only fourteen games into the 1978–79 campaign and was fired after his team compiled a 2-12 record.

Auerbach was desperate to right the Celtics ship, and he turned to his All-Star center, Dave Cowens, to take on the dual role of player-coach (for no additional money). Auerbach hoped that the task would bring out the best in the veteran, as it had in Bill Russell in his final years.

Cowens' leadership had an immediate impact. He took over the team on November 17, 1978, and the Celtics won their first two games under "Big Red." They went on to win eleven of the first nineteen games under Cowens, culminating in a victory over the Kansas City Kings in St. Louis. Following that game, however, things changed dramatically. During the ownership transfer the previous summer, Red Auerbach had warned John Y. Brown about Marvin Barnes. Barely a third of the way through the season, his worst fear about the player was coming to fruition.

Marvin Barnes was a man of singular talent. A three-time All-American at Providence College, Barnes signed with the Spirits of St. Louis of the ABA. He won the Rookie of the Year award in 1974–75 and was being compared to Julius Erving in all facets of the game. After a stint in Detroit in the NBA, he ended up in Buffalo and was subsequently included in the seven-player trade that was part of the transfer of franchises between Buffalo and Boston. When Barnes arrived in Boston, people were concerned that his past would create problems on an already-fragile team. While at Providence, he had been arrested for hitting a teammate with a tire iron, and rumors of his drug use and subsequent erratic behavior had preceded him to Boston. But Brown had always been wowed by a performance he witnessed in the ABA, when Barnes showed up at halftime and proceeded to score 40 points. Hoping he would recapture past magic, Brown held on to the oft-troubled star.

Although time and drugs had diminished his talents, Barnes was still a good player and well liked by his teammates. In the first months of the season, Boston fans saw a hint of the old Barnes, who could score, rebound, and block shots. That all came to end after that night in St. Louis, the city where Barnes had sowed his ABA roots and had lived his ABA lifestyle. Following the game, the team returned to the hotel, where a party was soon in full swing in Barnes' room. After his teammates retired to their respective rooms for the night, the music from Marvin's room continued to echo through the halls. When the other players awoke the next morning, the music was still playing and the party still in full bloom. Marvin missed the bus that morning, as he would many more buses. This lifestyle on the road was not only detrimental to his performance on the court, but it was also costly to the team. In the comfort of Celtics-paid hotel rooms, Barnes would often entertain friends old and new. The Celtics front office frequently received hotel bills for extended stays in Barnes' designated room, long after the team had left town. It was later explained that when Barnes would leave town with the team, he would leave the room key with his friends, allowing them to stay and enjoy the room for days at a time—compliments of the Boston Celtics.

Barnes missed ten games that season due to "illness." His drug use became so pervasive that on at least one occasion he snorted cocaine while sitting on the Celtics bench during a game by hiding his head under a towel. Teammate Tiny Archibald, who was sitting next to him, was so disturbed by the act that he immediately changed seats to the other end of the bench.

By January, Cowens had had enough. The two men approached the game from vastly different directions. Cowens was an overachiever who could only play the game at full throttle. Marvin Barnes was the consummate underachiever and an unreliable teammate. Following the St. Louis incident, the team went 3-11, putting their season record at 16-31. Barnes' behavior and disrespect for his gifts stirred the fury of his coach, and Cowens confronted Barnes in the middle of an Indiana Airport following yet another loss. The two went nose to nose for an extended conversation. Subsequent to the exchange between the player and his coach, Barnes was suspended for three games (the Celtics won all three of those games), and team physician Dr. Thomas Silva determined that the player was in "weakened condition."

On February 8, at the request of Dave Cowens, Barnes was waived by the Boston Celtics and left to his own devices to fend off the world. The team would pay his salary for the remainder of the season but voided the final two years of his contract. The players' union filed a protest, but more out of obligation than any concern for the player.

In the *Boston Globe*, Bob Ryan wrote about the tragedy known as Marvin Barnes:

> As for Marvin Barnes, hasn't it all been said? The man had the ability and instinct for the game to become one of the greatest players ever. He had everything going for him in Boston too—from ownership, to fan support to the extreme, to a special need for his particular service—and yet he blew it. Some say his story is not actually tragic because he has had every available opportunity to get help—the most since the day he walked onto the campus at Providence College. But when a man as universally liked as Barnes winds up like this, I believe we're talking about a tragedy.

Throughout the season, Cowens had to deal with disruption in the front office, multiple changes in player-personnel (eighteen different players donned the Celtic green), a preponderance of drugs, and an unqualified disrespect for authority and the tradition of the Celtics. When Curtis Rowe first came to Boston in the Paul Silas deal in 1976, he had stated that being a part of the Celtics organization was his ultimate dream. Soon, however, his unbalanced play and sporadic sobriety led to an embittered basketball player, about whom Red Auerbach would say, "I would have taken a toothpick for [him]." Following a Celtics loss, Rowe openly shared his lack of concern when he remarked to his teammates in the locker room, "Don't worry, they don't put W's and L's on your paychecks." Rowe generally would save his bemoaning for the shadows of the locker room, never daring to challenge his coach face to face or on the practice floor. But during one team meeting in which Cowens was telling the players to pull together and support one another, Rowe grew tired of the lecture and boldly recommended, "If you wanted someone to jump up and down, you should have drafted a fucking cheerleader."

Subsequent to Barnes' termination and Rowe's banishment to the bench, the Celtics began responding to Cowens' enthusiastic style. They won seven out of their next eight, including two straight against the rival Knicks in an away-home weekend series. For the first time in the entire season, the word *playoff* was being uttered in connection with the Boston Celtics. But such utterings would soon come to an end.

Unbeknownst to anyone else in Boston, John Y. Brown spent the weekend drinking whiskey, listening to his girlfriend, and trying to prove his preseason pledge that he could be an asset in the acquisition of talent.

Despite the team's success, the owner was discontent. The team on the floor could not be associated with his personnel moves. Since the third game of the year, Auerbach had been methodically chipping away at Brown's players and placing the team on his own charted course for resurgence. The relationship between Auerbach and Brown deteriorated badly, and Brown relished baiting the Celtics president, attempting to embarrass Auerbach. Bob Cousy talked about one such incident in his book *Cousy on the Celtic Mystique*. After a difficult loss, Brown walked up to Red's office, where Cousy, Red, and friends were discussing the game. When he walked into the office, Brown taunted, "Well, well, well, here comes our great leader. Now say something intelligent, great leader." Furious, Cousy was "tempted to punch Brown in the stomach," but he restrained himself.

Auerbach ignored the owner's taunts; he was getting revenge in his own way. Brown had been responsible for acquiring four players on the opening-day roster: Earl Tatum, Billy Knight, Marvin Barnes, and Tiny Archibald. All but Archibald had been removed from the roster, and the guard remained on the roster only because trade overtures to Houston Rockets and Chicago Bulls went unclaimed. Auerbach's raid on Brown's players wasn't simply an act of vengeance, however. Rather, Auerbach used these "assets" to bring in new talent and acquire the building blocks for another great team. The transactions had netted Chris Ford and Rick Robey, and the team acquired two additional first-round draft picks by trading the former-star-but-now-bitter Jo Jo White to Golden State and back-up center Dennis Awtrey to Seattle.

Though the team was back on course to building a competitive roster, Brown's ego was in a state of discontent. This was his team, and he wouldn't be cast aside. He had won a professional basketball championship—albeit in the ABA—and he could make trades just as effective as the "great leader." So while the Celtics traveled home to Boston to prepare for a Sunday matinee game against the Knicks, Brown and his woman friend, Phyllis George, stayed in New York for a late-night dinner.

Brown and George were the prototypical power couple: a rich, influential man with an attractive woman by his side. George was the 1971 Miss America and held the distinction of being the first pageant winner ever to drop the crown (breaking off jewels) during the traditional winner's runway walk. Born in Denton, Texas, the beauty remained in the American mainstream by serving as a largely uninformed pregame analyst for NFL games on CBS.

Joining Brown and George for dinner that night were Knicks General Manager Eddie Donovan and owner Sonny Werblin. As they consumed cordials and discussed team needs and desires, it was made clear that Brown and George were fascinated by Bob McAdoo.

The following morning, Jan Volk woke up to hear rumors of a potential trade between the Celtics and Knicks that would bring Bob McAdoo to Boston. Volk couldn't believe it. Such a trade had never been discussed or even entertained with him or others in the Celtics front office. Anxious, he arrived at the Garden early on Sunday morning, before the start of that day's game against New York, and made his way to Auerbach's office. The team president knew immediately why Volk was so agitated. Putting out his hands as if to say "hold on," Auerbach told his general manager, "I just got off the phone with John Y., and he assures me there is no deal."

Feeling relieved, the two made their way to the arena. Auerbach took his regular seat in section twelve situated at center court on the opposite side from the team benches. Seated in front of him was the owner and an excited Phyllis George. Throughout the game, George jumped up and down and cheered the Celtics victory—and probably for Knick Bob McAdoo.

Phyllis George had reportedly been a Bob McAdoo fan for some time, and after witnessing his 45-point gem against the Celtics at Madison Square Garden that Saturday night, she was roused to offer her input at dinner with the Knicks executives. Prior to the Sunday game, George came upon Celtics radio announcer Johnny Most and asked him, "How do you think Bob McAdoo would look in green?"

After the game, Volk and Auerbach met in Auerbach's office, as was the custom, and again the question came up as to whether there was any chance the McAdoo rumors were true. Lounging behind his desk, Red waved off the suggestion with cigar in hand. "No way," he told Volk. "I talked to John Y. again, and he assured me there's nothing to it."

The next morning, Jan Volk and Red Auerbach awoke to read that the Celtics had acquired Bob McAdoo in exchange for three first-round picks—the three picks that Auerbach had so carefully stockpiled during the season. (Knowing that the deal had been devised during the late-night dinner in New York, Red would refer to it as a trade "made over whiskey.") While Auerbach fumed in Boston, down in New York, Bob McAdoo lamented, "Anywhere but Boston."

🏀

During the franchise's entire history, the Boston Celtics have never had a player lead the league in scoring. It was contrary to the team concept that Auerbach had developed in building championship teams. In the five years prior to his arrival in Boston, McAdoo not only won the scoring title three times, but he averaged 23 field-goal attempts per game. During his last scoring-title campaign, in 1975–76, McAdoo averaged nearly 25 shots per game. In comparison, the Celtics' top scorer that season, Dave Cowens, put up fewer than 17 shots per game—and the Boston Celtics won the NBA championship.

McAdoo's game was a complete contradiction to the Celtics tradition of ball movement and finding the open man. McAdoo's dismay at being sent to Boston stemmed from two other concerns as well. First, he and Cowens were polar opposites in every way, and their differences dated back at least to the 1974 playoff match-up; a *Boston Globe* headline from 1974 summed up the essence of the two stars: "Big Mac Scores—Big Red Wins." The new Celtic's second concern was referenced in the book *The Selling of the Green*, in which McAdoo referred to Boston as a "racist city" and said that the Celtics organization, by rule, "just don't accept black talent." McAdoo was so disinterested in playing for the Celtics that he refused to make living arrangements during his stay but instead slept on Cedric Maxwell's couch in a one-bedroom apartment. He was going to make sure that his days in Boston were few.

🏀

Later that morning after the McAdoo trade was confirmed, Jan Volk made his way to the Telex machine at the Celtics offices. The Telex was the device used by teams to confirm in writing the terms of a deal, and a deal was only valid once like-communications are exchanged between the teams and forwarded to the league office for confirmation. Sitting on the machine was the Knicks' memo, which stated their understanding of the deal. Upon reading the memo, Volk's distress and concern only increased. The Knicks had included in the transaction all of McAdoo's deferred money, dating back to his Buffalo Braves' contract, which amounted to more than the current worth of the Celtics franchise. Volk immediately checked the outgoing transmissions and was relieved to find that Brown had not yet sent the Celtics' confirmation. Frantically trying to reach the owner, Volk called all known numbers, but there were no answers. Desperate, he decided to call the team's silent owner, Harry Mangurian, whom Volk reached at home. After explaining the added clause regarding the deferred income, the silent owner was no longer silent. "Fuck John Y! You make sure that's not part of the deal, or I give you permission to blow up the deal." With the backing of Mangurian, Volk held the Knicks' feet to the fire, and the language was removed from the transaction.

Volk's phone call wasn't the last one made to Harry Mangurian that week. Red Auerbach also called down to Florida, with both a proposition and a threat. The exchange was recounted in Johnny Most's book *High Above Courtside*. "Harry," Auerbach told the owner, "I can work for you, but I can't work for your partner. If you buy out his share of the ownership and give me complete control of the personnel moves, I can still save this franchise."

The silent owner began the process, but it would take time. Meanwhile, Bob McAdoo reluctantly donned the green, and the *Globe* reported that he was warmly greeted by a crowd of 8,069 in his first game as a Celtic on March 1. And though Dave Cowens sacrificed his starting position for the new teammate, the player-coach was not happy with the trade. Cowens had been excited about the direction of the team. He knew back in 1974 that McAdoo "never passes." He also knew that his style would disrupt the progress that the team had made. Cowens proved to be right. Their winning ways were reversed following the trade, as Boston lost 21 of the remaining 27 games of the season.

During a loss in Detroit, the Dick Vitale–coached Pistons would run and gun their way to an embarrassing 160-117 massacre of the Celtics. Piston Kevin Porter scored 30 points and dished out 25 assists, enjoying every last one of them at the Celtics' expense.

Following the game, Red Auerbach charged into the Celtic locker room. He had had enough. With the pent-up pain of losing and the negative feelings for the carpetbagger from Kentucky, he unloaded on his team. "Too many players have worked too hard to build this up! I guarantee you that players sitting in this locker room right now will not be coming back next year. There are three players on this team that care about winning: Dave Cowens, Chris Ford, and Jeff Judkins." Then he stormed out, slamming doors. In the corner of the locker room, Chris Ford slammed his shirt to the floor and said that the game was a "fucking disgrace." Rick Robey, who had won an NCAA title at the University of Kentucky, was disgusted by the lack of dedication from his teammates, seeing them laughing on the court when their manhood was being questioned.

In the following day's *Boston Globe*, Bob Ryan summed up the game as only he could. Under the headline "Celtic Pride Goeth Before Thee," Ryan wrote: "What occurred last night was the team's single darkest hour, if you had the stomach to watch the entire affair. . . . The Celtics brought total disgrace upon themselves."

⠀⠀✣

During this stretch of futility, John Y. Brown's only foray into the public eye was on March 17, when he married Phyllis George in New York. Guests at the ceremony included Walter Cronkite, Roger Staubach, Lou Wasserman, and Lee Majors. The reception was held at Central Park's Tavern on the Green, where his old Kentucky friend Muhammad Ali recited a poem to the bride and groom and Andy Williams serenaded them with a love ballad. On their honeymoon, Brown and George hatched plans to fulfill his father's wishes of seeing his son run for the Kentucky governor's office, devising the slogan, "Kentucky and Company: The state that's run like a business." His opponent, Louie Nunn, later commented to the voters, "Brown's campaign is in the same position as his ball team: neither will make it to the playoffs."

Soon thereafter, the newlyweds were guests at the White House and stayed in the Lincoln Room, where they conceived their first child, whom they named Lincoln. They would have two children in all. The run for the governor's office soon dominated their lives. Brown was now less interested in a losing basketball team and more interested in winning his election campaign. As a result, he sold off his interest to his partner Harry Mangurian, and he was gone. In the *Boston Globe*, columnist Ray Fitzgerald recommended that the people of Kentucky beware. If Brown became governor, Fitzgerald wrote, he would make the following trades: Secretariat traded to Florida for Flipper, Kentucky Derby traded to Holyoke for rights to St. Patrick's Day Parade, thirty-five thousand acres of bluegrass to California for Mojave desert, "My Old Kentucky Home" for "O Fair New Mexico," the contents of Fort Knox for autographed Yankee baseballs.

John Y. Brown was elected governor of Kentucky in 1979 and soon turned his eyes to the White House. But past demons ultimately derailed Brown's political aspirations. His penchant for baccarat tables in Las Vegas led to seven-figure losses, and ensuing wire transfers to a Florida bank were considered improper and drew the attention of federal investigators. His reputation was also sullied by his relationship with business partner James Lambert, who was later indicted on multiple drug charges. Wiretapping, deaths, and shootings all surrounded the scandal, and although Brown escaped indictment, his political career never recovered.

Prior to the final game of the 1978–79 NBA season, Dave Cowens announced that he would step down as coach and instead concentrate on just playing basketball. He also issued the following warning to the league: "I've seen a lot of smirks and smiles from a lot of these hot dogs around the league. . . . I remember who did it. They'll find out who they are when they try to drive the lane next year."

During warm-ups for the final game, the Celtics posed for the team picture. After the photograph was taken, both Curtis Rowe and Bob McAdoo announced that they felt ill and were unable to play. They changed out of their uniforms and left the Garden, never to play another game for the Boston Celtics. "Two things seem to happen when McAdoo leaves a ball club," Johnny Most later remarked. "Either the franchise goes to another city, or the team gets better."

For five burdensome months, a pall had been cast over the league's greatest franchise, but at the sounding of the final buzzer on April 8, 1979, it would finally be lifted. With two minutes left in the game, Coach Cowens pulled out a cigar to celebrate the closing of the season. Somewhat symbolically, the cigar would not ignite. Not until Assistant Coaches K. C. Jones and Bob MacKinnon came to Cowens' aid were they able to light the stogie. It was the first cigar smoked on an NBA bench since Governor John Volpe had prematurely lit Auerbach's cigar in 1966.

Sitting across the way, Auerbach could only smile as Cowens struggled to puff away on the cigar. But that wasn't the only reason Auerbach was smiling. One row in front of him sat the team's 1978 first-round draft pick, who had spent the season playing out his college eligibility. Now he sat in a half-empty Boston Garden watching the Celtics wrap up what was the worst season in franchise history. Above him, the flags of past glory almost apologetically hung from the rafters. It would be under these very flags that this "Hick" would find his destiny.

CHAPTER 17

"Those Are the God-damn Basketballs You're Getting"

ONE BY ONE, WHITE STUDENTS FILED OUT OF HYDE PARK HIGH SCHOOL IN PROTEST OF WHAT THEY PERCEIVED TO BE UNEQUAL TREATMENT. In the eyes of these students, efforts by the courts to even the playing field led to overcompensation at their expense. Unhappy, they staged a walkout to demonstrate their disapproval.

Hoping to quell the disturbance, Assistant Headmaster Robert Jarvis met with the students on the steps of the school. Their concern was singular: We want more white kids in the school.

While the issue of racial balance was at the crux of the desegregation movement, balance was no longer possible. The students' concerns were of great importance to them, but they lacked a viable resolution. It was an issue that Jarvis couldn't help them with. Boston had changed since busing started. No longer was white the majority; they were now a majority-minority. Jarvis knew his answer wouldn't satisfy the disenchanted, but he told them, "There aren't more white students in the school because there aren't that many white students in Boston."

❀

When the greatest generation returned from Europe in the mid to late 1940s, Congress had appropriated sufficient funds under the G.I. Bill to provide any veteran interested in attending college with the financial wherewithal to do so. In the September following the end of the war, eight million heroes showed up on college campuses with their $500-a-year grants and ignited the largest education explosion in American history.

Four years later, the prospective workforce looked to corporate America rather than trade industries and manual labor to establish careers. Within this employment evolution, an educated America reaped the benefits of greater means, which in turn led to more sophisticated goals. No longer was the top floor of a triple-decker the benchmark of success. Families wanted a yard, a second bathroom, and a driveway to call their own. As a result, family after family packed up their paneled station wagons and moved to destinations outside the urban borders to pursue their dreams. From 1950 to 1980, one third of Bostonians sought a new life in the suburbs.

YEAR	BOSTON POPULATION	VARIATION
1950	801,444	
1960	697,197	-13%
1970	641,071	-8%
1980	562,994	-12%

By the 1970s, "white flight" was a full stampede, sparked to a large extent by busing, as white families opted to move to suburban districts that were beyond the reach of Garrity's ruling. During the decade of busing, the city's overall population declined by nearly 80,000—but that number doesn't tell the whole story. In that ten-year period, the city's white population diminished by 135,583 (from 526,678 to 394,095). Even though Marvin Scott would comment that "the only white flight taking place in Boston occurred down at Logan Airport on a snowy day," the numbers were plain to see. The face of the city had changed.

For the white families that stayed in Boston, many scraped and borrowed and struggled to find the means to enroll their children in parochial or private schools. As a result of school transfers and white migration, the student body of Boston's schools changed in appearance and in numbers. During the busing crisis, the radical reduction of the student population forced the closure of 92 of Boston's 208 schools. The declining number of students and diminishing city funds led to massive layoffs of teachers and other school staff. This only further upset the white community, which was deeply affected by the loss of jobs, as the courts tried to balance not only the students but the teachers.

YEAR	MILESTONE	STUDENT	WHITES	%	NON-WHITES	%
1964	Racial Imbalance Study	91,800	70,703	77%	21,907	23%
1970	Decade	97,000	62,000	64%	35,000	36%
1972	Lawsuit filed	95,615	56,412	59%	39,203	41%
1974	Phase I	87,169	47,942	55%	39,227	45%
1975	Phase II	83,681	43,065	51%	40,616	49%
1976	Second year of Phase II	71,000	31,240	44%	39,760	56%
1979	Fifth year of busing	66,500	25,270	38%	41,230	62%
1980	Decade	68,000	24,000	35%	34,000	65%
1990	Decade	61,000	13,500	22%	47,500	78%

The radical changes occurring in the city and the schools, compounded by the city's growing financial constraints, aroused the concern of city officials and the courts. In an effort to empower the parents of the children who attended the declining schools, Judge Arthur Garrity conducted a survey that he hoped would provide him with a better understanding of the concerns and objectives of those most affected by the schools. The questionnaire was mailed out to seventy thousand students, parents, teachers, and school workers. Of those, only 31 percent responded. The one question that found consensus among all demographic groups was encouraging some involvement from the suburban schools.

Some responders to the survey chose not to answer the questions but instead took advantage of the comment section to voice their displeasure with the judge and his policies: "Ask Judge Garrity; he is the dictator"; "Ask Judge Garrity, only his answer counts"; "Please don't insult my intelligence by pretending I have a choice—Heil Hitler"; "Let Garrity fill out this form, not a mother whose opinion doesn't matter."

The complaints and concerns of the parents didn't compel Judge Garrity to diminish his scope; instead, he seemed to extend his role from judge to "czar" of the Boston public schools. In the words of one former law partner: "He knows what he thinks the law says and will go down the line for it." From 1974 until the end of the busing program in 1987, the judge issued 415 orders dictating school policy and operation, determining everything from where protestors could stand, what sporting equipment could be purchased, which racial epithets were outlawed within the schools, and where basketball teams could practice. Like Marlow in Joseph Conrad's *Heart of Darkness*, Garrity kept steering the desegregation mission farther down the river. By all accounts a fair, decent, conscientious man, Garrity had gone too far in search of his Kurtz as the city spiraled deeper to the point of no return.

In December 1975 Garrity placed South Boston High School in federal receivership. He determined that the school and those who oversaw it had failed in their obligation to assist the courts in desegregating the Boston public schools. Within his written decision, he copied a leaflet that was reportedly passed out to the white students of South Boston High School. It read: "Wake up and start fighting for your school and town. It's time you became the aggressor. Don't be scared by the federal offense threats. A fight in a school is not a federal offense. Be proud to be white and from Southie and show everyone that this is how you are going to keep it, no matter what."

Whether this was the work of a rogue resident or organized effort was never determined. Nevertheless, the contents of the leaflet were included in the written record to demonstrate the ongoing efforts of the people of South Boston to derail desegregation.

The Boston School Committee was outraged. The committee saw the receivership of one of its schools and the subsequent assignment of personnel as a violation of its powers, as granted by the city charter. Despite their opposition, committee members were compelled to sign off on the changes. At the subsequent meeting, the committee made the following statement: "We believe that this order is violative of our duties as elected officials, and we make the following vote under protest and under legal duress."

The committee believed that Judge Garrity's decision was an abuse of his powers, and it filed a motion of petition in the United States Court of Appeals, First Circuit. At the hearing, the court issued the following:

> The School Committee that took office in January, 1976, came
> to its task with the opportunity to demonstrate its fidelity to the
> law and to carry it out in the most effective way, whatever might
> be the personal convictions of its members. But the record of

the current year reveals to us a tactic of keeping a distance, of doing the minimum and then only by pressure of court order, and of limited and largely negative communication of its problems and suggestions to the court. It is not surprising that the court has felt that help, if sought, would not be forthcoming from the Committee.

Since 1965, South Boston High School had operated under the watchful eye of South Boston resident William Reid. As headmaster, Reid oversaw the school through Phase I and into Phase II, until the day Judge Garrity determined that the school's progress was deficient. Reid was dismissed, and Garrity approved the hiring of Jerome Winegar as the school's new headmaster and signed him to a two-year guaranteed contract. Winegar, who came to Boston from Missouri by way of Minnesota and was by most accounts a well-intentioned man, was expected to bring his Midwestern ideals of hope and optimism to South Boston. With his stringy curly hair and crumpled suit and tie, Winegar's disheveled appearance was somehow symbolic of the chaos that consumed the school. His plan was to implement a system of learning and discipline that would stabilize the school and build it into a thriving academic institution. Soon after Winegar arrived, his car was bombed. Winegar was placed under twenty-four-hour protection.

When the superintendent of the Boston Schools, Robert Spillane, came to the realization that Winegar was "in over his head," he attempted to terminate the South Boston principal. His request was denied by the court, which lent its full support to the headmaster. For Spillane, the relationship between Winegar and Garrity was made evident during a discussion about sporting equipment. Winegar had called the superintendent to complain that he didn't get the exact basketball of choice. Spillane was furious. Daily absences at the school exceeded attendance; students were dropping out at a tragic pace; and more students were going to prison than to college. The superintendent was outraged that the headmaster of this leaky school had the nerve to complain about what type of basketball the school received. In sharp rebuke, he snapped, "Those are the goddamned basketballs you're getting!" Winegar then informed the superintendent that he would go to Judge Garrity with his complaint, further illustrating to Spillane where the chain of command led.

Somewhere down the path toward desegregation, the essence of education had been sacrificed. More than $100 million had been spent to bus children from one neighborhood to another while schools were left in disrepair, classrooms were locked down, and hall monitors wore riot gear. When the biggest issue of the day was what type of basketball the school was getting, it became even clearer that the true problems of the Boston schools were not being properly addressed.

The horror. The horror.

CHAPTER 18

"I Would Have Played for Nothing"

FROM THE MOMENT THAT RED AUERBACH SUGGESTED TO WALTER BROWN THAT THE CELTICS SELECT CHUCK COOPER IN THE 1950 NBA DRAFT, MAKING HIM THE FIRST AFRICAN AMERICAN EVER CHOSEN IN THE NBA, IT WAS APPARENT THAT AUERBACH HAD AN INNATE ABILITY TO DISCERN SPECIAL QUALITIES IN AN INDIVIDUAL, LOOKING BEYOND NOT ONLY SKIN COLOR BUT ALSO JUMPING ABILITY OR HEIGHT. He looked for individuals who were able to work within a system that allowed the game to be played by a unit working collectively as a team with one common goal.

In Terre Haute, Indiana, in the late 1970s, there was a six-foot-nine-inch white kid who possessed old-school skills. He played the game beneath the basket where he applied his talent mixed with intelligence, strategy, and an intense passion for the game. Some saw shortcomings in Larry Joe Bird. Coach Joe B. Hall of Kentucky, who coached Bird on the College All-Star Team that played the Cuban national team in the summer of 1978, questioned the forward's ability to jump and get his shot off against bigger players. The legendary coach at the University of Indiana, Bobby Knight, allowed the shy player from French Lick, Indiana, to leave the Hoosiers program after just one season.

Outside of the Missouri Valley Conference, the junior forward on the Indiana State Sycamores was an enigma. In his sophomore season, Bird had averaged 32 points and 13 rebounds per game. Even though his team made it to the NIT tournament in 1976, Bird still lacked credibility. Indiana State was a small-time program, and the Missouri Valley was not a major conference, so the team's schedule was considered weak. Bird was voted an All-American during his junior season while leading his team with 30 points a game and 11 rebounds. People started to take notice. He exhibited an ability to assert his will on the court while enhancing the game of his teammates.

Bird was now on the radar of every NBA team in the league, including the Boston Celtics, who held two first-round selections in the 1978 draft. Because the class that Bird entered at his first school, the University of Indiana, was now eligible to graduate, by NBA rules the junior forward was eligible to be selected in the June draft. (At the time the NBA had strict rules about selecting underclassmen in the draft.) The team that selected him would maintain his rights for a year while the player had the option of either entering the NBA or returning to play out his final year of college eligibility.

The Celtics sent an array of scouts to Indiana to evaluate the dynamic forward and to judge whether his game would translate from the Missouri Valley Conference to the NBA. Assistant coach and former Celtic star K. C. Jones returned from his visit to Terre Haute convinced that Bird possessed a complete game, featuring both an outside shot and an inside game that were complemented by superior passing and rebounding skills. But Jones also described a skill that particularly caught Auerbach's attention: Jones said that Bird had "outstanding instincts." This was the type of intangible that excited Auerbach.

Later in the season, Assistant Coach John Killilea also traveled to Indiana to watch Bird. When he walked into Auerbach's office upon his return, he compared the college forward to a perennial NBA All-Star, calling him "the next Rick Barry." In the *Boston Globe*, Bob Ryan would later describe Larry Bird as "a six-nine sturdy blond-haired amalgam of Bob Pettit, Dan Issel, and Rick Barry"—three eventual Hall of Famers.

Prior to the 1978 draft, Bird announced that he would return to Indiana State for his senior year, as his mother requested. This meant that any team that drafted him would have a window between the selection and the following year's draft to come to a contract agreement with him. If the team and Bird were not able to come to terms, then he would return to the draft, thus voiding any rights the team had on the player.

The Celtics held the sixth pick in the draft, which was their own, and the eighth pick, which they had received from the Lakers in exchange for Charlie Scott. For most teams that held such high draft picks, it usually meant that the team had struggled during the previous season and thus the fans would be less inclined to be patient and would not want to wait a full year to reap the benefits of their draft pick. The Celtics had the luxury of being able to satisfy their fans with one selection that would bring immediate contributions to the team and another selection that they could use to invest in the future.

For the first time in league history, the NBA decided to make an event out of the draft. Each team was required to send a representative to the Waldorf Hotel in New York to issue their selections in person. Representing the Celtics was General Manager Jan Volk and marketing employee Steve Riley. At the Celtics table, Volk was connected by phone to Auerbach in Boston.

The first four teams to pick in the draft bypassed Bird in the name of instant gratification, as four elite senior collegians were taken to open the draft:

1. Portland Trailblazers: Mychal Thompson, University of Minnesota
2. Kansas City Kings: Phil Ford, University of North Carolina
3. Indiana Pacers: Rick Robey, University of Kentucky
4. New York Knicks: Micheal Ray Richardson, University of Montana

The holder of the fifth pick was the Golden State Warriors. Four years removed from an NBA championship, the team had spiraled to sixth place in the West with a roster that consisted of center Robert Parish and veteran guard Jo Jo White. At the table with the Celtics logo, Volk sat quietly, hoping against hope that Golden State would bypass the player that his team envisioned as the cornerstone of the future. Volk and Auerbach communicated their shared anxiety in silence across the phone lines. Finally, the Golden State representative handed the Warriors' selection to the NBA official, who in turn announced, "With the fifth pick of the 1978 NBA Draft, the Golden State Warriors take Purvis Short of Jackson State."

On both ends of the phone between New York and Boston, the relief was palpable. Auerbach lit his cigar and leaned back in his chair. Larry Bird was on the Celtics draft board and still available. Over the years, Auerbach had proven that patience served the organization well. In 1953, he snookered the other owners by selecting Kentucky stars Frank Ramsey, Cliff Hagan, and Lou Tsioropoulos, even though all three were returning for their final year of collegiate eligibility. In 1956, Auerbach traded two future Hall of Famers for the draft pick that would net the team Bill Russell, knowing that the NCAA champion center would not be available until midway through the season because of his commitment to the U.S. Olympic team. In 1969, Jo Jo White slid to the ninth spot in the draft after he was assigned to the Marines. Auerbach chose him anyway, which turned out to be a steal when Red used his vast network of connections in Washington to have his new guard assigned to domestic duty in the reserves.

Nine years later in New York, Volk anticipated Auerbach's preference, but he wasn't completely sure. He hoped that the Celtics president wouldn't get greedy and decide to wait to take Bird with the team's next pick at the eighth spot. Back in Boston, Auerbach savored the moment. He puffed smoke skyward, dictating tempo like one of his teams would. Finally after a painstaking moment, Auerbach communicated to Volk, "The Celtics select Larry Bird with the sixth pick in the draft."

At the table, Volk put down the phone and began to fill out the NBA form that indicated the Celtics' selection. When he looked down, his hand was shaking. For years he had negotiated contracts, argued legal cases, and represented the greatest franchise—but never did he remember being so overcome by sentiment. For months, management had gathered in Auerbach's office, committed to the prospect of making Larry Bird a Boston Celtic. And it was about to become reality. The once-great franchise would control the rights to a player worthy of Russell, Cousy, Havlicek, and Cowens. Volk steadied his hand sufficiently to write "Bird," and then he handed the form to the NBA runner, who brought it to the podium where the selection was announced. "With the sixth pick in the 1978 NBA Draft, the Boston Celtics select Larry Bird from Indiana State."

Two picks later the Celtics chose Freeman Williams, who was subsequently shipped to Irv Levin's San Diego Clippers as part of the franchise transfer deal. Bird's rights would remain with the Celtics for one year while he returned to Terre Haute to prepare for his senior season at Indiana State. Back in Boston, Auerbach fawned over his draft pick, "The kid is one helluva prospect."

As the city waited for its savior, the Celtics struggled throughout the 1978–79 season. Many fans temporarily transferred their allegiances to Indiana State, and their future star was getting plenty of national hype as well. The cover of the college basketball preseason issue of *Sports Illustrated* featured the blond forward from Indiana State with two Sycamore cheerleaders under the title "Secret Weapon."

On February 24, 1979, CBS Sports traveled to Terre Haute to televise Indiana State's game against Wichita State. Earlier in the year, TV analyst Billy Packer had called the Sycamores "pretenders" and was jeered by the home fans as he took his seat behind the microphone. Three months into the season Indiana State was undefeated, led by their amazing forward. Now viewers around the country would have the opportunity to see for themselves if the Bird hysteria was legitimate.

Larry Bird would indeed rise to the occasion. He scored 49 points and grabbed 19 rebounds in Indiana State's 109-84 victory. While the point total was impressive, Bird allowed the offense to come to him and didn't force the issue. He seemed as content to show off his passing game as much as his shooting touch. The nation now believed.

The Celtics were on the road in Los Angeles and had a day off before they had to travel to San Diego to play the Clippers. Dave Cowens hosted a party in his suite for teammates to watch the chosen one. They, too, believed.

Later in the season, Coach Cowens traveled with players Rick Robey and Jeff Judkins on a trip to Indiana State to watch their future teammate firsthand. They watched Bird score 27 points and collect 19 rebounds in a victory over West Texas, a game that clinched the conference title for the Sycamores.

Later that night, the Celtic trio took their draft pick out on the town for some dinner and refreshments. Terre Haute was Bird's town. Everywhere they went, beer and food were provided compliments of grateful fans.

During dinnertime conversation, Bird expressed concern over the Bob McAdoo acquisition. He was alarmed by what he was hearing about McAdoo's selfish play and its impact on the team, which seemed to be reflected on the

South Boston High School, seen here in October 1974, at times resembled a military zone more than an educational facility during the worst of the busing crises. A heavy police presence on school grounds was essential to maintain a semblance of order inside the school and out. *Lee Lockwood/Time & Life Pictures/Getty Images*

Many white students refused to show up for school when classes opened in the fall of 1974. Valerie Banks was the only student to show up for her geography class at South Boston High on the first day of court-ordered busing on September 12. *AP Images*

Despite the hostile and even violent response to the forced busing of students, the desegregation program entered its second year of implementation in 1975. On the first day of classes, September 11, white students and black students prepared for another potentially dangerous bus ride to South Boston High School. *AP Images*

Judge Arthur Garrity was the target for much of the wrath and frustration over the desegregation efforts, and in October 1974, protesters gathered outside of his Wellesley home to voice their opposition to his ruling. On at least a few occasions, the opposition took the form of death threats, and Garrity was provided with twenty-four-hour protection. *Boston Herald/AP Images*

Louise Day Hicks, shown here at an anti-busing rally in November 1977, was the chair of the Boston School Committee and the face of the anti-busing movement. Her obstinate support of the status quo, as well as that of her colleagues on the School Committee, pushed the issue of racial imbalance in the schools to the point of crisis. *Ted Gartland/Boston Herald*

On May 3, 1975, members of the Progressive Labor Party and others marched through Dorchester in support of busing to integrate the public schools (above). The marchers clashed with anti-busing demonstrators, many of whom came armed with bats, sticks, rocks, and other projectiles (below). At least ten people were injured and eight were arrested. *AP Images/J. Walter Green*

On June 8, 1979, Red Auerbach, Larry Bird, and Bob Woolf appeared together at a press conference to announce the signing of the former Indiana State player to a contract worth more than $650,000. Bird cracked up his new boss when he proclaimed that he would have played for nothing. *Steve Carter/NBAE/Getty Images*

The 1980–81 Boston Celtics. Front row (left to right): Chris Ford, Cedric Maxwell, President and General Manager Red Auerbach, Coach Bill Fitch, Chairman of the Board Harry T. Mangurian Jr., Larry Bird, Nate Archibald. Back row: Assistant Coach K. C. Jones, Wayne Kreklow, M. L. Carr, Rick Robey, Robert Parish, Kevin McHale, Eric Fernsten, Gerald Henderson, Assistant Coach Jimmy Rodgers, and Trainer Ray Melchiorre. Not pictured: Terry Duerod.

Larry Bird stands at the center of the Boston defense during the 1981 NBA Finals against the Rockets in Houston. Celtic guard Tiny Archibald (7) defends the ball while Robert Parish (partially obscured) boxes out Houston center Moses Malone (24). The Celtics won two of the three games on the road during the finals, including the clincher on May 14, to win the series in six games. *Jim Cummins/NBAE/Getty Images*

Larry Bird acknowledges the crowd at the Celtics' victory parade through Boston on May 18, 1981. Although it had been only six years since the last Celtic championship, it was a much-needed celebration for the city of Boston and its basketball team. *Boston Herald/UPI Photo*

Thousands gathered in front of City Hall to cheer as the Celtics hoisted the Larry O'Brien Championship Trophy following the 1981 NBA title. Only a few years earlier, near this very spot, a chance encounter at the Government Center ended in a violent, racially charged attack on Ted Landsmark—and now it was the place where Boston came together as one, black and white, young and old, rich and poor. *Mike Andersen/Boston Herald*

court, such as losses to San Antonio (149-119) and Detroit (160-117). Bird was still weighing whether to sign with the Celtics or to re-enter the draft in 1979, and the Celtic representatives did their best to put his mind at ease. Things would be different next year—they had to be.

Cowens, Robey, and Judkins returned to Boston to play out the schedule while Bird continued to carry his Sycamore team on his back, leading them to an undefeated regular season. He took his game up a notch in the NCAA tournament and helped carry Indiana State to its first (and only) Final Four visit in school history. That week, Bird again appeared on the cover of *Sports Illustrated*, this time under the title "Bird Takes Off: Indiana State Makes Final Four."

In the semifinals, Bird submitted a masterpiece. Making 16 of 19 shots, the blond forward scored 35 points against Mark Aguirre and DePaul University in a 76-74 victory, punching the Sycamores' ticket to the NCAA Finals. In the final game, Michigan State and Magic Johnson proved to be too much, and Indiana State's fairy-tale season came to an end in a 75-64 loss.

Bird's senior season was one for the ages. Following the tournament, he was voted to his second straight All-American team. Boston fans hoped this greatness would extend to the Garden. Both the Celtics organization and its fans were desperate. The team was in the midst of the worst season in franchise history and in dire need of revival.

🏀

For years, Red Auerbach had built the team with players who had character and pride. Many of the current players were guilty of soiling the Celtic legacy. Auerbach, as much as the owners, had allowed the team to stray; by all reports Larry Bird possessed the ingredients necessary to return the ship to its proper course.

As much as the team needed him, the city needed him. A successful Celtic team would provide the oppressed a much-needed distraction. In the eyes of

Celtic fans, the team had no choice but to sign Bird no matter the price. For years Boston had looked to the Boston Garden's parquet floor in search of a diversion from life's myriad difficulties. From the balcony, they cheered not just because a basket was made or a game won, but because the team in green gave them a reason to feel good, to say with pride that they were from Boston. More than ever, the fans needed the Celtics to win.

Back in Indiana, local businessmen formed a committee to interview potential agents for Larry Bird. In all they met with sixty-five prospects and in the end they chose Red Auerbach's nemesis, Boston agent Bob Woolf. Over the years, Woolf represented several Celtics, including John Havlicek. Not shy when with the media, it was said "the very sight of a red light on a camera was enough to arouse [Woolf] to the point of orgasm." Woolf and Auerbach had sat across from the table as protagonists many times in the past. Back in the late 1960s, when the ABA was attempting to hijack the NBA, Woolf had exerted his ABA bargaining chip to force the team to pay Havlicek the most lucrative contract in team history.

On the weekend of April 8, which was two months prior to the deadline to sign the draft pick, Bob Woolf flew his client Larry Bird to Boston to introduce him to the city. During his visit, client and agent were guests of the Boston Celtics at the Boston Garden where the team was playing the final game of the season against the New Jersey Nets. When Bird walked into the Garden, the crowd rose for an extended standing ovation. Following the game, the polished agent introduced his shy client to the Boston media. Surprising to the press, Bird was affable and engaging. His "backwoods" country persona didn't play "hillbilly" but instead "folksy." Any lack of polish was interpreted not as unsophisticated but instead as sincere. He seemed genuine and likable. His answers were direct but not threatening. That was Bob Woolf's job. When he was asked about being selected by the Celtics, Bird answered honestly: "Last year they drafted me. I was tickled to death just to be part of the Celtics because of the tradition. But you know if this doesn't work out here we'll have to go someplace else. Celtics took a chance on me. I gotta' love 'em and put my heart right into them. I owe them something and if things don't work, I feel for them."

While Bird did excite the gathering with talk of the possibility of future championships, he was careful to communicate that money would be a factor in his signing. His agent would expound upon this notion by estimating Bird's worth as the "franchise." Woolf would also communicate to the throng with pens and cameras that he would be meeting with Red Auerbach to establish guidelines for negotiations. This was his way of telling Auerbach that the player and agent had leverage (because of the time restrictions) and thus would dictate the terms of the process.

Not long thereafter the two men met to discuss Larry Bird and his contract demands. In the *Globe*, Will McDonough described the meeting as "expletive laden and profane." It was going to be a tug-of-war. Over the next two months the negotiations would be subtly waged in the newspapers while bluntly discussed behind closed doors where meetings were often boisterous and intense. As the deadline approached, the pressure mounted for both sides.

With just weeks to go, Auerbach had called off the negotiations, placing the blame on Bob Woolf and his outrageous demands of $1 million or more. Being sure not to insult Bird, Auerbach was clear to point out that the forward had yet to score a basket in the NBA and that his agent was demanding the most lucrative contract in league history.

In Larry Johnson's sports cartoon in the *Boston Globe*, an image of the Sesame Street character Big Bird was drawn with Larry's head on top while down below sat two bags of money at his feet under the title of "This turkey hasn't played a game yet."

The fallout from Auerbach's volley was felt throughout the Woolf camp and family.

Not soon thereafter, Bob Woolf called for a press conference where he claimed that he and his family were being harassed on the streets and at workplaces because of Auerbach, whom he called a "dictator." He accused Red of applying emotional and psychological pressure on him and his family and warned that if such intimidating practices continued he would file a complaint with the league and the players union. When Auerbach was asked about the possible filing of a grievance, the cantankerous Celtic president waved off the reporter with the rebuke: "Don't bother me with that crap."

By May, owner Harry Mangurian, who after taking over from John Y. Brown had pledged to find the money to sign Larry Bird, stepped in to serve as an intermediary. Soon the two sides began to move to the middle and finally had an agreement in principle. With just a week to go to the draft, the process was placed back in the hands of Auerbach and General Manager Jan Volk to finalize the language of the contract. With the general terms agreed upon, Auerbach and Woolf met one last time to confirm the agreement. In the middle of the meeting, Woolf pulled a piece of paper from his pocket. He then preceded to hand the page to Auerbach who read the contents with a curious eye. Disturbed by what he read, he asked Woolf what the meaning of the page was about. The agent, with his best negotiating face, answered that these were a list of bonuses, including a $25,000 bonus for making the all-rookie team, that he would like to have added to the agreed-upon contract. Auerbach's face went stark red before he asked, "So let me get this straight: We're going to pay Larry the largest rookie contract in the history of the league and for that he's not even going to make the all-rookie team? I think I'm making a mistake here." With that he tore up the list, threw it in the barrel, and then called an end to the meeting.

Eventually, the two sides came to a consensus. Terms were agreed upon, language mutually accepted. In Indiana, Larry Bird was coaching the West Vigo High School baseball team, which was in the middle of its tournament. He had no intention of leaving his team in the middle of the postseason. Though, he was eventually convinced to leave the team and come to Boston for the press conference to celebrate the signing of the contract. Bird did come to Boston and spent the night before the press conference at Bob Woolf's house in Brookline. The following morning, a nervous Bird went for a run around the neighborhood to release his pent-up energy. Midway through his run he realized he was lost. Concerned that he would miss his first press conference as a Celtic, he flagged down a stranger to help him find his way back to his agent's house. Only after several passes around the neighborhood did Bird and his newfound friend find the Woolf residence.

On the day of the signing, the three parties smiled and laughed as if the proceedings were smooth and unencumbered. As the principals fielded questions, Auerbach stated that the public opinion that he and Bob Woolf didn't get along was a misconception. When Bird was asked if he felt pressure, he shook his head and said, "Is it written anywhere in my contract that I'm going to be the savior? I'm just going to give 100 percent and I won't sit down if I have a broken toe nail." He then added with a charm that would further endear him to the masses, "I forgot to tell Mr. Auerbach that I would have played for nothing."

Auerbach laughed and then lovingly punched his new player in the arm. The franchise was signed. It was the first step in the Celtics rebirth and Red knew it. The city knew it.

CHAPTER 19

"It Was His Flock"

EVERY ATHLETE REMEMBERS HOW HARD IT WAS TO EARN HIS OR HER FIRST VARSITY START. Every practice you hustle and grind while the starters get all the repetitions. You carry the equipment that the older kids walk over. You feel like an outsider desperate to feel a part of the team. You continue to work in search of an opportunity that will allow you to show the coach, teammates, and yourself that you can play the game. But until that moment comes, you keep your head down and endeavor to improve and to impress while waiting for that tap on the shoulder telling you that your efforts have been rewarded.

When Jamaica Plain head football coach Tom Richardson finally tapped Darryl Williams on the shoulder, he couldn't have been happier. He was just a sophomore but had good hands and was showing promise at wide receiver. Standing five-foot-eleven, he was still adding to his 150-pound frame. He was a superior athlete who could already dunk a basketball and outrun most of his friends.

The game against Charlestown High School was supposed to be played at Jamaica Plain High School, but because their field wasn't ready the team would have to travel. Some of the black players were apprehensive about going to Charlestown, but not Williams. He was consumed by nervous excitement. He didn't care about the stories and rumors. He just wanted to catch the football.

On game day, Williams couldn't concentrate on his Friday classes or hardly eat lunch. He was too excited. When the final bell rang and most kids boarded buses for home to start the weekend, Williams ran for the team bus carrying his helmet and shoulder pads. On the bus he wondered what the day would hold. Would he score a touchdown? Make a great catch? He had dreamed of end zone dances and one-handed catches; now he had a chance. The coach believed in him. He was determined to prove him right.

When the team arrived at Charlestown it was unusually warm despite the overcast skies. The teams stretched out and threw the football before the game. The crowd, as with most city games, was sparse, but that was all right. The players played for each other. They played because they loved football. Soon, the captains met at midfield and a coin was tossed. The captains shook hands; the ball was teed up and kicked. The game was on. Williams was finally playing in his first game. When the offense was on the field, he lined up and ran his patterns and blocked downfield as the play called. He wanted to do everything right.

Toward the latter part of the first half, the coach called for a pass play. Williams' heart pounded. This could be it. He lined up. Across from him, the cornerback tried to read his eyes. Williams tried to appear casual and averted the glare, turning his attention to the quarterback, who crouched over his center awaiting the snap. When the ball was centered, Williams instinctively ran. When he arrived at the designated spot, he turned. In slow motion he saw the ball leave the quarterback's hand and head in his direction in a clockwise rotation. He stopped breathing, as all his senses focused on the one task of making the catch. When the ball had traveled half the distance, his hands went up as if they were preprogrammed. He then braced for the contact while maneuvering his hands to where the pass would arrive. When the brown leather ball sunk into his palms, he wrapped his fingers around it. It was his. Darryl Williams had caught his first varsity pass and no one could ever take that away from him.

At halftime Jamaica Plain was leading Charlestown 6-0, scoring on a drive set up by Williams' reception. During the intermission the team sat in the east end zone in the shadow of Charlestown's Newtown tenements. The muggy temperatures had made the locker room uncomfortable, leading Coach Richardson to spend the intermission outside hoping for a westerly sea breeze. During the break from play, the head coach and former professional player Tom Richardson talked about adjustments while his team caught their breath and took in fluids. At the end of the discussion, the players were ready for the second half. They rose to their feet and snapped chin straps to helmets. As they readied themselves to return to the sideline, they heard a "pop." Being from the city, the kids knew it was a gunshot. Screams of "hit it" and "get on the ground" were yelled as players dove for the cover of a coverless end zone.

As a team, they lay on the grass and waited for time to pass and safety to return. Only after a sufficient period of calm did they begin to climb to their feet. That was except Darryl Williams, who didn't move. He lay motionless. Somehow the lottery of tragic fate had chosen the player with number 44 on his back. The bullet had snuck between his helmet and shoulder pads, entering behind the left ear. Once inside, the bullet found its way around the arteries to the fifth cervical vertebrae where it lodged in the spine. When Darryl arrived at the City Hospital he was unconscious, lacking both brain and nerve action.

The shot had come from the rooftop of the adjacent housing projects, which were mostly boarded up and closed. The desolate surroundings made the area a popular location for kids to party and cause mischief. But now the partying would end. Charlestown would make sure of it. The people of the neighborhood were outraged. This was their town, and they were proud of it. They were Townies who wanted what their parents wanted and their parents before them. A place they could call their own. Nevertheless the hatred that had consumed some during the 1970s had now manifested itself in the form of a sad and senseless shooting. Charlestown, like South Boston, would forever be broad brushed.

They were, as a whole, God-fearing people who now banded together as a community determined to protect what belonged to them: their reputation. They opened doors when detectives knocked; they stopped and talked when police approached; they answered phones when the authorities asked. In a neighborhood where the violation of the "code of silence" was considered a capital offense, answers were usually scarce. But this time, people talked. They wanted to right the wrong, as much as was physically possible. Soon, police had three teenagers in custody. Stories of beer drinking and subsequent pigeon shooting were suggested but discounted by most.

When the shooters and victim awoke earlier that morning they were more alike than different. They were teenagers. Confused and curious at what life would hold for them. They existed in the moment hoping to be someone but not quite sure how to get there. Now three Charlestown teenagers were imprisoned behind bars while Darryl Williams was imprisoned by his own body's failings.

While the cloud of the Williams shooting hung over Boston, the city's mayor was desperate. Throughout his tenure as the chief officer, Mayor White's priority was to build Boston into a world-class destination. At times, the racial unrest had served as an impediment to his efforts. But he never allowed the mayhem in the schools and streets to force him off course.

But now the shooting of Darryl Williams had ignited a spirit of vengeance that threatened to implode the city. In the days following, a white language teacher at Roxbury High School was attacked by a group of blacks who kicked and beat him unconscious, knocking out teeth and breaking his nose. At Dudley Station, three white students that had been bused to Madison Park High School in Roxbury were being beaten by a group of blacks when a bus driver pulled his bus up next to the fight and opened up the doors of the transport to allow thirty other blacks to join in the attack.

☙

Neither black nor white were all guilty or all innocent. While a black man dropping off his wife in South Boston was chased by a gang of whites, a pair of white sisters were assaulted by marauding blacks only to be rescued by the Dorchester High football team; while black buses were stoned entering white neighborhoods, white students felt the same sting of broken glass in the neighborhoods they were bused to. Good people suffering because others failed to find compromise. No one won, only lost.

For Mayor White, the pall of the racial conflict couldn't have happened at a worse time. For months and months the city had been planning for two events of international concern. On the Monday following the tragedy in Charlestown, Pope John Paul II would land at Logan Airport on his first American visit since being named successor to Peter. A few weeks later, the John F. Kennedy Library was scheduled for its official dedication in the Dorchester section of Boston. The world would turn its attention to Boston, giving the mayor an opportunity to showcase his legacy.

The mayor did his best to bring calm to the streets. He commended the neighborhoods of Roxbury and Charlestown for their patience and peace, referring to the incident as an aberration. "We are coming out of our racial problems, but it's like a virus that you have for a long time," he said. "It recurs occasionally but it's most important to see how the body reacts. We're getting progressively stronger." While Mayor White felt Boston was progressing, Congressman Paul Tsongas saw the Williams shooting as a continuation of past problems and not a momentary lapse. Speaking in Boston he articulated these fears with a fierce warning: "Boston will be condemned to a self-created hell of despair until it confronts and eradicates the festering prejudice that propelled the bullet into Darryl Williams who was struck down by darkness and hatred."

Many in the black community agreed with Tsongas. They saw the shooting as a symbol of the peril blacks existed in as residents of Boston. One of their brightest had been shot down on a football field while defenseless and innocent. They had had enough. It was time to take a stand. Either the city would allow them to walk the streets and play in its parks in peace, or they would let the world know of the condition that plagued what Mayor White called a world-class city.

The forward voice for the black community was State Representative Mel King. For years the people he represented had lacked an advocate. King filled that void. He was tall and soft-spoken, steadfast and deliberate, undeterred and resolute. Ever since the shooting on Friday, King had carefully measured the options of response. In the past, calls to City Hall or boycotts or staged walk-outs had had marginal impact.

By Sunday, Mel King had decided to exploit the city's vulnerability by forcing the hand of one of the most powerful men in the world, Pope John Paul II. In King's eyes, "The Pope had to get *his* flock to do the right thing. He needed to speak to *his* people about the injustice."

It was late Sunday night, and Darryl Williams still lay in a City Hospital bed on the precipice of death. The clocks throughout the city were approaching midnight when the phone rang in the rectory at the Cathedral of the Holy Cross. The pastor, Father Walter Waldron, had already put in a long day preparing for the arrival of the Pope, who would visit his parish as part of the coming day's proceedings. It would be the finest moment in the long and storied history of Boston's Catholic Archdiocese. It would be Father Waldron's finest moment after years of sacrifice and giving.

As he picked up the phone he prayed the call would be brief. He was tired and weary and had hoped to get some sleep before the morning came. But he would soon realize that wouldn't be possible. On the other end of the phone was Mel King. The two men as community outreach workers had known each other and were friendly enough. Father Waldron knew King as a man of steely resolve. He knew that what he said he meant and what he meant he said.

His request was succinct. He wanted Father Waldron to serve as an intermediary between himself and Cardinal Medeiros, Boston's highest ranked cleric. He had a concern that had to be resolved this night at this moment, despite the late hour. Knowing that the man couldn't and wouldn't be moved off point, Father Waldron, as requested, connected King with Cardinal Medeiros. King had a quiet but unflinching ultimatum for the cardinal: "Either the Pope mentions Darryl Williams at the Mass on the Esplanade, or we will have no choice but to march and protest outside the doors of the cathedral tomorrow morning and use every peaceful means possible to disrupt the service at the cathedral."

This was Father Waldron's worst nightmare. For years he had worked the South End as the "Hippie Priest," caring for people of all races. The parish and the community were an extension of him. Over the last days he had worried himself sick over the visit. Between the Secret Service and the duties as a host he had feared the worst, and now the worst had just been presented. The thought of the national and international cameras filming protestors with blow horns and general disorder outside his parish would tarnish this lifetime event forever.

For almost three hours the men negotiated. It wasn't until sometime after two o'clock in the morning that they came to an understanding. The cardinal had pledged his word to Mel King that he would talk to the Pope about his request but couldn't promise or speak for John Paul II.

Hours later, the Pope arrived at Logan Airport to a hero's welcome. After walking down the stairs of the plane he dropped to two knees and kissed the ground. Rising to his feet, he was then greeted by President Jimmy Carter and his wife, Roslyn, and other dignitaries. Standing behind the dignitaries stood Cardinal Medeiros, who was desperate for the ear of the Vicar of Christ. Invited into his limousine for the motorcade ride through the city, the cardinal explained the dilemma to the Pope, who took the request under advisement before rising from his seat to greet the people of Boston through the sunroof of his car. The motorcade would travel down Day Boulevard in South Boston and through the North End on its way to the South End where they would arrive at the cathedral. It was the same streets that buses traveled every day, transporting students to their school of, not choice, but assignment.

In the sanctuary at the cathedral, Father Waldron was nervously arranging his vestments and readying the area when he was approached by the Pope's consigliore, translator, and the head of the Vatican Bank, Archbishop Paul Marcinkus. Marcinkus had just spoken with the Pope, who had agreed to mention Darryl Williams' name during the mass later that afternoon.

A big smile spread across Waldron's face. Immediately he ran from the sanctuary outside the church where Mel King and 1,800 other protestors had assembled. When he informed the state representative that the Pope agreed to mention Darryl during the later service, King true to his word spread the message that disruption was not necessary. And though King would have preferred to have met with the Pope to tell him what was going on in Boston, he would settle for strong-arming the most popular and powerful pope since St. Peter himself. (City Councilor Dapper O'Neal also wanted to get close to the Pope, but it was his hope "to ask him to pray for the *Boston Globe* and all those flaming liberals for they know not what they do.")

Father Waldron would greet John Paul on the steps of the cathedral, where they would exchange pleasantries. The service would be a beautiful moment in the church's history. At the conclusion of the service, the Pope marched outside and was not jeered by Mel King's assembly but instead cheered. Later in the day the Pope presided over mass at the Esplanade just blocks from the Boston Common, where Mel King marched with Martin Luther King in 1965, and where the statue for the 54th Regiment stands and the monument to Crispus Attucks resides. During the rainy but magical service, the Pope asked the people of Boston to embrace the "option of love and not violence." Later, during the prayers of intercession, the "complete recovery of Darryl Williams" was prayed for. The Pope was true to his word.

Weeks later, Ted Kennedy would visit with Williams and his mother on his way to the dedication of his brother's Presidential Library in Dorchester. He commended Williams on his courage and shared with Ms. Simmons, "I know how you feel." But he didn't. He was a man of almost infinite means capable of providing almost anything for his children, Edward Jr., Patrick, and Kara. They didn't have to board buses or walk hallways lined by the National Guard. They could choose where they wanted to go to learn and play. Boston students and their parents did not have that right. Williams had requested entrance into his neighborhood school of Madison Park but had been denied. Instead he was bused to Jamaica Plain High School. It was there that he would be forced to attend school and meet a tragic fate.

Soon Shirley Simmons would bring her quadriplegic son home to an empty house with no one to help. Where was Ted Kennedy when Darryl needed him? Kennedy had turned his back on the city a long time before. He could have been a part of the solution; instead, he left the city to its own resolution.

◉

Fall in New England is always a special time. The sight of turning leaves combined with the pleasant weather is one of the distinctive characteristics of the region. In 1979, the changing of the seasons brought hope to Boston. Pope John Paul II had energized a city that was starting to realize a unity between neighborhoods. While the city moved forward, albeit slowly, the Celtics were in the midst of training camp. Like the city that they represented, the Celtics were seeking a rebirth that would allow them to realize past glories. On the court was a blond forward who, for the first time, wore the shamrock and laced up black sneakers. There was hope on the streets and on the basketball court.

CHAPTER 20

"Never Seemed a Rookie"

WITH JUST A MONTH TO TRAINING CAMP, RED AUERBACH HAD TO FIND A WAY TO PURGE THE FORCES THAT HAD INFECTED THE BOSTON CELTICS DURING THE PRIOR SEASON. With the arrival of Larry Bird, the team needed to start anew. In the summer, the Celtics had signed free agent M. L. Carr of the Pistons. Carr was a high-energy player whom Auerbach saw as the perfect Celtic. During discussions with the guard/forward, Auerbach immediately established the role for Carr. Auerbach wanted him to be the "stopper." For years, Auerbach had built successful teams by compiling players who filled specific needs. Carr would serve one of those needs.

As mandated by league rules the Celtics were obligated to compensate the Pistons for the acquisition of their former player. In the Celtic offices, Red Auerbach and Jan Volk concocted a scheme that might allow them to both secure Carr's services while at the same time ridding the team of an unwanted player. The plan called for Auerbach to talk with the Pistons while

Volk traveled to the NBA offices in New York to research the compensation rules and precedents.

The coach and general manager of the Pistons was the loquacious Dick Vitale, who was enamored with Bob McAdoo and Auerbach knew it. When Vitale broached the topic of McAdoo as compensation, the wizard of the Boston Garden knew he had Vitale where he wanted him. "Are you kidding me?" Auerbach scoffed. "McAdoo is a great player. He's won three scoring titles. We think M. L. will be a fine addition to the team, but he's no McAdoo. If you want him, we're gonna have to get some draft picks or something."

Meanwhile, Volk was in New York reviewing old cases and transcripts of past free agent signings. Within those records he found the case of a player who had played for the Detroit Pistons but for whom the acquiring team was not obligated to compensate the Pistons because Detroit had failed to demonstrate an inclination to re-sign him. Volk knew this was a significant precedent. When he returned to Boston, he reviewed the tape that the Celtics had made of their original interview with Carr. During the conversation, Carr had informed them that the Pistons refused to pay him his bonus for the previous year until he signed a new contract. To Volk, this hinted of breach and was similar to the precedent-setting case. A brief was written and sent simultaneously to the commissioner's office and the Pistons.

When Auerbach was sure that Vitale was in possession of the legal brief, he called back, looking to exploit his leverage like only he could. The Pistons had two first-round selections in the ensuing draft. Auerbach said that if those picks were included in the deal, then they had an agreement and Bob McAdoo would be in a Pistons uniform. Vitale agreed (Bob Ryan would describe him as "giddy"), and the two teams had a deal. But before the trade could be announced, Auerbach, Volk, and Vitale agreed to remain silent until the commissioner and the league approved the transaction. Thirty minutes later Jan

Volk was driving home from the Celtics' offices when he turned on the sports talk show on WBZ Radio, "Calling All Sports." Host Bob Lobel was in the midst of breaking the story that the Celtics had agreed to send Bob McAdoo to the Pistons as compensation for M. L. Carr and two first-round draft picks. Vitale clearly could not contain his excitement about his new player.

With the shamrock now taken from McAdoo, the team looked to get a fresh start. In addition to Carr, the Celtics had signed guard Gerald Henderson from the Continental Basketball Association. Henderson was a shooting guard out of Virginia Commonwealth who had refined his ball-distributing ability while playing for the Tucson Gunners in the Western League. Chris Ford later nicknamed him Quick, and Henderson would fit into a guard rotation that would include Tiny Archibald, Ford, and Jeff Judkins. Archibald, who had come over in the bizarre franchise switch between John Y. Brown and Irv Levin, had worked hard in the offseason hoping to resurrect his career. A man of few words, he became obstinate during the previous season. He hated to lose, and this feeling had manifested itself in a failure to commit himself to practice or to a team with no chance to win. His quiet moods were described as "morose" and "malcontent" by the media. But now Archibald had a chance to win. At age thirty-two, he was nearing the end of his career and realized this could be his best chance to win. He didn't need to be the man; he already had been the man. As a star with the Kansas City Kings, Archibald once led the league in both scoring and assists in the same year.

Along with the new faces on the court, the Celtics would be led by a new coach, Bill Fitch. In every season since 1950, a member of the Celtic family had coached the team. The failures of the past two seasons had led Auerbach to look outside for a cure to the disease that consumed the team. Fitch, a former Marine and a known taskmaster, had led the Cleveland Cavaliers to the 1976 Eastern Conference Finals only to lose to the eventual-champion Boston

Celtics. He was named Coach of the Year in recognition of his efforts and, in the process, established himself as a builder. He was a workaholic and self-proclaimed dictator who was unwilling to compromise. He was a perfect fit for an up-and-coming team in Boston.

At the start of camp, much anticipation surrounded the newly signed Larry Bird. Although he was an unproven commodity at the professional level, he was being paid the unheard-of sum of $650,000 as a rookie. In the book *Selling of the Green*, Celtic forward Cedric Maxwell said that his first thought upon Bird's arrival was, "Here comes this white punk—he can't play." Then, it "didn't take long to realize he could." M. L. Carr later commented that Bird's abilities were evident after two times down the court during his first training camp.

Still, the veteran players were quick to test the hotshot rookie. On the first day of camp, Bird was ordered to fetch water for the other players, as was a Celtic tradition for newbies. Larry Bird was a proud man who didn't expect anything from anyone and in turn didn't expect to serve as anyone's caddy either. As the call for water lingered, Bird seized on the opportunity to make his position clear. "Go fuck yourselves," he told them.

From that moment forward, Larry Bird became a leader of the team. He endeavored to out-work and out-hustle not only his opponents but also his teammates. The first to practice and last to leave, he was unwilling to fail and open to suggestions for improvement. The Fitch preseason camp was the most difficult that any of the players had ever participated in. On the first day, Curtis Rowe, who in the past had shown a disinclination to practice hard, complained of soreness. Fitch ordered him to leave the court and the gym all together. Rowe would never again be seen in a Celtic uniform.

The camp took its toll on Bird as well, who was sick and sore but never stopped. In Coach Fitch's early assessment of his rookie, he was pleased with the prize student's willingness to work hard: "It wasn't an easy camp for him, but that's good he struggled some days. He really struggled with his health, but he never missed a day. He has proven he has the intangibles. He's very coachable. He listens and asks questions and doesn't sulk when you say something to him." Soon the rookie would have the opportunity to measure himself against the NBA's best.

In the Celtics' first preseason scrimmage in the Bird Era, they were matched up against the strength of the East: the Philadelphia 76ers. Bird scored 18 points in the game, leading Sixers forward Julius Erving to assess, "I have a very favorable opinion of him as a player. . . . I guess the best thing to say is that he can play."

During training camp and the preseason, the team's chemistry was galvanized by a shared will to win as well as a common dislike for their hard-driving coach. The young Bird continued to acclimate and improve. Against the Knicks, he submitted his first professional masterpiece, scoring 36 points and pulling down 15 rebounds despite sitting out most of the fourth quarter. When the Celtics went to Indiana State to play at Bird's alma mater in an exhibition game, he scored 17 points and grabbed 16 rebounds. A week later, he accounted for 19 points and 19 rebounds in a rematch with the Knicks.

Bob Ryan wrote in the *Globe*, "Lord, how lucky we hoop freaks have been in this town. From Russell to Cowens in one year, and now from Havlicek to Bird. We are truly the Hoop God's Chosen People."

By opening night, the team and the city were consumed with anticipation. The Boston Garden was sold out, which was a rarity during the previous two seasons. And the hometown team didn't disappoint, beating the Houston Rockets 114-106. Bird scored 14 points and grabbed 10 rebounds while playing in foul trouble, as he would for much of the first month. Boston opened the season by winning its first 4 games and 10 of the first

12. They leapt into the top spot in the standings and held it throughout the entire season.

In addition to holding a superior record, the Celtics beat the rival 76ers in the Pete Maravich sweepstakes. Philadelphia thought it had signed Maravich and consequently had shirts made up with his name on the back, only to find that the Celtics had secured his rights.

At season's end, Boston had edged out Philadelphia for the Eastern Conference Title. The Celtics' record of 61-21 was not only good enough to win the East but also was the NBA's best. The record for the 1979–80 season as compared to the previous season's mark represented the biggest turnaround in league history up to that point.

The players were proud of their accomplishments. After the season's final game, they high-fived and yelled and sang in the locker room. That was until Red Auerbach walked into the locker room and brought the party to an abrupt halt. "We don't celebrate anything here except championships," he reminded them

The Celtics earned a first-round bye in the playoffs and then faced the Houston Rockets in the Conference Semifinals. Boston swept the series in four straight, winning every game by at least 18 points. The win set up a meeting with the playoff-tested 76ers. In the end, the veteran team from Philadelphia, led by the likes of Julius Erving, Caldwell Jones, and Maurice Cheeks, was too much for the upstart Boston team. Philadelphia won Eastern Conference Finals in five games, including two wins on the Garden parquet. Ray Fitzgerald eloquently recounted the closing seconds of the elimination game:

> Bird broke from a cluster of players near the Philly foul line and headed for the Celtics' bench, and the noise began. All around the beat-up Boston Garden, home of King Rat and obstructed-view seats, the fans stood and applauded and stamped their feet.

Disappointment sat on these people like Poe's raven, but in the midst of that disappointment, they wanted to let this most remarkable young basketball player know they appreciated what he'd accomplished in his rookie season.

But, of course, Larry Bird had never seemed a rookie, not from the time he showed up here for his first press conference and told the media it was nice of Red Auerbach to give him the half-million but that he'd have been happy to play for nothing with the Boston Celtics.

Bird finished his first postseason having averaged a team-high 21 points and 11 rebounds in the nine games while chipping in nearly 5 assists per game.

❦

The historic season had come to an end. The rookie Larry Bird proved to be more than anyone had hoped for. He not only made the All-Rookie team but also was named the league's Rookie of the Year, beating out Magic Johnson by a 63-3 vote.

With Bird, the team was reborn. Dave Cowens, re-energized with his duties limited to just playing the game, made amends for past disappointments; Cedric Maxwell, in his third season in the league, applied his diverse skills around the basket; Tiny Archibald led the team with his deft passing and attacks on the basket; Chris Ford stretched defenses with his outside shooting; off the bench, Rick Robey served as a perfect back-up for an aging Cowens; M. L. Carr brought an infectious energy; and the young Gerald Henderson improved with every game.

Bill Fitch was named Coach of the Year, earning his second award with a second team. The sharp-tongued coach was effective in getting his point across to his players, helping them to improve while cutting them down at the same time. He possessed a sharp intellect and diabolical wit that often manifested itself in ridicule and hurtful demonstrations. During the 1980–81 season, Fitch would embarrass back-up center Rick Robey in front of teammates and fans alike in an open display of mockery. It occurred after Robey had allowed his opponent to get past him and to the rim. The coach immediately substituted for his burly reserve. When Robey came to the sideline, he took a seat at the end of the bench to avoid the reach of his unhappy coach. But Fitch would have none of it. He summoned Robey to take a seat next to him. Reluctantly, Robey walked past his teammates and sat down next to his coach. Fitch put his arm around his center and ordered him to take off his sneakers. Robey did as asked and sat there in his stocking feet. When there was a break in play, Fitch turned to his center and asked, "Now, son, I have to ask you, do those sneakers have fucking nails in them?" Robey shook his head no, inducing Fitch to finish his point with, "Well, you weren't moving your feet so I just wanted to know if there was a reason for your horseshit defense. At least I know it wasn't the sneakers."

The self-absorbed Fitch used whatever means necessary to gain any advantage from his players, and while the players didn't always appreciate it, they knew in their heart of hearts that they needed him. But in the end, as the 1980 season and playoffs came to an end, the Celtics weren't there yet. To be able to beat Philadelphia when it counted most, they needed to improve as a team. Once again, Auerbach would apply his draft-day magic and make the most of the two first-round picks that he had pilfered from the Pistons.

In Bob Ryan's season recap, he quoted the blue-collared Larry Bird: "If anything, we'll have to work harder next year. We had a tough training camp, and we got off to a good start this year, which was essential. Next year's will be even tougher. If I think I did a good job this year, well, I'll be even hungrier next year."

CHAPTER 21

The Covenant

ON THE FIRST MORNING BACK TO SCHOOL FOLLOWING THE DARRYL WILLIAMS SHOOTING, JAMAICA PLAIN HEADMASTER DONALD SPRATLIN ADDRESSED THE STUDENT BODY OVER THE PUBLIC-ADDRESS SYSTEM. "I will not allow Darryl's tragedy to become a tragedy for all of us. It's clear the only direction that will benefit all of us is the one we collectively decide to take. . . . We want Jamaica Plain High School to continue its pace and become the great high school we all know it can be. I ask you now to join in a moment of silent prayer for Darryl."

While football coach Tommy Richardson described the shooting as a scar that would last a lifetime, he also spoke to the need to keep living. For the first time in years, the city was in consensus. As a victim, Darryl Williams was not white or black. He was what Boston politician Joseph Timilty called "the son of everyone in the city." Every child who had ever run on a field or played in a playground shuddered over the shooting; every parent could feel for Darryl's mother, Shirley Simmons, who sat by his bedside wondering why. She had dreams and hopes for her child. But now she only hoped for him to live so she could tell him she loved him.

Despite her pain and fears, she found it within herself to speak to the city as a parent would speak of her child. She saw the good in Boston and its wonderful potential. She didn't hold ill will toward any people or neighborhood. Instead she saw the incident as the act of misguided individuals who didn't represent anyone but the constraints of their own hearts. She didn't elect to march or beat her chest, blaming the city and thus dividing it further. Instead, she chose to serve as a uniting force: "My only hope is that we can become a city where everybody can walk safely in the streets—blacks and whites. Where everyone can walk without fear. Is that too much to ask of a city? I'm not interested in marches and protest. I'm not interested in the politics. We need to love each other."

For the first time, a neighborhood from "one" community sought out the neighborhood from the "other" community. At the weekend service at Shirley Simmons' place of worship, the Eliot Congregational Church in Roxbury, Charlestown priests Father Ernest Serino and Father Robert Boyle asked if they could address Ms. Simmons and the congregation as representatives of the neighborhood they served. Their request was granted, and the two priests were given the pulpit. They read a letter to the congregation that was written and signed by people of Charlestown:

> In our shock and sense of disgrace that we feel over the mindless savage shooting of your young son, Darryl, we the undersigned residents of Charlestown wish to extend to you our prayer-filled condolences during these most difficult hours and days. We

pray for you that your wounded mother's heart may find some solace and peace. We pray for your family and for Darryl's teammates and for all who love him and who experience or share the agony of this terrible event. And we pray for healing and forgiveness of all the racist madness that consumes the hearts of the few who bring dishonor and debasement to all people of good will and over the city of Boston. We feel utterly helpless and speechless in the face of the suffering. In this moment we only hope you will accept our faltering efforts to diminish in some small way the darkness of your grief.

At the conclusion of the service, the clerics from both churches met to discuss the crisis and how to remedy the ills that infected the city. Father Serino and Father Boyle were asked to plead with the archdiocese's lead cleric, Cardinal Humberto Medeiros, to play a bigger role as a unifying force among the city's neighborhoods.

❦

Humberto Sousa Medeiros was born in the Azores in 1915 and came to Fall River, Massachusetts, with his family as an immigrant, no different than many of the families that occupied the triple-deckers. Prior to returning to Boston, he had served as an intermediary between the migrant workers and established communities of Brownsville, Texas. This experience may have been viewed by some as an asset in dealing with the situation in Boston's neighborhoods.

Medeiros was named Archbishop of Boston in 1970 to succeed the wildly popular and charismatic son of South Boston, Cardinal Richard Cushing. In 1973, after being elevated to cardinal, Medeiros was cheered like a hero as he walked the streets of South Boston in the St. Patrick's Day Parade, but soon he was no longer welcomed on those streets. Medeiros alienated the people of

South Boston and other members of the church when he spoke out against those in power who had failed to desegregate the schools. "They've had nine years to do it," he said, "and have done nothing." He further proclaimed that Catholic schools would "not be used as a haven for those who seek to circumvent the court order."

Throughout the busing crisis, the Catholic Church had been a divisive entity. People from outside the church had long called for it to assume a stronger voice in pushing for the desegregation efforts. Many parishioners, by contrast, expected the church to use its power and influence to forestall the radical change that had been cast upon them.

Medeiros' comments reinforced the belief of many churchgoers that the archdiocese was failing in its role to serve as a support base for those most affected by the desegregation order. They felt that by placing the blame for the continuing status quo at the feet of elected officials, he was also branding the citizens who had voted for those officials as culpable in the city's growing racial crisis.

Now considered an outsider by the people who attended his churches, the cardinal was hurt by their misconception about his purpose in speaking out in support of the desegregation program. Medeiros was increasingly concerned with the violence that was enveloping the city, which he depicted as an extension of the crucifixion: "Christ's agonizing on the cross has been continued on the streets in this archdiocese and in the schools of our city."

In the face of this division within the Catholic Church, as well as continuing criticism from outside the church that Boston's Catholic leadership was not doing enough to end racism in the city, the shared outrage surrounding the shooting of Darryl Williams provided an opportunity to unite people across neighborhoods and faiths. From this common concern, an initiative was born. Representatives from Catholic, Jewish, and multiple Protestant denominations gathered to discuss ways to bring the city together. Together they devised a contract, called the Covenant, by which individual citizens were to be held responsible for upholding the principles of justice, equality, and harmony. Priests, rabbis, and ministers were directed to promote the Covenant among their constituents and urge them to sign the document, pledging to uphold the sanctity of these principles.

Although the creators of the Covenant had great faith in this tactic, they also were realistic. They knew it was not a panacea but rather a spark for discussion, thought, and reflection. They wanted to encourage people to search their own hearts and those of their families for what they truly wanted for their community. At an assembly held on the Boston Common to support the Covenant, Cardinal Medeiros beseeched the gathered: "Root and stem and branches must now and forever drive racism out of the hearts and minds, out of the living rooms and neighborhoods, and out of the social atmosphere and institutions that make up Boston."

In all, 275,000 people signed the Covenant. And while the document had its detractors in both white and black communities, it was an important step in the rebirth of a city that for nearly a decade had been on the brink of all-out catastrophe.

At City Hospital, the renewed spirit of unity in the city buoyed Shirley Simmons when she most needed it. "It's been an unbelievable experience," she said. "I never knew there were so many good people, so many people willing to give and help. I wish everybody could feel the emotion that I feel, and the good feeling that I know Darryl feels."

The tide was turning in Boston. No longer were people willing to sit back and let forces from without and within divide the city. A moving example of this was recounted by William Looney, a famous Boston lawyer and an associate of Judge Arthur Garrity in the state attorney general's office. He also was and is a passionate protector of his alma mater, Boston Latin School. Latin is the city's premier exam school and the oldest learning institution in the country; it was attended by five signers of the Declaration of Independence. In the days when the courts were making decisions for the public schools, Looney was assigned the task of insulating Boston Latin from such matters. The friends of Boston Latin hoped that the courts and the subsequent unrest would not infiltrate their campus. This goal was only realized through the compassion and vigilance of the headmaster and students themselves, as described by Looney:

> Somehow twelve white hooligans, who didn't attend the school, had gained entry to its hallways and sought out the first black student they could find. When they came upon a diminutive seventh-grader, they unleashed their fury of hatred upon him. Fortunately, the captain of the football team, who happened to be white, came upon the scene. After scaring off the attackers, he picked the victim up in his arms and carried him to the nurse's office, where he was attended to. When the headmaster, Wilfred O'Leary, was informed of the senseless attack, he gathered the senior boys around him and gave them a directive. "Your school day is over. Your assignment is to find the twelve trespassers and by whatever means necessary expel them from these grounds."
>
> The seniors, as instructed, searched the halls until they discovered the twelve antagonists. They then proceeded to remove them from the school. Boston Latin was never again affected by racial unrest.

CHAPTER 22

"Even the Liberty Bell Is Cracked"

BILL FITCH LOVED TO WATCH VIDEO. On the television screen he could come to understand the nuances and tendencies of his team and his opponents. He was so captivated by the power of the technology that he occasionally got lost in the video and ignored what the naked eye was telling him. His reliance on such a tool flew in the face of the old-school instincts that Red Auerbach used to read and understand the game. Auerbach called Fitch's affinities "cockamamie," and he later nicknamed him "Captain Video."

By the conclusion of Fitch's first season with the Celtics, friction was growing between coach and president, two headstrong and possessive men. Fitch wanted it made clear that the Celtics were his team, without interference. During the Celtics' ill-fated playoff series against Philadelphia, Fitch had raised some eyebrows when he asked Auerbach and owner Harry Mangurian to wait outside the locker room in the hallway while he addressed his team. Later that year, when Auerbach commented to the press that he had allowed his coach great latitude, Fitch responded, "I'd like to thank Mr. Warmth for reminding me that I'm on a multiple-day contract."

Following the 1980 playoffs, the Celtics turned their attention to the NBA draft, which 76ers General Manager Pat Williams had dubbed the "Dick Vitale Sweepstakes" in reference to the one-sided trade that the Detroit coach had made with the Celtics. In the previous season the Pistons had compiled a record of 16-66, thus making the Celtics eligible for a coin toss between them and the Utah Jazz for the first pick in the draft. When the Celtics won the toss, Auerbach pounded the table in exultation. He knew that his team would be complete once he convinced seven-foot-four center Ralph Sampson of the University of Virginia to declare for the draft. When Sampson denied the Celtic president's overtures, Auerbach was furious and would hold a grudge for years to come.

Still, the Celtics possessed the first and thirteenth picks in the draft, and they proceeded to set their sights elsewhere. Elsewhere happened at the 1980 U.S. Olympic tryouts in Kentucky. There Auerbach and Fitch spent a late night with Golden State Warriors management Scotty Stirling and Pete Newell. The Warriors had finished the prior season with a disappointing 24-58 record. Stirling and Newell believed that the draft was deep enough that they could trade their sometime-unhappy leading scorer and rebounder Robert Parish and the third overall pick in the draft in exchange for Boston's two first-round selections.

The meeting concluded with an understanding that the two sides would conduct their due diligence, and if both were still interested, they would revisit the matter prior to the draft. When the Celtic brass returned to Boston, Fitch proceeded to watch as much film as possible of center Robert Parish. Parish's game was primarily on the periphery, but he had the length that the Celtics had lacked against a Philadelphia frontcourt featuring two six-foot-eleven-inch towers, Darryl Dawkins and Caldwell Jones.

Golden State was interested in selecting center Joe Barry Carroll of Purdue University with the Celtics' first pick. Utah, who held the second pick, was enamored with the exciting Louisville guard Darrell Griffith, who had wowed the country with his leaping ability and earned the nickname "Dr. Dunkenstein." This left the Celtics to choose among the likes of Mike O'Koren, Mike Gminski, Kiki Vandeweghe, Andrew Toney (whom Philadelphia coveted), and a gangly, six-foot-ten forward out of the University of Minnesota named Kevin McHale.

A native of Minnesota, McHale had stayed home to play basketball even though the program was under NCAA sanctions. McHale, who would later be named the greatest player in the school's history, led the Gophers to an NIT Finals appearance in his senior season while averaging 17.4 points, 8.8 rebounds, and 57 percent shooting from the field. His potential and diverse skill-set intrigued the Celtics. This interest was further piqued when Bobby Knight, who had coached McHale in the Pan-American summer games, gave him a ringing endorsement.

The night before the Celtics were to make their decision, Fitch and Assistant Coach Jimmy Rodgers watched tape of all the potential prospects. By three in the morning, "Captain Video" wanted to watch just one more tape before deciding whom the Celtics would take with the number-three pick if they were to make the trade with Golden State.

The tape was a game between Minnesota and Purdue. In the game, Kevin McHale dominated the projected number-one pick, Joe Barry Carroll. Fitch was convinced; the Celtics management was convinced. So convinced were they, that they concluded that even if they didn't make the trade, they were going to take McHale with the first overall pick in the draft.

The Celtics did make the trade and took McHale with the number-three pick. After the trade was announced, Auerbach accepted the accolades of the masses, ignoring the significant role that Bill Fitch had played in facilitating the transaction with Golden State. Just as Auerbach had received credit for everything that went right during Tommy Heinsohn's coaching tenure, Fitch was now being consumed by the same shadow. But Fitch wasn't Heinsohn. He felt no loyalty to Red or the Celtics. In fact, he didn't even subscribe to the whole Celtic mystique. He coached the team as if there were no past, only the present to prepare for the future. Nevertheless, the rift between coach and president grew wider.

In the newspapers there was great debate over the trade. McHale was a relative unknown, and Parish had failed to raise the pulse of those who had seen him over his first four seasons in the league. Ray Fitzgerald wrote of the Celtics' new center: "The last time I saw Parish—wait a minute and I'll hum a few bars—he did not remind me of Kareem or Artis Gilmore or even Rick Robey. He lah-de-dahed through a televised game from the Coast, a seven-foot invisible man. Phlegmatic is a good word, and also disinterested, and lethargic makes three."

Bob Ryan, in his article, quoted one NBA coach as saying, "I've never been a Parish fan. I've always wondered about his motivation. But guys have a way of turning around when they get into that Celtic green."

Now—with Parish, McHale, Cowens, Bird, Maxwell, and Carr—the Celtics had a frontcourt to match that of any NBA team. Maxwell, McHale, and Archibald, however, had yet to be signed prior to training camp. Maxwell eventually inked a four-year deal reportedly worth a million dollars. When he showed up at camp that September, the Celtics were disappointed to see that he had put on twenty pounds in the offseason. Fitch quipped, "Thank God we're not paying him by the pound." Maxwell never was concerned with offseason conditioning. He gradually played himself into shape, allowing him to continue his routine of ordering a hot dog with everything on it before taking the floor each night.

The Archibald and McHale negotiations were more contentious. Tiny wanted the security of years; McHale wanted his perceived value. When the Celtics didn't share his assessment of that value, the Minnesota forward and his agent traveled to Italy, where they seriously entertained playing overseas for a year. Back in Boston, Auerbach was not moved by this ploy to gain leverage in the negotiations. He didn't anticipate that the rookie forward would play a major role with his established front line, so there was no urgency to sign the first-round pick. In Auerbach's mind, McHale could go to Europe and play, but if someday he wanted to play in the NBA, it would be with the Celtics, who would retain his rights. The two sides eventually met in the middle, and McHale was signed just three weeks before the season opener. It took two more weeks before Tiny Archibald settled for a one-year contract.

With all the players signed and accounted for, Coach Fitch proceeded to impose a boot-camp regimen for the preseason preparation. Robert Parish struggled to keep up, and both his abilities and his desire were being called into question. In Will McDonough's weekly column in the *Globe*, he wrote, "People around the club are concerned about Robert Parish. The big center, acquired from Golden State, has not been the force they thought he would be when they made the trade."

It was Fitch's goal to coach not only the most talented team in the league but also the best conditioned. With the combined passing skills of Archibald, Bird, and Maxwell, the team was tailor-made for an up-tempo offense that could push the ball up the court. The problem was that Parish's game was not conducive to such a style. In Golden State, he had played the high post and thus floated up and down the court. In the Celtics system, he was making it only as far as the free-throw line before the possession was reversed, and thus he was always behind the play. After days of not having his center involved at either end of the court, Fitch felt it was time to drive home his point.

During one practice session, Fitch waited for what he felt was an egregious effort by Parish. The coach blew his whistle and brought practice to a halt. All around the court, players were bent over with hands on hips while Fitch reprimanded his center in front of his teammates. "Robert, you're running like an elephant. Can't you run any faster?" Exhausted and frustrated, Parish knew that things weren't going as planned, but he had never had to run like this before or been at a camp this demanding. Looking at Fitch, he retorted, "What the fuck do you want from me?"

Fitch sent everyone home for the day and shut down practice. At the next practice, it was said that Parish wasn't running like an elephant but instead like a gazelle. The center had received the message loud and clear: Fitch and the Celtics meant business and would not stand for anything less than the best.

As camp wore on, Maxwell was getting back into shape, and McHale was exceeding expectations. With Parish now beating his teammates up and down the court, Fitch needed a new whipping boy. Surprisingly, he turned his wrath on one of the great NBA players of all time, and maybe the greatest college basketball player of all time, Pete Maravich.

One of the reasons Maravich had chosen Boston over Philadelphia in the bidding war for his services the previous season was that his father, Press Maravich, was a friend of Bill Fitch's. In the closing months of the 1979–80 season, Fitch used Pete sparingly, much to the dismay of not only the player but also team president Red Auerbach, who years later expressed his disappointment: "If I was coaching, there's no doubt I would've used him a lot more minutes. But Fitch didn't see it that way,"

Heading into the 1980–81 season, Maravich came to camp in shape and with the intention of earning the starting off-guard position, which Chris Ford now occupied. Maravich suffered through camp but had survived and now was thriving. Fitch, however, continued to harass the guard to the point that

Assistant Coach K. C. Jones felt sad for the superstar. "It pained me to see Bill treat Pete that way because Pete busted his ass on both offense and defense," Jones said. "I just felt bad for Pete because he was a great player and I appreciated the way he was playing. He just had an issue with the coach."

The constant wrath of the coach was starting to wear on Maravich. When he had signed with the team, he said he had waited ten years to play for the Celtics. Now he was contemplating giving it all up. One night after practice, he called former Celtic Jeff Judkins, who was now with the Utah Jazz. Maravich shared with his old teammate that he was contemplating retiring. Judkins was shocked. "What are you talking about? You're on a great team. It's your dream to win a championship." Pete couldn't be persuaded. "You don't understand," he said. "The guy has ripped the spirit of the game out of me. I'm not having fun. It's not the basketball I love." (Maravich wouldn't be the last Celtic to feel this way about Fitch. Even Larry Bird, who was a Fitch supporter, confessed in a later year that he would play out his contract and leave the Celtics if Fitch remained the coach.)

The following night during an exhibition game, Maravich sidled up next to Cedric Maxwell and shared his decision. "Cedric, this is the last game I'm ever going to play in, and you're the first to know." The Celtics were surprised, but not completely. Everyone was aware of the pressure Fitch was placing on the star and that the player was unhappy with the situation.

In an effort to get Maravich to change his mind, the Celtics sent veteran Dave Cowens to talk to Pistol Pete. When Cowens returned, not only had he failed to convince Maravich to return, but Maravich had convinced Cowens to retire, too. The two men were kindred spirits who loved to play the game, but Cowens, like Maravich, had had the fun of the game taken from him.

Cowens called Auerbach and informed him of his decision. Auerbach knew that his redheaded center wouldn't change his mind. He was that kind of person.

Cowens' final wish before leaving the team was that Kevin McHale wear his number. Instead, that February, the Celtics retired number 18, and Cowens took his rightful place among the legends of Boston Celtics basketball.

❀

The Celtics would now open the season having lost two players who would later be named among the top fifty players in NBA history. The onus now fell on Robert Parish to be the anchor in the middle that Cowens had been. The Celtics realized this, and in the opening game against Cleveland they made a point of forcing the offense to him in the early possessions to get him involved from the start.

The Celtics started the season with a win, but their play was erratic for the remainder of the opening month. They trailed the 76ers by 6½ games in early November, and the crowds at the Boston Garden were getting anxious. But then the team began to gel. They won 36 of 40 games beginning on November 9, including a remarkable run of 25 wins in 26 games between December 9 and January 28. In a Christmas Day victory over the Knicks on national television, Bird scored 28 points and grabbed 20 rebounds. In one game during this stretch, M. L. Carr broke his foot, but before coming off the floor he received a pass and shot the ball. Afterward he said, "The Duke would be proud of me. I went down shooting."

The team was getting contributions from the entire roster. McHale was regularly taking over games in the fourth quarter, earning him the nickname the "Animal" from the media for the way he ate up opponents in the final minutes. And while Robert Parish, Tiny Archibald, and Larry Bird earned invitations to the All-Star Game, Cedric Maxwell was having his best season as a Celtic. He allowed the offense to come to him while also being charged with guarding the opposing team's best forward on the defense end.

Fitch's recipe of obsessive coaching and a roster filled with determined players yearning to win had transformed exhibition-season turmoil into a championship-caliber team.

After eighty-one games played, the Atlantic Division title had yet to be determined, with the 76ers sitting a mere one game ahead of the Celtics with one game to play. The regular-season finale was a scheduled match-up between the two powerhouses at Boston Garden. It was reported that more than 18,000 fans attended the game, even though the arena had a seating capacity of 15,320, obstructed seats included.

The rivalry was reaching a crescendo. For years, Boston and Philadelphia had waged war on the basketball floor, two hard-edged Northeast cities with fan bases desperate for a world championship. Over the history of the rivalry, more often than not it was the Celtics who came out victorious, with Russell winning while Chamberlain scored. In 1980, the trend had been reversed when the Julius Erving–led 76ers eliminated the Celtics in the Eastern Finals. But now the Celtics had added size and defense and more scoring. Both teams were hungry—the Sixers hoping to overcome the previous year's disappointment in the NBA Finals, and the Celtics looking to exact revenge and reassert their place as the league's best.

The season finale was played not simply to determine the division title and home-court advantage in playoffs, but also to establish a message for the inevitable playoff meeting between the two teams. In the previous year's playoffs, M. L. Carr and Julius Erving had exchanged words after a hard Carr foul, inducing Carr to quip, "Get the Doctor a lawyer." But that was Carr's job. Red Auerbach was paying him to be a stopper, and that he did. He didn't care what people thought of him or said about him. For years Carr was on the outside looking in. He had been cut by several teams, including the Celtics, but he never lost the belief that he could play in the NBA. He traveled across the globe to play in Israel. He worked at Lewisburg Federal Penitentiary in Pennsylvania during the day and drove across the state at night to play in the Eastern League. He was willing to do whatever it took to keep his dream alive.

In the game against Philadelphia to close the season, Carr had another mission: send a message to their sharp-shooting rookie Andrew Toney. During the game, Carr bodied Toney to the ground while running around a pick. Toney jumped to his feet, and the two squared off. Cooler heads prevailed and further altercations were avoided, but in the end the Celtics won the game 98-94 to earn the Atlantic Division title and home-court advantage in the playoffs. In the process, Carr had delivered his message to the 76ers and then would deliver one to their fans: "Boston is better than Philadelphia in every way. Even the Liberty Bell is cracked and the steak and cheeses are sloppy."

The line had been drawn.

CHAPTER 23

"All Are Here Alike Welcome"

DAN REA WAS FIELDING PHONE CALLS ON HIS NIGHTLY TALK SHOW AT WBZ RADIO WHEN A CALLER WAS BUZZED IN. After being greeted by the host, the caller identified himself as a black person from Boston and stated his reason for calling: "Every person in South Boston is a racist." Rea immediately rebuked the caller's broad-brushed accusation. "You can't say that about one group or neighborhood." The caller clarified his claim. "Dan, as you drive across the bridge into South Boston, there is graffiti on a wall that reads, 'Niggers not welcome.'" The caller then paused, letting the power of that image sink in, and then he continued, "You see, you can't get in and out of South Boston without seeing these words. The fact that no one has done anything about it means to me that they must approve of the message."

The call ended, but Rea had trouble letting it go. The next morning he contacted South Boston politician Louise Day Hicks and asked if she was aware that the wall leading into the city was branded with a racial epithet. She confirmed that she knew of it but followed with, "What do you expect me to do about it?" Rea, unsatisfied with the response, hung up the phone and called City Councilor Ray Flynn and asked him the same question. Flynn pledged to immediately rectify what he characterized as a misrepresentation of South Boston's beliefs. The next day he gathered some neighborhood kids, grabbed some paint, and proceeded to cover over the words of hate in an act that would symbolize where Boston was headed.

In neighborhoods throughout Boston, the old refrains of hate and antagonism were now being seen as counterproductive to the city's mission. The shooting of Darryl Williams had led to a collective epiphany. People wanted the city's leadership to lead Boston in a new, more collaborative direction. For twelve years, Mayor Kevin White ran the city on a platform of development and expansion. His attention to the business community had led to the building of bridges and buildings that would make Boston a desirable destination for corporations to lease and for conventions to gather. During his time in office, he oversaw the restoration of Faneuil Hall into a popular tourist destination and the addition of thousands and thousands of commercial square feet to the Boston skyline. But people in Roxbury and South Boston weren't concerned with how many Elks could fit in the Hynes Auditorium; they wanted peace on their streets and sanity in their schools.

In the 1980 mayoral race, White was finally challenged to face these demands. His opponent, Joseph Timilty, compelled the mayor to listen to his constituents' needs and wants. The voters didn't want to be dictated to but instead wanted to be partners in the process of change. Timilty had promised such cooperation to the citizens, which drew the attention of many of White's supporters. This shift was reflected in poll numbers, and consequently, Mayor White's political machine made adjustments. Attention was now being paid to all corners of the city. Priorities were refocused to bringing peace and stability to the streets.

White ran the city from City Hall, but at his offsite office in the historic brick townhouse known as the Parkman House in Beacon Hill, the mayor held secret meetings to discuss how best to address the city's problems. Community leaders like South Boston's Jimmy Kelley and black leaders such as the Reverend Michael Haynes and Deputy Mayor Clarence Jeep Jones were summoned at the mayor's request. At night, White would be driven in unmarked cars to Charlestown and snuck in a side entrance at St. Mary's Church to meet with leaders from the community and call on them to be accountable.

The city was moving in the right direction. The power of the Covenant and the words of peace and responsibility that were being spoken from pulpits in churches and temples throughout Boston made people conscious that they were part of the solution.

The amended priorities of Kevin White's campaign proved to be vital to his survival as mayor. Five weeks after the Darryl Williams shooting and Pope John Paul II's cry for Boston to "embrace love," White earned 55 percent of the vote and was elected to his fourth term as the city's mayor. In his acceptance speech he spoke of his hopes for the city:

> We will always differ as a people in this city, but no longer can the city be divided as a people. We hold old friends and welcome new coalitions. . . . Remember that this is a great city. It is our city. It belongs to everyone who lives in it, works in it, and loves it.
>
> The primary goal is that anyone can walk anywhere in the city without fear of violence. . . . I can't wipe out hypocrisy or bias or bigotry, but I can guarantee with some authority that anyone can walk in any section of this city regardless of his color or national origin. That I'm going to guarantee. I won't do it overnight. But I will do it.

Mayor White's speech built on the progress that was being made throughout the scarred city. Collectively, citizens from all neighborhoods realized that resistance to change was counterproductive, and the city's diverse population was inching toward common ground.

When Augustus Small accepted the keys to South Boston High School in 1901 as its headmaster, he pledged to "educate both sexes of all races and religions without partiality, with malice toward none and charity for all. All are here alike welcome, from him of the greatest pedigree to the lowest immigrant, from the child for the oldest faith to the one belonging to the latest discovered truth." Seventy-five years later, all of Boston was starting to embrace that same pledge.

CHAPTER 24

"We're Bringing It Back to Boston"

GOING INTO THE 1960 NBA SEASON, THE BOSTON CELTICS HAD WON THREE OF THE LAST FOUR CHAMPIONSHIPS AND IN THE PROCESS WERE CAPTIVATING THE ATTENTION OF SPORTS FANS THROUGHOUT THE UNITED STATES. The league, still relatively young compared to the other team sports, looked to build on the attention that the team had garnered by asking them to barnstorm across the county and promote the league and the sport as they prepared for the upcoming season. One of the stops on the tour was Marion, Indiana.

When the Celtics arrived in Marion, they were greeted as guests of honor at a luncheon hosted by the city, after which the mayor presented each member of the team with a key to the city. The players thanked the city for its hospitality and then headed to the high school to play the exhibition game.

Following the game, the Celtics made their way to the lone restaurant that was still serving food in the town center and asked for a table. They were told that everyone on the team could be accommodated except Bill Russell and K. C. Jones, since the restaurant did not serve blacks. As a group, the team was outraged. Standing together, they refused to eat and left the restaurant. They went back to the hotel and retrieved the keys to the city that they had been given earlier in the day. They then hailed two cabs and asked the drivers to take them to the mayor's house. By the time they got to the residence, it was two in the morning. One by one, the players piled out of the taxis and marched up the front steps and knocked on the door. When the door was finally opened by the half-asleep mayor, the Celtics explained their snub at the restaurant and then handed their collection of keys back to the mayor.

Dating back to the 1950 NBA draft, the Boston Celtics established that they were a color-blind organization. Despite warnings from other owners about selecting an African American, owner Walter Brown drafted Chuck Cooper, the first black player to be drafted in league history. "I don't give a damn if he's striped or polka dot or plaid," Brown defiantly declared. "Boston takes Charles Cooper of Duquesne."

Not only were the Celtics the first team to draft a black player, they were also the first to start five black players and the first professional sports organization to hire a black head coach, as they did when they made Bill Russell player-coach in 1966. The only thing that mattered to the Boston Celtics was winning. And win they did, more than any other basketball franchise in history. In April 1964, after the Celtics defeated the San Francisco Warriors to capture another NBA title, K. C. Jones walked over to teammates Jim Loscutoff and Frank Ramsey, both of whom had just played their final game, and shook their hands. Jones then said, "Maybe it sounds funny because I'm black and you're white, but the Celtics are a family. I'll feel your losses deeply."

The 1981 Celtics team was built from the same blueprint as past Celtic champions, where talent and drive, not skin color or ethnicity, were the measures of a basketball player. The Celtics of 1981 carried themselves with the same swagger that past squads had.

<table>
<tr><th colspan="4">1980–81 BOSTON CELTICS ROSTER</th></tr>
<tr><th>NO.</th><th>PLAYER</th><th>POSITION</th><th>HOMETOWN</th></tr>
<tr><td>00</td><td>Robert Parish</td><td>center</td><td>Shreveport, Louisiana</td></tr>
<tr><td>7</td><td>Nate "Tiny" Archibald</td><td>guard</td><td>New York, New York</td></tr>
<tr><td>20</td><td>Wayne Kreklow</td><td>guard</td><td>Neenah, Wisconsin</td></tr>
<tr><td>30</td><td>Michael (M. L.) Carr</td><td>forward-guard</td><td>Wallace, North Carolina</td></tr>
<tr><td>31</td><td>Cedric Maxwell</td><td>forward</td><td>Kinston, North Carolina</td></tr>
<tr><td>32</td><td>Kevin McHale</td><td>forward-center</td><td>Hibbing, Minnesota</td></tr>
<tr><td>33</td><td>Larry Bird</td><td>forward</td><td>French Lick, Indiana</td></tr>
<tr><td>40</td><td>Terry Duerod</td><td>guard</td><td>Highland Park, Michigan</td></tr>
<tr><td>42</td><td>Chris Ford</td><td>guard-forward</td><td>Atlantic City, New Jersey</td></tr>
<tr><td>43</td><td>Gerald Henderson</td><td>guard</td><td>Richmond, Virginia</td></tr>
<tr><td>45</td><td>Eric Fernsten</td><td>center-forward</td><td>Oakland, California</td></tr>
<tr><td>53</td><td>Rick Robey</td><td>center-forward</td><td>Coral Gables, Florida</td></tr>
</table>

In an article in the *Boston Globe*, Larry Whiteside discussed with guard Chris Ford the team's diverse composition:

> The Celtics have a racial makeup of six whites and six blacks, which Ford will tell you is about the last count anybody connected with the organization would ever make. They admire the family concept. Nate Archibald has come up with a theme song which tells you a lot about each other. It is simply called "Ain't No Stopping Us Now." . . . Chemistry: twelve guys who can work

together. Twelve guys who have a feeling for one another, that's what makes a great team.

The team was not only composed of a balanced racial mix but also represented all corners of the country. There were players who hailed from urban backgrounds, from the Midwest, from the West Coast, and from the South. The team was in many ways a model for American society on how to function as one. But the Celtics were oblivious to the societal implications of their composition. They just wanted to win.

✪

Chicago-Bulls Head Coach Jerry Sloan sat in the locker room and shook his head at the very thought of Larry Bird. "That's what he's all about," Sloan said. "He does it when the game is on the line. In all my time of basketball, he's the most complete player I've ever seen."

The Celtics had taken the momentum from the end of the regular season and carried it into the first round of the playoffs. The Celtics swept Artis Gilmore, Reggie Theus, and the Chicago Bulls 4-0 behind Bird's brilliant play. In Game Three, Bird put forth a most impressive 24-point, 17-rebound, 10-assist performance, which writer Bob Ryan described as "Havlicekian." In Game Four, he submitted a 35-point masterpiece in the 109-103 clincher in Chicago. After the game, rookie Kevin McHale was underwhelmed by his first playoff experience: "People say things change drastically in the playoffs. I didn't notice it."

He soon would.

It was perhaps inevitable that Boston and Philadelphia would meet in the Eastern Conference Finals. But before the dream match could arrive, the 76ers struggled against the Milwaukee Bucks in their conference semifinals series. The Milwaukee Bucks and Marques Johnson fought hard before succumbing to the 76ers in seven games. The much-anticipated battle of the Eastern titans had finally arrived.

One year earlier, the size of Philadelphia's Caldwell Jones and Darryl Dawkins had proved too formidable for Boston. This year, the Celtics had the seven-foot Robert Parish at center and the six-foot-ten Kevin McHale coming off the bench as the sixth man.

The Celtics' victory over the 76ers in the final regular-season game had earned Boston the home-court advantage. The team had struggled in previous contests at the Spectrum in Philadelphia, and it was imperative that the Celtics maintain their home-court advantage in the series.

Game One at the Boston Garden was a hotly contested affair. The lead exchanged hands back and forth until the final possession. With just seconds left in the game and the Celtics leading 104-103, Philadelphia put the ball in the hands of their rookie scoring sensation, Andrew Toney. At draft time, while the Celtics were busy acquiring Kevin McHale and Robert Parish, Bob Ryan wrote that the 76ers were practically suicidal in their obsession with the guard from the University of Louisiana–Lafayette. Their obsession was well placed. In his first season, Toney showed time and again that he had the ability to rise to any occasion. He earned the nickname "The Boston Strangler" for his repeated success against the Celtics, and the nickname would be apropos again in Game One. As the clock ticked down, Toney beat his man off the dribble to gain the baseline. Cedric Maxwell rotated over in an effort to help defend Toney, but he got to the baseline a step late. Maxwell bumped Toney and was called for the foul. Two free throws later, the Celtics' home-court advantage was gone. Game Two was a must win.

The second game of the series was played the very next night. The Garden crowd was maniacal as always but now concerned as well. Alleviating their diminished confidence, the crowd was treated to a Bird masterpiece in Game

Two. He scored 23 points in the first half and ended up with 34 for the game. When he was substituted for late in the fourth quarter, the crowd rose to its feet and cheered wildly. The cheers rained down on Bird until Bill Fitch went over to him and asked him to acknowledge the crowd. Bird obliged with a wave, which encouraged the crowd to roar further. The Celtics won the game 118-99 to even the series at one game a piece with the teams heading to Philadelphia.

Two days later, when the team arrived at the Spectrum, Celtic GM Jan Volk was informed by the Boston radio team that announcer Johnny Most and their operations had been moved from their usual location close to the court to a lofted position a significant distance from the action. Opponents and their fans hated Johnny Most as much as they did the Celtics themselves. For three decades, this Celtics icon had broadcast games from Philadelphia uttering descriptions of the 76ers players' high crimes and victimizing of defenseless Celtics. The change in location was an attempt at gamesmanship by 76ers General Manager Pat Williams, which infuriated Red Auerbach.

On hearing of the planned relocation, Volk immediately sought out Williams in an effort to "save" him from the wrath of Auerbach. When they met Volk suggested, "You need to take care of this and this is why—and this isn't my decision—this will come from Red. When your broadcast team comes back to the Boston Garden, Red will put them so far from the court that they will need oxygen, coats, and mittens." Following this conversation between general managers, Most and the broadcast team were returned to their usual Spectrum perch.

The controversy over where Johnny Most would sit was the only contest that the Celtics would win on this day. The 76ers dominated in Game Three and earned a 110-100 victory. Robert Parish, who was struggling with back pains, shot an erratic 1-for-14 from the field, leading his grouchy coach to call him out in the press. "I'm not excited yet about the way he's played in the series," Fitch said. "We need double figures from him on offense, and we need double figures in rebounds."

What made the public censure of his center's play noteworthy was the fact that Fitch had for the most part eliminated any contact or communication with the press. By the end of his second season, Fitch had succeeded in alienating himself from players, the press, and Auerbach. The coach almost reveled in his ability to make the media's life more difficult. Many in the press found him to be more than just cantankerous. Some found him to be sneaky and vengeful, which they often recognized in his inability to sustain eye contact with the questioner.

With the Celtics now trailing 2-1 and the 76ers in possession of home-court advantage, the pressure was squarely on the shoulders of Boston. Prior to Game Four, the usually understated 76ers Coach Billy Cunningham warned, "If they [the Celtics] don't win on Sunday, I'd say they're in trouble. I don't see how they could expect to defeat us three straight times."

This warning/threat from the opposing coach didn't seem to motivate the Celtics, who again allowed the 76ers to build a significant first-half lead. But as was the character of the team all year, they refused to give up. With seconds remaining in the game and the 76ers' lead reduced to 107-105, the Celtics had possession with a chance to tie the game. Dribbling up the court with the ball in his hands was the man who had been the engine of the machine all season and all game: Tiny Archibald. Deciding not to call timeout, he pushed the ball from his basket toward midcourt, when he spotted Larry Bird streaking to the right of the key toward the basket. Over the last two years, Archibald had witnessed firsthand the value of getting the ball into the hands of Bird. Archibald crossed over the center line and pushed a long chest pass to his teammate. But the 76ers' star defender, Bobby Jones, had just one thing on his mind: find Bird. He, like everyone else, knew that Bird would be the likely target. He anticipated just such a pass and beat Bird to the spot. Jones intercepted the basketball and secured the victory to give Philadelphia a 3-1 series advantage.

The teams headed back to Boston for Game Five. For the Celtics, each game was an elimination contest. In the locker room prior to taking the court, Bill Fitch did his best to diminish any pressure that his players might be feeling: "We only have to win one game—that's it. We win one game and everything changes."

But even with Fitch's efforts to put his players in the proper state of mind, the team trailed throughout the game. The 76ers were quicker to gather up loose balls and secure critical rebounds. With two minutes remaining in the game, the Celtics were trailing 109-103. In the runway leading to the locker rooms, Philadelphia General Manager Pat Williams was accepting congratulations and wishes of good luck in the upcoming finals. But suddenly, the complexion of the game began to change. Fitch had turned to a defensive-minded backcourt of M. L. Carr and Gerald Henderson, who harassed, annoyed, and forced turnovers.

The 76ers turned the ball over 22 times in the game, including 6 by Julius Erving, one of which was picked up by M. L. Carr, who in turn was fouled by the forward with twenty seconds remaining on the game clock. Carr, who had been signed by Red Auerbach to be the "stopper," now stood at the foul line ready to shoot the biggest free throws of his life. After Carr made the first free throw, Billy Cunningham called a timeout, hoping to unnerve M. L.—initials that Bob Ryan said stood for "Mighty Loose."

Carr calmly walked over to the bench when Cedric Maxwell sidled up next to him and offered his thoughts on the pending free throw. "M. L., no pressure brother. If you hit the free throw, we keep playing. If you miss it, we go home and our season is over."

Carr hit the free throw and the Celtics lived to play again. After the game, Kevin McHale described the 111-109 victory like only he could: "It's like we were on death row and walking to the electric chair and they tell you have a couple more days left. It's like a reprieve." Carr said it was the best defense he had ever played and called his two rebounds and free throws the biggest of his career.

In the runway, Pat Williams was in shock. His team had completely dominated the Celtics all game, but somehow the men in green still had a pulse.

The series now returned to the Spectrum. The Celtics had lost eleven straight in the building, and Fitch was concerned with how the streak was affecting his team mentally. He wanted to reverse the negative karma that was contaminating the players. To accomplish this, the team would change everything they had done in past visits to the Spectrum. The players were assigned different lockers than they had for previous games. As they headed out for pregame warm-ups, they used the 76ers' tunnel to gain access to the court and then proceeded to warm up on the 76ers' basket. The Celtics were desperate to change their luck.

One of the few sellout crowds of the year, including the playoffs, had come to the Spectrum to watch the home team eliminate the once-great Boston Celtics. The Friday-night crowd smelled blood. Cheering wildly throughout the pregame, they were brought to a fever pitch by jazz great Grover Washington's rendition of the National Anthem on his saxophone. The patriotic salutation was followed by the introduction of the starting lineups by beloved public-address announcer Dave Zinkoff, who saved the team captain for last, as was the ritual: "Julius 'The Doctor' Errrrrving." Later in the game, the Celtics would take note of another Zinkoff announcement.

All the reverse-jinx hijinks by the Celtics appeared to have little effect on the Spectrum curse. By the fourth quarter, the home team was ahead by 17 points and in complete control of the game. During a timeout, the Celtics staggered to the bench, confused and frustrated. Over the public-address system,

Dave Zinkoff announced that tickets to the NBA Finals would go on sale after the game. Behind the bench, where General Manager Jan Volk was seated, a 76ers fan looked both apologetic and concerned. For years, the Celtics had proven that they were dead only when they were dead. Didn't Zinkoff and the Sixers know about the celebratory balloons tied to the ceiling in the Los Angeles Forum in 1969, never to be released? Didn't they remember, back to 1968, when the 76ers were leading the Celtics three games to one and six teenagers stuck a sign in Red Auerbach's face that read, "Your old men are dead," thus kick-starting another amazing Celtic comeback?

On the bench, the players heard the announcement. Cedric Maxwell decided that he had to do something to change the tone of the game if the opportunity availed itself. Nicknamed Cornbread by friends at home, Maxwell was an affable, fun-loving player who was admired and loved by his teammates. His contributions to the Celtics had been quiet but steady. He lived in the shadow of Larry Bird but continued to thrive while defending the other team's best forward every night. He had been drafted by the Celtics with the twelfth pick in 1977 out of the University of North Carolina at Charlotte, where he, much like Bird would two years later, led his team almost single-handedly to the NCAA Final Four. When the Celtics drafted Maxwell, he was actually disappointed. The Atlanta Hawks were the holders of the fourteenth pick and were much closer to home for Maxwell. Not to mention, the gangly forward, like many around the country, had heard stories about Boston and its "acceptance" of blacks.

Moments after the timeout, Maxell got his opportunity to help turn the tide of the game. Fighting for a rebound against the mammoth 76ers center Darryl Dawkins, Maxwell fell out of bounds into the crowd. As he walked back onto the court, he was overcome by an out-of-body experience. From up above he watched as he inexplicably ran back into the crowd after a verbose fan. It was out of character for him, but he knew deep in his subconscious that the game couldn't continue as constituted. Yelling and pointing and pushing ensued, causing the crowd and security to surge. Maxwell looked behind him to find his teammates lined up in support. It was at that moment he knew anything was possible. Standing together as a team, the Celtics were ready to take on not only the 76ers but also the entire Spectrum.

From that moment, the Celtics chipped away at the lead, hitting baskets and increasing their defensive intensity. Possession after possession they stopped the 76ers while converting on the offensive end. Then, with just over a minute left in the game, Larry Bird hit a clutch shot that bounced high off the back of the rim into the air before dropping through the net. The basket gave the Celtics a 98-95 lead. But like in Game One, the situation was tailor-made for "The Boston Strangler," Andrew Toney. As they had all season, the 76ers gave the rookie license to take over the game. With the ball in his hands, Toney worked off picks and around the Celtics defenders, freeing himself for a jump shot. He hit the shot and the lead was down to one. Then, in the closing seconds, Toney stole the ball from Bird, setting the scene for another chance at heroics.

With the ball and the fate of the Celtics in his hands, Toney dribbled to the left of the free throw line. The Celtics immediately sent both Carr and Tiny Archibald at him. Toney beat them off the dribble, giving him an open lane to drive to the hoop unimpeded. When he got to within five feet of the basket, he suddenly encountered fellow rookie Kevin McHale, who had rotated off of his own man, Darryl Dawkins, and now stood between Toney and the basket. As Toney laid the ball up in the air, McHale rose and extended his elongated arms to block the shot. But he didn't just block it. In the tradition of Bill Russell, he blocked it to himself, retaining possession of the ball and the game. Seconds later Maxwell would sink clutch free throws, and it was over. The teams would have to play a Game Seven to decide the series and see who would go on to play in the NBA Finals.

The Celtics had beaten the 76ers in the Spectrum and subsequently celebrated as if they had won the championship. All the way to the locker room they hugged and jumped and high-fived. Kevin McHale extended his arms to the 76ers fans with his index finger raised, letting them know who he believed was superior. Before the game, Julius Erving had called Game Six the championship game. Maybe he was right. In the locker room afterward, McHale called the win the "most joyous occasion of my life."

They had switched lockers, they had trailed by 18 points, they had gone into the crowd as a team to protect one of their own, and they had proven wrong Zinkoff's announcement about the sale of tickets for the NBA finals.

When the Celtics returned home later that night, they were greeted at the airport by thousands of zealous, slightly inebriated Celtic fans who came to welcome their team home and wish the players good luck in Game Seven.

The series had now reached a crescendo. Pat Williams called the game "pressure on top of pressure." Chris Ford later confessed that the intensity of the series and the stress that accompanied it had caused him and his wife to lose weight from worry and anxiousness.

The Boston crowd was delirious before the game. Similar to Game Five of the 1976 Finals against Phoenix, the temperature at the Garden seemed to be affected by the passion of the Celtic fans. This free flow of adrenaline was felt on the court, where in pregame warm-ups the players treated their crowd to a dunking display, including a rare jam by the vertically challenged Chris Ford.

It was just like it used to be in the Garden before John Y. Brown, Curtis Rowe, and Bob McAdoo latched on to the team and sullied the Celtic mystique. It was only fitting that Game Seven of the most intense series in team history would be waged on the storied parquet floor of the Boston Garden.

As the two teams prepared for the opening tip, Celtic fans sat anxiously in front of televisions at home with the volume muted but the radio on to allow Johnny Most's voice to narrate the events. From loge seats and balconies inside the Garden, fans cheered and rarely sat. They had invested so much in this team. They needed them to win. Boston needed them to win.

The game unfolded like the entire series had (except for Game Two). The 76ers, who had never beaten the Celtics in a Game Seven, controlled both tempo and momentum as they built a lead to as much as 11 points in the second half. With just over five minutes remaining, Philadelphia was up by 89-82. Then the energy of Celtics-past seemed to rise from the parquet. Suddenly the pressure, the heat, the unique smell that enveloped the Garden on warm days, started to choke the visiting team.

Pat Williams could not bear to watch. Instead of taking his usual spot in the runway leading to the locker rooms, the general manager hid in a broom closet in the hallway as the Celtics yet again chipped away at the lead. Over the next seven possessions, the 76ers committed six turnovers and failed to score a basket.

With just over a minute left, Darryl Dawkins had possession of the ball on the left side of the basket. He made a strong, two-handed move to the hoop but was harassed by three Celtics, causing his molested shot to come off the backboard and into the hands of Larry Bird. Bird's moment was upon him. He dribbled down the left side with his right hand, calculating his options while accounting for teammates and defenders. When he arrived at midcourt his mind was made up. He continued his dribble to the elbow of the foul line.

It was at this very spot on the same parquet floor that in 1969 Sam Jones ran around the picket fence in Game Six before hitting the game-winning shot. It was here that an injured John Havlicek floated through Phoenix Suns defenders to bank in his famous shot in the 1976 Finals. It was here that Larry

Bird would join them in Celtic greatness. He picked up his dribble and squared himself to the basket. He jumped and released the ball from his hands above his right shoulder, electing to bank his shot like Havlicek. From the broom closet, Williams heard the roar and knew.

Celtic fans overcome by anticipation filed to the edge of the basketball court ready to charge the parquet in celebration. But there was still one second left on the clock and the 76ers had possession of the ball ready to inbound at half court. Deep in their subconscious, Celtic fans fought images of a Jabbar skyhook or a Gar Heard turnaround jump shot. The Celtics couldn't lose this time. It was destiny.

As the crowd chanted, "Here we go, Celtics, here we go," the official handed Bobby Jones the ball on the left sidelines at half court. Jones waited for teammates to work off picks and fight to free themselves. With time limited, Jones lofted an alley-oop pass toward Julius Erving on the right side of the basket, but it was too high. It bounced off the backboard. It was over.

The greatest comeback in Celtic history, the greatest series win in Celtic history. At the top of the key, Larry Bird covered his head with his two arms and jumped up and down with all the innocence and unrestrained excitement of a child. Around him, the fans consumed the floor. It was their win, too.

It had been a long and painful five years for the Celtic organization and its supporters. Meddling owners and selfish players had led the team astray. But now all was forgotten. This Celtic team honored the parquet, the jerseys they wore, the flags that waved above, and the fans who so desperately needed them. On the court they jumped and hugged and exulted while in the stands and living rooms they cheered and shared the moment with friends and neighbors.

Standing in the balcony ten rows behind the perch of Johnny Most was a season-ticket holder who held a unique perspective on the ultimate value of the Celtics' victory. He had suffered just like all the other fans, but he never gave up hope. Night after night he came and waited for this moment, and now it was here. He smiled—not just at the Celtic win but also at the joy of the city. He, as much as anyone, understood the pain of change and unrest—as both a Celtic fan and a Bostonian. Ted Landsmark had been through so much. Now he celebrated his team's victory and the rebirth of a city. They had come a long way.

In the visitors' primitive locker room, Coach Billy Cunningham was inconsolable. Drawn and almost catatonic, he stared ahead, unable to explain. Julius Erving claimed that the Milwaukee Bucks were better, while Darryl Dawkins complained that the lack of a foul call on his shot was "bullshit."

In the Celtics' locker room, the emotion was palpable. A relieved Chris Ford said he wouldn't have been able to face the Boston fans if they had lost. Even Fitch gave thanks. But no one was more profoundly affected by the emotion than Larry Bird. Never had he realized such a level of joy and accomplishment. All the hard work, the days on the hardtop back in French Lick, all the lonely jump shots, the whispers that the attention bestowed upon him was somehow a function of his skin color and not his game—it all culminated in this moment. The words he spoke were not in summary of the game he had just played but a reflection on his life and all that he had overcome: "I never give up. Too many people give up."

🏀

Back in February, Rockets center Moses Malone returned to Houston after the All-Star Game, and he was not happy. He felt that the coach of the West All-Stars, Pat Riley, had disrespected him by using him sparingly in the game. Consequently Malone was bitter and more determined than before. When he arrived in the Rockets' locker room prior to their first game after the break, he walked over to the television and turned it off, and then he turned off the stereo. Malone had the undivided attention of his teammates. Referring to himself in the third person, he proclaimed, "Big Mo is tired. If you don't want to play hard tonight, then stay the fuck in the locker room." And with that, Malone proceeded to lead his team on a mission.

Despite a 40-42 regular-season record, the Houston Rockets earned the final playoff spot in the West. They were matched up against the Los Angeles Lakers in the first round, offering Moses a chance to exact vengeance on them and their coach, Pat Riley. Houston shocked the defending-champion Lakers, defeating them two games to one while earning both victories at the Forum in Los Angeles. The Rockets went on to upset George Gervin and the San Antonio Spurs in round two and then defeated the upstart Kansas City Kings in the Western Conference Finals. In all, the Rockets won 7 of 10 games on the road in the playoffs, including all 3 clinching games. Because they disposed of the Kings in just 5 games, they had the luxury of waiting for the winners of the Celtics-76ers series that would go 7. The Rockets collectively expected and were looking forward to the prospect of meeting the 76ers in the Finals. They felt confident that they matched up favorably against Philadelphia and fully assumed that they could continue their unexpected run of success.

When the Celtics finally eliminated the 76ers, earning an invitation to the NBA Finals, Houston forward Robert Reid couldn't get Larry Bird out of his mind. Before the 1976 Finals, Phoenix Suns rookie center Alvan Adams had set one goal for himself: keep Dave Cowens from winning the Finals MVP award. Five years later, Reid sat in his Boston hotel room with similar thoughts running through his head. The six-foot-eight defensive specialist, who was a virtual unknown when he came out of St. Mary's University as a second-round draft pick, would be called upon to use his great athletic skills to cover one of the game's best. Before departing for the Boston Garden, Reid got to his knees: "Lord, I never ask you for anything but for the two teams to play hard and be safe. But, Jesus, I am calling on you today. I need your help. Jesus, Jesus, Jesus, please don't let Larry Bird win the MVP."

Whenever the Celtics and the Rockets played each another, Robert Reid found himself connected to Larry Bird. In 1985, the Celtics hosted the Rockets on St. Patrick's Day in a nationally televised game at the Boston Garden, and Bird was in one of his patented grooves. Coming out of the break between the third and fourth quarter, Bird walked up to Reid and pointed out, "Hey, Reid, do you know I have 38 points?" Reid ignored him. Undeterred, the Celtic forward continued: "I'm putting 50 on you right here on national television."

On the opening possession of the fourth quarter, Bird hit a long jump shot to give him 40. The next time down the court, he drained another jumper, giving him 42. Fifty points seemed inevitable. But Reid was determined that he wasn't going to allow Bird to accomplish this task at his expense. The next time down the court, Reid knocked down one of Bird's teammates to earn a foul. On the next trip, he again fouled one of the Celtic players. A third time he ran at Kevin McHale and put a body on him, but there was no whistle. Following a break in play, referee Darrell Garretson approached Reid. "We heard what Bird said to you," Garretson told him. "And there is no way we're going to let you foul yourself out."

With Bird sitting at 46 points, and no chance of fouling out, Reid called upon the scouting report that he had been given, hoping for insight into how to stop his opponent's quest for 50. Reid knew that when Bird had the ball on the right side he would play two-man basketball with McHale, who would set up on the low post. On the left side, Bird would work the pick-and-roll with Parish. Trying to read Bird's teammates, Reid overplayed him to one side. But Bird outthought him and took the ball right down the middle and shot. While the ball was in the air, Bird yelled "Reid!" just in case he might miss the 47th and 48th points. Bird ended the game with 48 points, and Reid was there for every one of them.

✇

Robert Reid and the rest of the Rockets were confident heading into the NBA Finals. "We're the matadors," Reid said. "Let the bull out because we're going to stick him." The Rockets didn't fear the Celtics. They showed up ready to play and win. But playing on the parquet floor in the playoffs is a different experience than the regular season.

Prior to the first game, Reid found himself fighting the urge to look up into the rafters where the championship flags hung along with the retired numbers of past Celtics. During the National Anthem he couldn't help himself and snuck a peek. He then looked in the crowd and realized he had made a mistake. "You would see those flags with all those retired numbers on them. And then you would look in the crowd and see those very same players. It was like you had to beat them too."

Even though it was the NBA Finals, the Celtics and fans found the series anti-climactic following the intense battle with Philadelphia. Houston entered the playoffs with a sub-500 record. It was the first time since the Minneapolis Lakers in 1959 that a team made it to the NBA Finals with a record of more losses than wins.

In the first half of the opener, the Celtics allowed the confident visitors to gain a 14-point lead. It was not until the fourth quarter that Larry Bird was able to push his team ahead. He grabbed 21 rebounds in the game, none bigger than the offensive board he pulled down with seven minutes left and his team clinging to a 1-point lead.

Bird had the ball on the right wing and was searching for Cedric Maxwell in the low post. Maxwell's defender fronted him, so Bird passed to Parish at the free-throw line and received the ball back from his center. Bird then put the ball once to the floor with his left hand and arrived at the right side of the top of the key, where he shot a jumper over defender Robert Reid. Reid turned to watch the ball's flight, assuming that the shooter also was captivated by the rotation of the basketball. Instead, Bird had instantly reacted. With the ball only halfway to the basket, Bird configured flight, speed, and direction, using his brilliant basketball mind to calculate that the ball would land on the rim short and to the right, thus sending the rebound parallel to the baseline. When the ball hit the rim and caromed exactly where the Celtic forward had figured, he was there to meet it. Then, in a moment of NBA greatness, Bird caught the ball in the air and, while falling out of bounds, switched it from his right hand to his left hand and finger-rolled the ball around the backboard and into the hoop. Red Auerbach called it one of the greatest plays he had ever seen.

In addition to being one of the greatest plays in NBA history, Bird's brilliant maneuver was pivotal to a team that had played the whole game without a pulse. The Celtics barely held on to beat the Rockets 98-95. After the game Maxwell confessed, "It was a little hard for us to get up for this game." Although Houston had competed basket for basket with the Celtics, whispers of sweep made their way into the newspapers and onto radio talk shows. This disrespect would draw the ire of Moses Malone.

Most observers assumed that the Rockets had gotten their chance in Game One and blew it. But that wasn't the case. The Rockets shocked everyone except themselves and beat the Celtics in Game Two at the Garden. During halftime, Bill Fitch was so infuriated with this team's lax play that he punched a hole in the chalkboard. At the postgame press conference, the Celtic coach again called out one of his players in front of the media, placing blame on the injured Tiny Archibald. The guard, who had been playing with leg ailments since the Philadelphia series, missed a crucial last-second jump shot that would have tied the game. "Tiny hasn't had many falls in the last few games," Fitch said. "He's been given the outside shot but hasn't hit it."

The series now shifted to the Summit in Houston. In Game Three, 16,121 excited Rockets fans were disappointed by the home team, who managed only 71 points, including just 30 in the first half. Cedric Maxwell and Chris Ford led the Celtics with 19 and 17 points, respectively.

In Game Four, the Rockets got the Celtics' attention, much to the delight of the Summit crowd. Guard Mike Dunleavy was virtually unstoppable, scoring 28 points on the day. At one point in the game, Fitch sent in his defensive stopper, M. L. Carr, with strict orders to put the clamp on Dunleavy. Carr, who was used to employing his aggressive physical talents to intimidate opponents, opted for another method to distract the red-hot Rocket. Standing next to Dunleavy, Carr started up a conversation with the Rocket guard during a break in the action: "Isn't this great? Here we are playing in the NBA championship on national TV. I'm so happy, I think I'm going to kiss you." Carr then leaned over to kiss Dunleavy, who ducked away and ran back on defense. Carr followed him, grabbing his butt but not cooling him down. The Rockets won Game Four 91-86, tying the series at 2 games to 2.

In the victory, Robert Reid held Larry Bird to just 8 points for the second straight game, making the most of his athletic body and a scouting report to slow down the Celtic forward. Earlier in the series, people in the Rockets organization came to learn that Bird was playing with an injured thumb on his right hand. As a result, Reid took every opportunity to overplay Bird on his right side, forcing him to his left and slapping the thumb whenever Bird shot, passed, dribbled, or ran. This so infuriated the Celtic that he squared off with Reid to reclaim his turf. Reid grabbed Bird's shirt with his left hand and cocked his right fist. (The scene would be captured in a Leroy Neiman painting.) Reid would later say that he restrained himself from throwing the punch because a voice inside his head told him, "Robert, if you hit this white boy, you'll never play in this league again."

Houston Coach Del Harris had made a point of simplifying the game for his team in Game Four. He only used six players. Center Moses Malone played all forty-eight minutes, scoring 24 points while grabbing 22 rebounds. After the game, the usually reticent Malone suddenly became loquacious. Standing in front of his locker, the Rockets center welcomed microphones and tape recorders and proceeded to offer unprecedented bulletin-board material for his opponents. "I don't think they're all that good," he said. "I think they get a lot of publicity because they play back East. But I think we're a better team. . . . I respect the old Celtics, the ones who won thirteen championships. But I don't think that much of this club because I don't think they can stop us from doing what we want to do." Moses finished by saying that he could beat the Celtics with four guys from the streets of his hometown of Petersburg, Virginia.

At Logan Airport the next day, the Rockets were walking through the terminal when Mike Dunleavy looked to his right and caught a glimpse of the front page of the newspaper, on which Moses' comments were emblazoned. He shook his head in disbelief. He knew in his heart that the series was now essentially over. "We could have just got back on the plane," he later remarked. Dunleavy caught up to Reid and asked him if he had seen the paper. Reid just nodded and replied, "This isn't going to be good."

Game Five was never in doubt. The Celtics led by as many as 29 points and never looked back. The star of the game was Cedric Maxwell, who tallied 28 points and 15 rebounds, including 9 offensive boards. Bird described Maxwell's aggressive play as "the best football game I've ever seen Cedric play." During the game, Maxwell had made a point to slide over to Moses Malone and recommend, "You better get those four guys from Petersburg because these four you're playing with aren't working out that well." Afterward,

Maxwell commented that the team had responded to the taunts of its opponent and rose to the occasion. "The man threw down the challenge," Maxwell said, "and this is a team that responds well to challenges." In the Houston locker room Moses responded, "They're still chumps."

Heading back to Houston for Game Six, the Celtics would have the chance to secure the championship on their opponents' floor, which would mark the fifth straight time they clinched a title on the road. In front of another sellout crowd at the Summit, the Celtics built a 17-point lead that the Rockets would reduce to just 3 with ninety seconds left. But Larry Bird took over the game at that point, hitting a knockout three-pointer on the way to a 102-91 victory. The Boston Celtics had won their fourteenth NBA championship.

Cedric Maxwell was named MVP of the series. It had been a long journey for the talented forward, but he finally was getting some recognition. At the age of twenty-five and in his fourth season in Boston, Maxwell was the senior member of this team. He had been with the Celtics at the franchise's lowest and now was able to experience it at its highest. Sometimes forgotten and under-appreciated in Celtic lore, Maxwell was a realist. He understood that the team belonged to Larry Bird, but that didn't mean that he couldn't carry the team on his back when it needed him. "The big thing is that I'm considered as just the other forward on this team," Maxwell said. "I understand that it's because Larry Bird is an excellent basketball player, but I have pride, too, and everybody wants notoriety."

One by one, the team filed into the locker room with cigars in hand. In the middle of the celebration, Bill Fitch called the team together and offered thanks. "We played together and prayed harder together," the coach said. "We thank God for all the blessings we've had. Now, we gotta walk out that [locker room] door and pick up a trophy. Let's go. Let's go get it. Let's go get it!"

During the presentation, Red Auerbach accepted the Walter A. Brown Trophy on the Celtics' behalf with Larry Bird standing next to him. Bird and Auerbach had a special relationship similar to that between Auerbach and Russell. It was Bird who had prompted a smile and a loving punch from the Celtic president at the press conference announcing his signing when Bird said he "would have played for nothing." It was Bird who would lighten the grind of practices by bowling a ball to the feet of Auerbach whenever he fell asleep in his sideline seat, rousing the senior citizen and eliciting cheers from teammates. And now, as Bird stood next to his mentor on the championship stage and proceeded to help himself to Auerbach's cigar, he puffed away in celebration, prompting another classic smile from the great coach. Behind them, the Celtics jumped and smiled and hugged and just reveled in the moment. There was something so genuine about this celebration. From the back, M. L. Carr yelled, "We're bringing it back to Boston. That's where we're bringing it."

The celebration eventually moved from the Summit locker room to the Azalea Room at the Stouffer Hotel in Houston. The players partied all through the night and into the early morning hours. The next day, in reward for the team's great victory, the dictator known as Bill Fitch would allow the bus to leave late for the first time all year.

In the lobby that morning, a weary Mike Dunleavy, who also stayed at the hotel, was checking out. He looked up to see the Celtics still supporting one another, as several players carried a "spent" teammate to the bus for the ride to the airport. He figured they had a nice time.

Winning a championship has a way of changing one's perspective. Even Bill Fitch was moved by the moment. Fitch, who never bought into the whole Celtics mystique ideal, now started to see what it was all about. "You've always seen those thirteen flags on the ceiling," he reflected. "You see 'em every day, but you don't think that much about 'em. Then, when you win, you realize how much went into those thirteen flags. I think everybody on this team realizes that now."

✦

The world-champion Celtics were greeted by thousands of well-wishers at the airport upon their return to Boston. A few days later, the team was formally honored with a parade through the city. Mayor Kevin White declared it Celtic Day. In Washington, Senator Ted Kennedy issued a proclamation on the Senate floor: "Today, all the members of the U.S. Senate express their admiration for the Boston Celtics, who have made basketball history once more by winning their fourteenth world championship. We all strive for excellence; the Boston Celtics have shown surpassing excellence over the course of three decades."

Police estimated that more than 1.5 million people came to Boston on May 18, 1981, to celebrate the championship. The victory parade ended at City Hall, where the players were introduced to the assembled and where Boston gathered to celebrate, again, as one. It was on the grounds of the New City Hall that, in the 1800s, William Garrison advanced the effort of Emancipation; where, following the end of World War II, Boston came to celebrate in Scollay Square; and where Ted Landsmark was attacked by a flag-wielding teenager in a sad representation of the discord that had overtaken the city. It had been a long and arduous road, but finally the world would see the city in a new light, unified by a basketball team whose only interest was the same as it always had been: winning.

In the crowd, a fan named Don Hockman was asked what the Celtics' victory meant. His answer spoke to the value that a sports team has for the people it represents and to the power of a team's successes (and failures): "Well, I think maybe at this time the important thing is that it gives the people of Boston a positive thing to hold on to in a world of negatives. It's an event that brings people together."

The parade wound down Boylston Street and over to Tremont before arriving at City Hall for a private gathering in Mayor White's office. There, many of the same politicians who had failed in their duties over the last decade, ate cake and sought autographs from their basketball heroes. In the corner of the mayor's office, Boston School Committee member Pixie Palladino was furious with Larry Bird because he had failed to sign his first name but instead marked the paper "L Bird." The days of Pixie getting what she wanted were long gone.

Out on the balcony, Johnny Most introduced the players to the sea of people below. The Celtics were awestruck. Just a decade before, Red Auerbach had chided the Boston Chamber of Commerce for not doing enough to advance the team in the city's eyes. Now it seemed that the entire city had come to Government Center to cheer and recognize the team. The applause lasted more than five minutes.

When Larry Bird appeared at the microphone, the crowd's collective voice reached a crescendo. They could relate to him. He rolled up his sleeves and gave an honest day's effort. He dove on the floor, caromed into tables, refused to be held down. He came from a humble upbringing. But he, like the city he now represented, persevered. Nothing was taken for granted but instead cherished.

Down below, the people were standing shoulder to shoulder, unified and happy.

CHAPTER 25

Epilogue

IN 1994, NEARLY TWO DECADES AFTER HIS HORRIFIC AND UNFORGET-
TABLE ENCOUNTER ON THE PLAZA OF BOSTON'S GOVERNMENT CENTER,
TED LANDSMARK WAS SITTING IN HIS OFFICE WHEN HIS ASSISTANT
WALKED IN AND INFORMED HIM THAT AN UNANNOUNCED VISITOR WAS
IN THE LOBBY HOPING TO MEET WITH HIM. Having no pressing matters,
Landsmark asked his assistant to show the man in. Soon, a white man, who
seemed nervous and ill at ease, entered the office. Landsmark offered him a
seat across the desk and asked the mysterious visitor what he could do for him.
"Mr. Landsmark," he said, "you don't know me, but I'm one of the kids that
attacked you at City Hall some years ago." He reached into his pocket, pulled
out a photograph, and handed it across the desk to Landsmark. The man continued, "I want you to have this picture of me and my son. I know that I have
made mistakes in my life, and I'm sorry." Pausing for a breath in the midst of
this cathartic moment, he added, "I want you to be assured that I will teach my

son to do the right thing, to respect others and not be like I was. I was going through some tough times then, but I'm here today to move forward and ask you to find it within yourself to forgive me."

Landsmark was taken aback. Since that day on the bricks of Government Center, the pain that he felt was more for those attackers than for himself. Bruises and breaks of the body heal, but limitations of a person's soul sometimes cannot. But here in front of him sat a contrite man who had come to realize his faults and took a courageous step to face them. The moment was as powerful as the day the two men first encountered each other, under very different circumstances. Overcome by a spirit of compassion, Landsmark stood up from his seat, reached across his desk with his black hand, and shook the white hand of the repentant man. It was there in the clasp of two men that the new Boston was personified.

❀

From the day that John Winthrop and the Puritan settlers landed in Boston nearly four centuries ago, a way of life was forged and subsequently molded with each passing generation. The city of Boston is where the first shots of the American Revolution were fired. There in the streets, white men and black men stood side by side in a fight for personal liberty and the rights of a nation. The city was shaped and formed on the principle that opportunity would be provided for one and all so that its people could thrive and prosper.

The book *Old Charlestown* recounts a celebration that was held throughout the town in 1826 to commemorate the fiftieth anniversary of the signing of the Declaration of Independence. During the day, the townspeople were treated to patriotic readings and performances by the town choir. Church bells rang in the background as the Artillery Company of Charlestown fired their muskets into the sky in salute of those who had sacrificed in the name of their country. At a dinner later that night, two Charlestown natives who had fought in the Battle of Bunker Hill, Timothy Thompson and Thomas Miller, each offered their sentiments to generations of Bostonians to follow. Thompson proclaimed: "The first town which fell a sacrifice on the altar of Liberty, but now, phoenix-like rises from its ashes and becomes a nursery of freemen." Miller offered, "The rising generation—may they be well educated in the principles of a true government, of morality, and of religion; remembering that righteousness exalteth a nation."

Although the city at times has lost its way and fallen short in its role as a nursery of freemen and righteousness, Boston is still and always has been a special city. After a difficult, tumultuous period, it has again found its way. The city forever owes a debt of gratitude to people like Shirley Simmons and Ted Landsmark, who spoke of peace and not division; to that mother in South Boston or Charlestown who marched the streets with rosary beads in hand and pain in her heart as her right to decide the fate for her precious children was taken from her; to that generation of school children who were sacrificed because others failed on their behalf—you are the heroes of Boston. These people symbolize the strength, courage, and compassion that the city was founded on.

When I embarked on this project, I was carrying some level of preconceived notions. I had always held the courts responsible as the main culprit in the chaos that enveloped the city during this period. In truth, the main culpability falls on those members of the Boston School Committee and status-quo politicians who turned their backs on not only the Supreme Court and the Constitution but also the very people they were sworn to serve. I now know that Judge Wendell Arthur Garrity was a good person at heart with every good intention. His ruling on the need to desegregate Boston's schools was the only decision that could have been rendered. His interpretation of the Constitution could not be argued, which was validated twenty-two times by appellate and supreme courts. Where the judge faltered was in the application of the remedy.

To attempt to alter the makeup of communities, which had been formed over generations, in an eleven-week period and with minimal input by the people most affected was, simply put, foolhardy. Garrity's decision to compel the immediate desegregation of Boston's schools through forced busing was, ultimately, a failure—there is no other way to say it. The purpose of the desegregation movement had been to balance what was imbalanced. When all was said and done, the racial mix of the schools was not blended but instead washed. As many predicted, white citizens fled the city, causing irreparable harm to many neighborhoods that were at the heart of Boston.

In retrospect, alternative and complementary strategies likely would have better served the city as a whole, enhanced the quality of education, and ensured the equitable division of resources. Perhaps a system of faculty rotation would have guaranteed the same quality of teaching for every school district. If there were no option but to bus students between districts, could it have been done incrementally, beginning with younger grades that would have grown with the process? Instead, the implementation of desegregation was employed like a sledgehammer and in neighborhoods where change would be most difficult.

Charles Glenn, the chief author of Phase I of the desegregation efforts, later came to realize that rather than identifying imbalances based on race, they should have identified students instead by economic class. James Coleman, the sociologist who had originally conceived of the idea of busing as a remedy to racial imbalances in education, also came around to hold this view in later years. To have achieved this more complete approach to rebalancing the schools would have required going beyond the borders of

Boston to include suburban communities—the very suburbs where Judge Garrity, members of the State Board of Education, and other so-called experts lived.

Prior to Phase II of busing, launched in 1975, Father William Joy organized an open house at Charlestown High School for black parents whose children would be attending the school in the coming September. As he led tours around the facility, he was struck by the collective shock of the parents. They had assumed that the school would be superior to their children's current school. Instead, they found an outdated facility in disrepair. Not only had the Boston School Committee blatantly disregarded the rights of all, but they had allowed the entire school system to regress into a stagnant institution wallowing in decay. Not only should the five Boston School Committee members have been castigated for racial discrimination and neglecting the interests of the poor and disenfranchised, but for allowing the quality of education in the schools to sink so low.

⁂

In a column in the *Boston Globe*, writer Charlie Stein referred to August 18, 1992, as Black Tuesday. It was on that day that Larry Bird retired from the Boston Celtics; it also happened to be the day that one of Massachusetts' biggest employers, Wang Laboratories, filed bankruptcy. It was a virtual day of mourning for many.

Ever since the day that Bird had returned from the Olympic Games in Barcelona, there was constant speculation about whether he would come back to play another year or retire. There was some talk that maybe he would play just home games and avoid the plane rides, which had become so taxing on his ailing back. But the agony was evident and the outcome inevitable. There were even stories of people seeing Bird pulled over on the side of the road and lying on the sidewalk in a desperate attempt to alleviate the pain that riddled his vertebrae. The signs were obvious that, at thirty-five years old, Larry Legend was not going to return for a fourteenth season with the Celtics. Only the fans were in denial.

On the night of Larry Bird's very first game in Boston in 1979, my friends and I took the Orange Line to the Garden. Like any true Boston teenager, we tried our hardest to sneak into the arena so that we could say we were there on that night. But sadly, our efforts were thwarted at every door, fire escape, and potential opening. Desperate not to miss his baptism into Celtic lore, we hustled home to watch the game on television. From that day forward, I followed his career with unreserved admiration.

I am not, by nature, an idol worshiper. When everyone in Boston was crazy for Carl Yastrzemski, my favorite Red Sox was Reggie Smith. But there was something special in Larry Bird's game that captivated me along with everybody else. Maybe it was just the sincerity of his effort. Maybe it was his ability to perform when so many others would give up. Whatever it was, it was a treat to grow up with Larry Bird.

I remember every moment of greatness: when he won the three-point shooting contest on the last ball and then stuck his mangled index finger into the air to signify victory before the ball even reached the rim. The night he hit 60 points against the Atlanta Hawks in New Orleans, and three Hawks players were fined for enjoying every one of the 60, falling out of their chairs and covering their faces with towels. The game in which he told the Washington Bullets, with just seconds left on the clock, that he was going to catch the ball in front of their bench and hit a three-pointer and win the game, and there was nothing they could do about it. In Dallas, after getting poked in the eye and his team being down by two, he put up a three at the end of the game and hit the winning shot, even though he was seeing two rims. The afternoon playoff game in 1987 when the Celtics were trailing the Pistons late in Game

Seven at the Garden and a pigeon flew onto the court during a timeout, stirring the crowd into a chant of "Larry, Larry, Larry." When the Celtics returned from the timeout, Bird ignited a comeback to carry his tired and injured team to victory. The Sunday afternoon playoff game against Indiana when he cracked his face on the parquet and returned from the locker room to toast Chuck Person and the Pacers. The first game that he faced Julius Erving after their fight, when he took the ball on the opening possession, beat Erving on the baseline, and proceeded to submit a reverse dunk. The night he threw a behind-the-back pass three-quarters of the length of the court for an assist, as an homage to Magic Johnson, who earlier that day had announced he had AIDS. And, of course, his steal against Detroit in Game Five of the 1987 Eastern Conference Finals. In my mind, the best part about that steal was not the steal itself but rather the fact that on the preceding play when the Celtics lost the ball, Bird had been knocked on his backside all the way in the far corner in front of his bench. All seemed lost, but he pulled himself up and put himself in position to steal the pass from Isiah Thomas. As he said following the series against the 76ers in 1981, "I never give up. Too many people give up."

To this day I still hold my wife responsible (even though she had no say in the date) for the fact that her wedding shower, which I had to attend, occurred at the same time as Game Seven of the 1988 Eastern Semifinals, when Atlanta's Dominique Wilkins and Bird waged one of the great duels in NBA history. Wilkins scored a Chamberlain-like 47 points while Bird countered with 34 in the Boston victory. As Brent Musburger said that day, "You are watching what greatness is all about."

When Bird first laced up his black sneakers for the Celtics, I was a sophomore in high school. When he called it quits, I was a professional banker still enamored with number 33. On the day he retired, I went next door to a restaurant and watched the proceedings in sad dismay. I just couldn't believe that no longer would I see number 33 wipe his hands on the bottom of his sneakers and treat us to his special gifts.

In *Cousy on the Celtic Mystique*, which was written in 1988, Bob Cousy remarked, "Let's just hope that when he [Bird] goes, he doesn't take the Celtic Mystique with him. We have all been very, very spoiled." When Bird did go, he did take the mystique with him, and yes, we had been spoiled. In Bird's farewell press conference he said, "I gave my heart and soul to the Celtics." That he did.

⊛

From the dust and brick piles of Scollay Square, much was promised. The pledge of "urban renewal" caused neon signs to be extinguished and the echoes of music to go silent. From the dust rose New City Hall with a pledge to serve the people. But somehow, the walls of the Brutalist Modern building and the bricks of its courtyard were part of a widening chasm between black and white, rich and poor. It was not until that May afternoon in 1981 when Larry Bird called out in defiance of Moses (Malone) that the city truly came together as one, unified again in belief and purpose. On those very bricks still stained from the blood of discord, the spirit of Scollay Square rose again as the city celebrated together as champions.

It wasn't the intention of the 1981 Boston Celtics to lead the city from division to harmony. It was a team of six black men and six white men playing the game at the highest level with regard for only one thing: winning. But in that pursuit of excellence, they galvanized a city. The team in green allowed the city's inhabitants to connect with one hope and purpose. It was simple and pure. It was basketball. The Celtics' magical ride and return to distinction served to bond communities and individuals that had drifted apart.

In Mayor Kevin White's final inauguration speech, he had one wish for the city: "The primary goal is that anyone can walk anywhere in the city without fear of violence." White's dream is now largely a reality. Boston, a center of education, research, and culture, is a beautiful, vibrant city featuring a mosaic of people who live and thrive in the "city on the hill." And the Boston Celtics are world champions once again.

Bibliography

BOOKS

Allison, Robert. *The Boston Massacre*. Beverly, Mass.: Commonwealth Editions, 2006.

Araton, Harvey, and Filip Bondy. *The Selling of the Green: The Financial Rise and Moral Decline of the Boston Celtics*. New York: HarperCollins, 1992.

Bird, Larry, and Bob Ryan. *Drive: The Story of My Life*. New York: Doubleday, 1989.

Bird, Larry, and Jackie MacMullan. *Bird Watching: On Playing and Coaching the Game I Love*. New York: Warner Books, 1999.

Bjarkman, Peter. *Boston Celtics Encyclopedia*. Champaign, Ill.: Sports Publishing, 1999.

Bulger, William. *While the Music Lasts: My Life in Politics*. Boston: Houghton Mifflin, 1996.

Carey, Mike, and Jamie Most. *High Above Courtside: The Lost Memories of Johnny Most*. Champaign, Ill.: Sports Publishing, 2003.

Chapman, Jay John. *William Lloyd Garrison*. Boston: The Atlantic Monthly Press, 1862.

Cousy, Bob, and Bob Ryan. *Cousy on the Celtic Mystique*. New York: McGraw-Hill Publishing, 1988.

Dauwer, Leo P. *I Remember Southie*. Boston: Christopher Publishing House, 1975.

Denton, Sally. *The Bluegrass Conspiracy: An Inside Story of Power, Greed, Drugs, and Murder*. New York: Doubleday, 1990.

Heinsohn, Tommy, and Joe Fitzgerald. *Give 'Em the Hook*. New York: Prentice Hall Press, 1988.

Heinsohn, Tommy, and Leonard Lewin. *Heinsohn Don't You Ever Smile?: The Life and Times of Tommy Heinsohn and the Boston Celtics*. Garden City, N.Y.: Doubleday, 1976.

Horton, James Oliver, and Lois Horton. *Black Bostonians: Family Life and Community Struggle in the Antebellum North*. New York: Holmes and Meier Publishers, 2000.

Kruh, Thomas. *Always Something Doing: Boston's Infamous Scollay Square*. Boston: Northeastern University Press, 1999.

Levine, Hillel, and Lawrence Harmon. *The Death of an American Jewish Community: A Tragedy of Good Intentions*. New York: Touchstone, 1993.

Lukas, J. Anthony. *Common Ground: A Turbulent Decade in the Lives of Three American Families*. New York: Vintage Books, 1986.

Lyman, Theodore. *Papers Relating to the Garrison Mob*. Cambridge, Mass.: Welch, Begelow, and Co. (Printers to the University), 1870.

O'Connor, Thomas. *The Boston Irish: A Political History*. Boston: Northeastern University Press, 1997.

———. *The Hub: Boston Past and Present*. Boston: Northeastern University Press, 2001.

———. *South Boston, My Hometown: The History of an Ethnic Neighborhood*. Boston: Quinlan Press, 1988.

Powers, John. *The Short Season: A Boston Celtics Diary 1977–1978*. New York: Harper and Row, 1979.

Quirk, James, and Rodney Fort. *Pay Dirt: The Business of Professional Sports*. Princeton, N.J.: Princeton University Press, 1997.

Russell, Bill, and Taylor Branch. *Second Wind: The Memoirs of an Opinionated Man*. New York: Random House, 1979.

Russell, Francis. *A City in Terror: Calvin Coolidge and the 1919 Boston Police Strike*. Boston: Beacon Press, 1979.

Ryan, Bob. *Celtics Pride: The Rebuilding of Boston's World Championship Basketball Team*. Boston: A Sports Illustrated Book, Little, Brown and Company, 1975.

Sawyer, Timothy. *Old Charlestown: Historical, Biographical, Reminiscent*. Boston: James H. West Company, 1902.

Schneider, Mark. *Boston Confronts Jim Crow, 1890–1920*. Boston: Northeastern University Press, 1997.

Shaughnessy, Dan. *Ever Green: Boston Celtics, A History in the Words of Their Players, Coaches, Fans, and Foes, from 1946 to the Present*. New York: St. Martin's Press, 1990.

Sullivan, George. *The Picture History of the Boston Celtics*. Indianapolis: The Bobbs-Merrill Company, 1982.

Wesley, Dorothy, and Constance Porter. *William Cooper Nell: Nineteenth-century African American Abolitionist*. Baltimore: Black Classic Press, 2002.

Whalen, Thomas J. *Dynasty's End: Bill Russell and the 1968–69 World Champion Boston Celtics*. Boston: Northeastern University Press, 2005.

Whitehill, Walter Muir, and Lawrence Kennedy. *Boston: A Topographical History*. 3rd ed. Cambridge, Mass.: The Belknap Press of Harvard University Press, 2000.

NEWSPAPERS AND PERIODICALS

Boston Globe

Mike Barnicle, Jack Barry, Anne Beaton, Bud Collins, Jack Craig, Dick Dew, Ray Fitzgerald, Bill Fripp, Harold Kaese, Clif Keane, Al Larkin, Michael Madden, Steve Marantz, Will McDonough, Leigh

Montville, Brian Mooney, Jeremiah Murphy, Jerry Nason, Marvin Pave, Herb Ralby, Matthew Richer, Ernie Roberts, Francis Rosa, Bob Ryan, Bob Sales, Dan Shaughnessy, Neil Singelais, Larry Whiteside

Boston Herald (Herald American, Herald Traveler, Record American)
Sam Brogna, George Brooks, Steve Bulpett, Joe Cashman, Jack Clary, Dan Cohen, Jean Cole, Bob Duffy, Joseph Fitzgerald, Ed Gillooly, Buck Harvey, Joe Heaney, Tim Horgan, Pat Horne, Clif Keane, Nat King, Murray Kramer, Bill Liston, Joe Looney, Earl Marchand, Jack McCarthy, Bill McSweeney, Leo Monohan, David Moore, Martin Norm, Alex Scahare, George Sullivan, Mary Sullivan, Cliff Sundberg

Christian Science Monitor

Houston Chronicle
Michael Murphy

Los Angeles Times
Thomas Foley

The New York Times
Wendell Rawls Jr., Thomas Rogers

South Boston Tribune

Sports Illustrated
Peter Carry, Frank DeFord, Curry Kirkpatrick, Barry McDermott, Leigh Montville, George Plimpton, Gilbert Rogin, Bill Russell, Jeremiah Tax

Celtics Chatter, a Boston Celtics Publication, September 1969

The Final Game: Official Commemorative Game Program and Magazine.
April 21, 1995
Hal Bock, Joe Fitzgerald, Norman Moyes, B. P. Newhouse, Bert Rosenthal, Joe Sullivan, David Zuccaro

LEGAL CASES AND GOVERNMENT DOCUMENTS

Massachusetts State Advisory Committee to the United States Commission on Civil Rights, "Report on Racial Imbalance in the Boston Public Schools." January 1965. www.lib.neu.edu/archives/freedom_house/full_text/racial_cover.htm

Sarah C. Roberts v. The City of Boston, 59 Mass. (5 Cush.) (1850). brownvboard. org/research/handbook/sources/roberts/roberts.htm

Tallulah Morgan et al. v. James W. Hennigan et al., 379 F. Supp. 410 (D.C. Mass., June 21, 1974). www.blackpast.org/?q=primary/boston-bussing-case

Tallulah Morgan et al. v. John J. McDonough et al., 548 F.2d 28 (United States Court of Appeals, First Circuit, Jan. 26, 1977). bulk.resource.org/courts. gov/c/F2/548/548.F2d.28.76-1426.76-1239.76-1121.html

WEBSITES AND ONLINE RESOURCES

Bernick, Michael. "Will Boston Schools Ever Desegregate?" *The Harvard Crimson*, January 17, 1973. www.thecrimson.com/article. aspx?ref=250158

Boston History & Innovation Collaborative. www.bostonhistorycollaborative.org

Bowen, Ezra, with Joelle Attinger. "Almost Free in Boston. *Time*, April 12, 1985. www.time.com/time/magazine/article/0,9171,1048431,00.html

Brennan, Sandra. "Irving H. Levin." *All Movie Guide*. www.allmovie.com/cg/ avg.dll?p=avg&sql=2:99498.

Celtic Nation. Unofficial Web site of the Boston Celtics. www.celtic-nation.com. databaseBasketball. www.basketballreference.com.

Famous Sports Stars. "Arnold 'Red' Auerbach: Abrasive Personality." sports. jrank.org/pages/214/Auerbach-Arnold-Red-Abrasive-Personality.html

Historic Roxbury/Boston National Historical Park. "Roxbury During the Siege of Boston, April 1775–March 1776." www.nps.gov/bost/forteachers/upload/roxbury.pdf

History Place, The. "Irish Potato Famine: Gone to America." www.historyplace.com/worldhistory/famine/america.htm.

Hughes, David. "Larry Bird: Basketball Legend Gave City "A Place on the Map."' *Tribune-Star* website. specials.tribstar.com/terrehautestop40/stories/bird.html.

"A Judge with Guts." *Time*, June 23, 1975. www.time.com/time/magazine/article/0,9171,879597,00.html.

Kallmann, McKinnell & Wood. "Boston City Hall: 1963–69." www.owlnet.rice.edu/~arch315/boston_kallmckwood.pdf.

Kruh, David. "Scollay Square." www.bambinomusical.com/Scollay.

Kubatko, Justin. Basketball-reference. www.basketball-reference.com.

Liberator Files, The. www.theliberatorfiles.com.

Massachusetts Foundation for the Humanities. Mass Moments. www.massmoments.org.

Massachusetts Historical Society website. www.masshist.org.

McClellan, Michael D. "Training Days: The Frank Challant Interview." Celtic-Nation.com. www.celtic-nation.com/interviews/frank_challant/

Murphy, Michael. "Former ABA teammates Barnes, Gerard living proof of evils of drugs." www.remembertheaba.com/ABAArticles/MurphyArticleBarnesGerard.html.

National Basketball Association official website. www.nba.com.

"New Coleman Report." *Time*, June 23, 1975. www.time.com/time/magazine/article/0,9171,913200,00.html

New York State Archives, States' Impact on Federal Education Policy Project. "The Johnson Years: The Coleman Report—Equal Educational Opportunity."

www.archives.nysed.gov/edpolicy/research/res_essay_johnson_
cole.shtml.

O'Sullivan, Tim. "The Doom of McAdoo." HoopsHype. hoopshype.com/
articles/clippers_osullivan.htm.

Professional Basketball Transactions Archive. www.prosportstransactions.
com/basketball/index.htm.

"Pure Gold in the Corn Belt: A pair of aces at Indiana State." *Time*, February 26,
1979. www.time.com/time/magazine/article/0,9171,920185-1,00.html

Richer, Matthew. "Boston's Busing Massacre." *Policy Review*, November/December
1998. findarticles.com/p/articles/mi_qa3647/is_199811/ai_n8809228

Theodore Landsmark Press Conference, April 7, 1976. openvault.wgbh.org/
ton/MLA000846/index.html.

WBUR. "Boston at the Crossroads." www.wbur.org/special/bostonatc.

Workable Peace Project. "Boston Busing: Integrating Schools in
Massachusetts." www.workablepeace.org/pdfs/busing.pdf

Index